1745
A MILITARY HISTORY
of the
LAST JACOBITE RISING

For Susan

1745
A MILITARY HISTORY
of the
LAST JACOBITE RISING

by
Stuart Reid

SPELLMOUNT
Staplehurst

British Library Cataloguing in Publication Data:
A catalogue record for this book is available
from the British Library

ISBN 1-86227-130-5

First published by Spellmount Limited in the UK in 1996

This edition published in the UK in 2001 by
Spellmount Limited
The Old Rectory
Staplehurst
Kent TN12 0AZ
United Kingdom

3 5 7 9 8 6 4 2

Typesetting by Rowland Phototypesetting Ltd
Bury St Edmunds, Suffolk

Printed in Great Britain by
Mackays of Chatham, Chatham, Kent

Contents

List of Maps

All maps © Derek Stone

List of Illustrations

All illustrations © Stuart Reid

Introduction

The battle of Culloden is, arguably, the most famous episode in Scottish history and yet, at the same time it is also perhaps the least well recorded of all the British army's campaigns. Indeed some partisan historians contrive to avoid referring to the British army at all, preferring instead to call it the *Hanoverian* army. In reality the Hanoverian army was in Germany where it belonged, or campaigning in the Low Countries. It was British soldiers (including all but two of the Scottish regiments) who defeated the rebels and their French allies.

My aim in writing this book has been to provide a factual and above all impartial study of the military aspects of the campaign. This draws not only on the familiar Jacobite sources, but also upon the British army's own records and the letters written at the time by its officers and soldiers. Naturally enough this approach has thrown some new light on several episodes, but it is by no means a history of the rebellion as seen from the British army's point of view.

In particular, one matter which is re-assessed is the rather fraught relationship between the Jacobite Lieutenant-General, Lord George Murray and Colonel John Sullivan, the Adjutant-General. Murray has invariably been portrayed by historians as the quintessential hero of the uprising, a military genius at odds with the incompetent Sullivan. Yet his contemporaries saw Murray very differently and for long afterwards there was a strong tradition that he was a traitor. Conversely, Sullivan actually appears to have been a very great deal more able than his modern critics will allow.

A book like this can never be an unaided effort and I should like above all to thank Martin Windrow, who by publishing my earlier study of the battle of Culloden, *Like Hungry Wolves* set me fairly on the way to writing this broader study of the rebellion. The staff of Aberdeen Public Library did their bit, as did those of the libraries of Newcastle-upon-Tyne and the Newcastle-upon-Tyne Literary & Philosophical Society, the Scottish United Services Museum, the National Army Museum, the Public Record Office at Kew, and last but by no means least David Grant, who read the manuscript, corrected my atrocious punctuation and pointed out the odd frayed edge.

Stuart Reid
North Shields
1996

CHAPTER 1

The Prince and the Slavers
Preparations for the Rising

Early on the afternoon of the 16th of April 1746 the last Jacobite army was famously and bloodily defeated on Culloden Moor outside Inverness, thus bringing to an end not just eight months of rebellion but half a century of intermittent religious and political conflict.

Arguably it had really begun even earlier with the bloody descent into the Great Civil War of the 1640s which tore the Highlands apart, but the immediate cause of the crisis was the death of King Charles II in 1685. Since he left no legitimate heir (if one excepts the ill-fated pretensions of the Duke of Monmouth) the throne duly passed to his autocratic younger brother James and James, although a far abler soldier and administrator than his brother, was a Catholic and so regarded with some uneasiness if not downright hostility by the greater part of the population both north and south of the border.

In November 1688, therefore, James's impeccably Protestant son-in-law Prince William of Orange invaded England at the head of a Dutch army. King James quickly mustered superior forces to meet him on Salisbury Plain, but then suffered a catastrophically complete nervous collapse and fled to France. Resistance to the Dutch invaders and their rather rag-tag Protestant rebel allies thereupon collapsed equally swiftly. Ever realistic, the English parliament hastily acquiesced in this 'Glorious Revolution' by inventing the curious legal fiction that James had abdicated. By this means they successfully invested the hasty accession of both William and James's Protestant daughter Mary to the throne with sufficient, albeit dubious, legality to avoid the awful spectre of another civil war.

In Scotland, by contrast, a much more robust approach was taken to the matter. On the 4th of April 1689, the Scottish Estates, or parliament, roundly declared that King James VII had 'forfaultit the Croun', and stoutly underlined this announcement a week later on the 11th by the formal adoption of the 'Claim of Right'.

This 'Claim of Right' asserted that by transforming a limited legal monarchy into an arbitrary despotic power (and worse still a Catholic one) King James VII had violated the Scots constitution. Such a firm

1

stance would doubtless have horrified the King's grandfather, James VI, who had done so much to formulate the concept of the Divine Right of Kings, but in effect, by this 'Claim of Right', echoing as it did the yet more famous 'Declaration of Arbroath', the Scots stoutly repudiated such high-flown nonsense. The King did not rule by divine right, but only by the will of his people and if he misused the powers with which they entrusted him, he could lawfully be deposed and the crown then offered to another.

Nevertheless, there was still some considerable residual loyalty to James in Scotland, and William's commander-in-chief there, General Hugh MacKay, was badly defeated by a Highland army at Killiecrankie in 1689. Another three years of often brutal warfare followed, both in Ireland and Scotland, culminating in the infamous (if rather overblown) massacre at Glencoe. But by the end of it Dutch William was firmly in control of all three kingdoms.[1] Consequently, when William died suddenly in 1702, he was very smoothly succeeded by his sister-in-law, Anne Stuart, another of the deposed King James's Protestant daughters.

The most significant moment in her twelve-year reign was the forcing through in 1707 of an Act of Union, firmly binding together the hitherto still independent kingdoms of Scotland and England.

Objectively perhaps, most Scots could hardly be expected to look back upon the final hundred years of the Stuart dynasty as a golden age. They were filled by religious and political strife which broke out time and again into open warfare with all its attendant horrors. And above all, those years were characterised by the family's marked reluctance even to clap eyes upon Scotland. Nevertheless, under the Stuarts, Scotland had for good or ill still been an independent country and it is very hard to escape the impression that 18th-century Jacobitism was not primarily an expression of ancient loyalty to the royal house of Stuart, but rather a convenient focus for opposition to the Union.

An early attempt by the Jacobite heir, the titular King James VIII, was made to capitalise on this widespread opposition by landing in Scotland early in 1708 and had he actually succeeded in doing so, all the indications are that the country would have gone over to him. At the time Britain was embroiled in the War of the Spanish Succession, and thanks to the military genius of the Duke of Marlborough, was on the point of victory over France. The French King Louis XIV desperately needed to avert the imminent threat of invasion and sought to do so by providing James with the ships and men which he needed.

A French fleet commanded by the Comte de Forbin duly arrived in the Firth of Forth on the 12th of March, carrying James and thousands of regular troops. At once they were approached by large numbers of fishing boats and enthusiastic offers of assistance to effect a landing. There was nothing whatever to oppose such a landing had the opportunity been seized and a triumphant Jacobite entry into Edinburgh was only hours away. Queen Anne's Commander-in-Chief Scotland, the Earl of Leven, gloomily reported that same day that he had so few troops at his disposal that a French landing would oblige him to abandon Edinburgh and retire immediately towards Berwick.

Fortunately for the Government, the French Admiral had completely misread his instructions and convinced himself that the expedition was no more than an elaborate bluff. At this critical point, therefore, he perversely refused to land either James or any of the French troops which he carried and instead fled northwards pursued by the Royal Navy.[2]

Six years later however another, and in many ways much more serious, crisis developed. In 1714 Queen Anne died and, like her uncle Charles II, she left no immediate heir. This time the succession was disputed by her own half-brother, the would-be James VIII, but he was a Catholic and as such by now in law firmly barred from the throne.

A Protestant heir was required and, although James still had his supporters, they failed to act swiftly enough so that the crown passed instead to the Elector of Hanover who, although a foreigner, had the great good fortune to be both an undoubted Protestant and a great grandson of King James VI. He also had the equally good fortune to have served in the Allied army under the Duke of Marlborough. Consequently, the newly crowned King George I had already acquired sufficient good contacts within the British army to be assured of its firm support when his Stuart cousin's supporters raised the standard of rebellion in September 1715.

This was just as well for, although the recently concluded peace treaty with France had seen the withdrawal of French support for James (and indeed would eventually see him exiled from France to Rome), the rising was strongly supported throughout most of Scotland and, more worryingly still, in the north of England. Not surprisingly, and in spite of remarkably poor leadership, it produced some very anxious moments before being fatally checked at Preston and at Sheriffmuir on the 13th of November. Not even the rather unprepossessing appearance on the scene of James himself could retrieve the situation and he soon departed from Scotland as unobtrusively as he had arrived, leaving his hapless followers to make the best terms they could.[3]

Scarcely disturbed by an improbable Swedish invasion threat in 1718 and an actual Spanish-backed fiasco which quickly came to grief at Glenshiel in the following year, Britain enjoyed over twenty years of peace after the rebellion of 1715 and in those long years Scotland grudgingly began to realise some benefit from the Union. Slowly Jacobite support became more and more marginalised and to some extent chiefly associated with the Scottish Highlands.

It is one of the great paradoxes of the Jacobite period that the Stuarts should in the end have come to depend so very heavily upon Highland support, given that family's long and virtually unbroken record of brutal repression of the Gaelic peoples. Yet it is a paradox easily explained inasmuch as the Highlanders were not the first or most important allies to whom the Stuarts turned but rather their last remaining ones.

While it is relatively easy to chart the decline in support for the Stuarts in lowland Scotland, and even easier to do so in England, explaining why comparatively strong support was still to be found in the Highlands in 1745 is much more difficult.

In the first place the lowland Scots Jacobites had done themselves no good at all in 1715. It was they rather than the clans who had borne the brunt both of the government's counter-insurgency measures and an ill-judged scorched earth policy carried out by the Jacobites themselves as they retreated northwards after Sheriffmuir. They therefore had a somewhat livelier appreciation than their Highland counterparts of the likely consequences of another rising.

On the other hand, despite the improving efforts of the more progress-ive chiefs such as Cameron of Locheil, the economically-backward High-lands gained least from the Union and nationalist sentiment there was consequently little tempered by new-found prosperity. Nevertheless, a fortunate escape from retribution in 1715 and simple economics alone will not account for this otherwise eccentric loyalty.

Nor, as is sometimes argued, was the Highland rebellion a despairing last stand by a Celtic civilisation. Although its Highland division was undoubtedly the chief strength of the last Jacobite army, it is evident even from a most superficial study of the rebellion that Jacobite loyalties were not determined by the Highland line, by Gaelic culture or even to any great extent by religion. Not only was a significant proportion of the army made up of lowland units, or at the very least contingents raised in the eastern Highlands, but by the time it was all over there were as many clansmen in arms against the Pretender as were found following his banner.

The Campbells famously remained loyal to the government, but they were not alone in doing so and during the '45 stood shoulder to shoulder with such unlikely allies as the MacDonalds of Sleat. They, together with the Mackays, Munroes, Sutherlands, Grants and the other so-called 'Whig' clans, evidently considered loyalty to the government to be more important than any nebulous notions of Gaelic solidarity. It was in any case the clan chiefs who determined whether their followers should be pulled out on to the heather willingly or not and they, from Cape Wrath to the Mull of Kintyre, were solidly anglicised and actuated more by worldly concerns than cultural ones.

4

Consequently, active support for the Stuarts in 1745 was principally found in Lochaber and elsewhere around the Great Glen, largely following the old patterns of allegiance originally established during the Great Civil War of a century before. While it is certainly the case that some Catholic clans such as the McDonnells of Glengarry joined in the rebellion, some other equally staunch Catholics further out in the Hebrides conspicuously failed to do so.

The great majority of the rebels were Protestants, albeit for the most part of the Episcopalian variety, although there were a few Presbyterians amongst them too. Nevertheless, while the conflict was by no means a religious one per se and at no time ever really threatened to turn into one, it is undoubtedly significant that Jacobites and Episcopalians were virtually synonymous since that church had most heartily embraced the old nonsense of the divine right of kings. Dr Archibald Cameron, Locheil's younger brother and de facto Lieutenant-Colonel of his regiment was only one of many Jacobites to cite 'Christian loyalty' as a major factor in his decision to follow the Prince.

Outside the Highlands the position looked even bleaker for the Jacobites. Although a strong but diminishing tradition of personal loyalty to the Stuarts was maintained in some quarters – not least in the strongly Episcopalian north-east – by 1745 it had become increasingly difficult to generate real enthusiasm for a family which had not sat on the throne for over fifty years.

This was particularly true in England where the Stuarts were themselves comparatively recent (and foreign) incomers. After all, a bare 85 years separated the accession of King James VI to the English throne in 1603 and his grandson's ignominious flight from it in 1688. Moreover, twenty of these years had been taken up with a particularly bloody civil war and interregnum. It was a very shaky foundation upon which to base an appeal for loyalty to the rightful lawful king. The wonder is not that so few joined the Stuart banner in 1745, but that any turned out at all.

The actual incumbent of the British throne – who by 1745 was King George II – might have enjoyed no great popularity in Scotland it is true, particularly after the introduction of excise duties, and the repressive measures which followed the infamous Porteous riot in 1737 led to something of a nationalist revival. Nevertheless, translating ancient loyalty and grumbling unpopularity into a full scale armed insurrection on behalf of a virtual stranger from Rome was to be no easy matter.

Without that still extant opposition to the Union, it would probably have been quite as impossible to raise appreciable numbers of men in Scotland as it soon turned out to be in England. Even this opposition, two generations after the Union, was in some measure beginning to fade in the face of the growing prosperity which the Union appeared to have brought.

Glasgow was perhaps the most striking beneficiary of the Union. After 1707, the removal of trading barriers meant that Scots merchants at last enjoyed legitimate access to the English colonies in North America and the Caribbean. Glasgow was ideally situated to take advantage of this trade and under the 'Tobacco Lords' grew dramatically in size, wealth and importance. A combination of stout Protestantism and commercial success ensured that in 1745 its citizens were in no doubt whatever as to where their best interests lay. It is no coincidence that the Glasgow Volunteers was to be one of the more active Loyalist units.

India too began to attract Scottish capital. The ill-fated Darien venture of the 1690s – Scotland's attempt to open trading links with the Indies – had in part been stifled by the opposition of the rival English East India Company, but now Scots entrepreneurs began buying their way into its successor, the United East India Company and ironically, by the end of the century they had turned it into something akin to a Scottish mafia. Inter alia such close identification with 'English' commercial interests ensured a corresponding shift away from the more traditional Franco-Scots trading alignment.

All of this was well recognised even at the time and the Jacobites themselves were only too well aware that should another generation pass without a Stuart restoration, the cause would be lost forever. In the wake of the nationalist revival in 1737 a veteran Jacobite, John Gordon of Glenbucket, was commissioned by McDonnell of Glengarry and others to seek James's permission to undertake a rebellion, with or without foreign assistance. James, quite sensibly turned down Glenbucket's scheme since he was unable to produce any real evidence of support for the venture in Scotland and James was in any case convinced that it would require the assistance of some 10,000 to 12,000 regular troops. At that point however there was absolutely no realistic prospect of obtaining them from France or anywhere else.

King Louis XV of France had little or nothing to gain and a great deal to lose from active intervention in British politics at this point. Britain and France had been at peace for over twenty years and, although that peace might not be a particularly amicable one, it was still not to be thrown over lightly. There was however a potential source for conflict in the colonies especially after 1739 when Britain went to war with Spain in the Caribbean. Once again therefore, in 1741, the Jacobite chiefs rather optimistically offered to raise 20,000 men if they could first be joined by 6,000 regulars from the famous Irish Brigade. But French priorities at this time were still essentially Continental and the offer was politely declined.

Lying on the western edge of Europe and surrounded by water, Britain could afford to take a reasonably detached view of Continental politics. France on the other hand with her long land frontier could not and in that same year became involved in the War of the Austrian Succession.

The origins of this particular conflict need not detain us here. Suffice it to say that the Imperial crown fell vacant and the principal claimant was Charles Albert, a Bavarian. France was Bavaria's long-standing ally, indeed Bavaria was virtually a client state, and readily provided French troops to support Charles Albert's pretensions.

However, another and much more legitimate claimant was the Hapsburg Maria Theresa of Austria and amongst her supporters was numbered the Elector of Hanover. He of course also happened at the same time to be King George II of Great Britain and not surprisingly British soldiers were soon sent to bolster Maria Theresa's troops. Initially they were shipped across to the Austrian Netherlands [modern Belgium] in 1742, but in the following year they joined George's Hanoverian regiments in southern Germany. Thus at Dettingen on the 27th of June 1743 a largely British army, led by King George in person, took on a French army and beat it although neither country was at the time officially at war with the other.

Thus far all the Jacobite overtures to the French government had been ignored or deflected, initially for diplomatic reasons and latterly because the necessary troops were much more urgently required in Germany. Now, with the war going badly, French priorities suddenly changed and Louis XV like his father before him resolved to mount a massive diversionary attack on Britain.

The plan was at once simple and potentially highly effective. Without even the minor courtesy of a formal declaration of war, some 10,000–12,000 men led by Marechal Saxe, one of the foremost soldiers of the day, were to land at Maldon in Essex and immediately march on an undefended London. Meanwhile a further 3,000 men, led by a Jacobite exile, George Keith, the hereditary Earl Marischal of Scotland were to be sent northwards to that kingdom. Both forces were confidently predicted to be joined on their arrival by large numbers of Jacobite sympathisers.

The rather startling notion that the county of Essex was stuffed full of Jacobites ready to rush to arms at the first appearance of French 'liberators' was quite laughable. Otherwise the plan was at least workable, and if it succeeded in toppling the government and placing James VIII on the throne of his ancestors, Britain would be at once changed from an implacable foe into a close ally. Even if this highly desirable result proved impractical however, the very least which could reasonably be expected was a temporary or even permanent British withdrawal from the Continent in order to deal with the crisis.

The sudden appearance of James in Paris would have fatally compromised operational security, so instead his then rather less conspicuous son Charles Edward duly arrived post haste from Rome to join the expedition, only to see it utterly collapse at the last minute.

At the beginning of March 1744 Saxe began embarking the twenty battalions destined for Essex. According to Lord Elcho, who was intending to join the expedition armed with the Prince's commission as Colonel of Dragoons, the following units were ordered to be assembled at Dunkirk; four battalions of the Regiment Navarre [one of the oldest in the French army], three battalions of Monaco, two each of Gondrin, D'Eu, Diesbach and La Cour au Chantre, and one battalion apiece from the regiments Beauffremont, Royal Corse, Royal la Marine, Soissonois and Languedoc. In addition there were two dismounted cavalry regiments, Mailly Cavalerie and the Dauphin Dragoons. All except the blue-coated Royal Corse and Diesbach's red-coated Swiss were French units.[4]

In accordance with earlier requests from the Scottish Jacobites, the Irish Brigade was earmarked to go to Scotland with the Marischal, though one cannot help but feel that their red coats would have received a better welcome in Essex than the French King's white coats.

Nevertheless, this expeditionary force was, by any reckoning, a serious threat to the British government or at least it would be were it ever allowed to land. By now the plan was to disembark the troops at Blackwall, just a few miles down the Thames estuary from London. Dunkirk was notoriously difficult to blockade, but in order to ensure that the crossing went smoothly Amiral de Rocquefeuil was ordered out of Brest with twenty-two ships of the line. His orders were to lure the British fleet commanded by Sir John Norris into a battle somewhere off the Isle of Wight. Win or lose, with the Royal Navy safely out of the way, Saxe ought then to be able to get his men across the Channel and safely ashore without undue interference.

Instead Rocquefeuil, having reached Spithead without finding any sign of Norris, blithely assumed, for no discernable reason, that old Sir John lay safely out of harm's way at Portsmouth and so decided to join Saxe instead. Norris however, having been forewarned by the British intelligence service, was actually cruising off Dungeness at the time, patiently waiting for Saxe to poke his nose out of the Dunkirk Roads. The two fleets therefore bumped into each other off Dungeness on the 6th of March, but with night and dirty weather coming on fast, both Admirals dropped anchor and waited for morning. As the night wore on the wind turned into a strong gale, perhaps even a hurricane and Rocquefeuil, who was in any case badly outnumbered, gratefully took the opportunity to run before it back to Brest.

The storm also dispersed Norris's fleet thus briefly uncovering

Dunkirk. There Saxe had begun embarking his men on the 5th of March, but it was necessary to ferry them some distance out to the transports in small shallow draught boats called *bijlanders* and this process was desperately slow. Nevertheless by the following night he had succeeded in getting sixteen of his infantry battalions and the Dauphin Dragoons (without their horses) aboard the ships anchored in the Roads. With the right combination of wind and tide Saxe and his men might then still have been successfully lifted across to the Thames without Rocquefeuil's dubious assistance.

Fortunately, the same violent storm which dispersed the battle-fleets also succeeded in sinking or driving ashore twelve of the invasion ships. There was considerable loss of life, and after a second storm on the 11th sank some more of the transports, Saxe decided that he had had quite enough of maritime adventures. Louis agreed and little more than two weeks later he formally declared war on Britain and ordered a much relieved Saxe and his men northwards into the Netherlands and eventual victory at Fontenoy in the following year.[5]

This abrupt switch in priorities was partly a return to the traditional French policy of aggressively defending her land frontiers at the expense of foreign adventures, and partly the price of an alliance with Frederick of Prussia. Anxious as he was to see pro-Hapsburg British troops neutralised or even withdrawn from Germany as a result of war with France, Frederick was even more anxious that the French troops whose assistance he craved should not follow them to England.

Thus abandoned by their French patrons as swiftly as they had been embraced, the Jacobites might have been forgiven for despairing, but Louis, perhaps by way of insurance, allowed Prince Charles Edward to remain in Paris where he naturally became the focus of considerable intrigue.

For a time the Prince had to be forcefully dissuaded from joining the French Army in Flanders, but denied this, his thoughts turned once more to regaining the British throne for his father. Understandably dismayed by the prospect of the Prince alone turning up on their doorstep, a number of Scottish Jacobites despatched John Murray of Broughton to warn him that without at least 6,000 French regulars to back him up, (and £30,000 in gold) he could not count on their support.

There was nothing new in this entirely reasonable demand but Charles remained intent on going it alone if he had to. Broughton thereupon assured him that if he did so he would be lucky to raise 4,000 men in the Western Highlands – a prediction which eventually turned out to be remarkably accurate. At the same time however he spoilt the effect by falling in with the Prince's plans to the extent of arranging the assembling of supplies of arms.

In any case a far more pressing difficulty facing the Prince at this time was a simple shortage of hard cash. Limping by with a French pension and the odd bank loan from sympathetic Scots exiles to cover his everyday expenses (and purchase some cheap broadswords), he suddenly had a stroke of luck.

Early in 1745 Lord Clare, the commander of the Irish Brigade, introduced Charles to a consortium of émigré Irish ship-owners based in Nantes and St Malo. Before the war they had made their considerable fortunes by shipping slaves from Africa to the Caribbean. Now, with that odious trade temporarily interrupted by hostilities they had just as successfully turned to privateering or licensed piracy.

The consortium therefore commanded both the money and more importantly access to the shipping which Charles desperately needed if he were finally to set foot on British soil. Conversely, financial and practical support for the Jacobite cause at this stage would clearly reap considerable later rewards for the slavers in the event of a second Stuart restoration. One of them, Antoine or Anthony Walsh therefore agreed to carry the Prince to Scotland in his 16-gun frigate *Le du Teillay*.

The little frigate required an escort of some kind in case it was intercepted by the Royal Navy and for this purpose another of the Irish slavers, Sir Walter Ruttledge, chartered an elderly naval vessel of 64 guns named *L'Elisabeth*. Ostensibly, she was to be sent privateering in the Caribbean, not gallivanting off to Scotland, and although the old battleship was patently too large and too slow for service as a corsair, it may well be the case that the French Minister of Marine, the Comte de Maurepas, was geniunely deceived by this all-too-transparent cover story. It is somewhat more likely, however, that the apparent subterfuge merely served to allow Maurepas (and perhaps even the King himself) a comfortable degree of deniability in the event of things subsequently turning out badly.

Thus it was that bereft of official (if not clandestine) French backing, Charles Edward Stuart sailed from Belle Isle on the 5th of July 1745. The *Le du Teillay* carried 1,500 firelocks, 1,800 swords and £4,000 in gold, while the *L'Elisabeth* freighted a further 2,000 firelocks, 600 swords, and in an almost pathetic gesture towards the 6,000 regular troops demanded by the Scottish Jacobites, 60 marines recruited by Lord Clare, clad in blue coats turned up with red and rather intriguingly named the 'Compagnie Maurepas' after the French minister who allegedly knew nothing of their intended destination.

Late on the 9th and a hundred miles west of the Lizard this shoestring invasion force was intercepted by Captain Percy Brett's HMS *Lyon*, of 58 guns. Unable to outrun her, Captain Dau of the *L'Elisabeth* fought the *Lyon* instead and both ships proceeded to pound each other into floating wrecks. As usual the French gunners fired high and Brett afterwards reported the loss of his mizzen-mast and a great deal of other rigging besides many shots through the hull which left 45 men killed and 107 wounded. On the other hand 56 of Dau's men were also killed and 176 wounded before night brought the engagement to a close.[6]

Walsh, aboard the *Le du Teillay*, kept the Prince safely out of the fight, despite Dau's request for assistance and the shattered *L'Elisabeth* limped back to Brest that night still carrying the surviving marines and those vital 2,000 firelocks. Undaunted, Walsh doggedly sailed on northwards. Despite the setback Charles Edward was still resolutely determined to raise his father's standard in Scotland. In any case, too much of the slavers' money had already been invested for Walsh lightly to abandon the enterprise now. In the event he made his landfall unmolested and after a decidedly lukewarm welcome on Eriskay, he landed the Prince and at least nine companions on the shores of Loch nan Uamh, in Arisaig on the 25th of July 1745.

The Jacobite chiefs had tentatively committed themselves to a rising only on the firm understanding that they would be armed and supported by a considerable French expeditionary force. Indeed as late as May 1745 they had hurriedly despatched yet another message to that effect. Not surprisingly Charles Edward's sudden arrival with no money, very few arms and worse still not a single French grenadier at his back inspired more alarm than rapture amongst his putative followers.

The powerful Skye chieftains, Norman MacLeod of MacLeod and Sir Alexander MacDonald of Sleat flatly refused to join him and they were not alone in this, but eventually support was promised by Ranald Mac-Donald, younger of Clanranald, Donald MacDonnell of Scotus, representing Glengarry, and by Alexander Macdonnell of Keppoch. All three men raised regiments for the Prince, but without the eventual, albeit reluctant, adherence of Donald Cameron of Locheil it is unlikely that any real headway would have been made.

Sources

1. See : Paul Hopkins *Glencoe and the end of the Highland War*, Edinburgh 1986.
2. See : J.S. Gibson, *Playing the Scottish Card*, Edinburgh 1988.
3. See : John Baynes, *The Jacobite Rising of 1715*, London 1970.
4. Elcho, *Affairs of Scotland*, p. 230.
5. McLynn, F. *France and the Jacobite Rising of 1745*, p. 24.
6. Gibson, J.S., *Ships of the '45*, p. 11–12.

CHAPTER 2

A Tour in the Highlands
Cope's March North

Although soon aware that something was up, the British army's Commander-in-Chief Scotland, Lieutenant General Sir John Cope, faced certain difficulties. In the first place the reported insurrection was remote from his headquarters, and in the second place his initiative was severely limited by the fact that he was constrained to follow the advice or rather orders given to him by his immediate political superior the Secretary of State for Scotland, John Hay, 4th Marquis of Tweeddale, but he, alas, was safely esconced in London and hopelessly out of touch with what was actually happening.

Not the least of the problems facing Cope was a shortage of sufficient men capable of undertaking any effective military operations. In his evidence to the subsequent inquiry into the defeat at Prestonpans, he recalled:

'As much as I can remember on the 2nd of July the troops in Scotland were quartered thus;
Gardiner's Dragoons at Stirling, Linlithgow, Musselburgh, Kelso and Coldstream.
Hamilton's Dragoons at Haddington, Duns and the adjacent places.
N.B. – both regiments at Grass.
Guise's Regiment of foot at Aberdeen, and the Coast-Quarters.
Five Companies of Lee's at Dumfries, Stranraer, Glasgow and Stirling.
Murray's in the Highland Barracks.Lascelles' at Edinburgh and Leith.
Two Additional Companies of the Royals at Perth.
Two Do. of the Scottish Fuziliers at Glasgow.
Two Do. of Lord Semple's at Cupar in Fife.
Three Do. of Lord John Murray's Highland Regiment at Crieff.
Lord Loudoun's Regiment was beginning to be raised; and besides these, there were the standing garrisons of invalids in the castles.' [1]

The more closely this list is examined, the less prepossessing it appears.

Neither Gardiner's 13th nor Hamilton's 14th Dragoons had ever been in action before and as Cope points out they were widely dispersed in their quarters. Their horses were also at grass and although ordered to be rounded up on the 3rd of August they were consequently soft-backed and therefore quite unfit for much in the way of hard work. At the same time the troopers themselves will have been spending the summer going through the infantry part of their training cycle – practising platoon-firing rather than cavalry drills. Between them, according to figures published at the time by the *Scots Magazine* the two regiments mustered 567 rank and file at Prestonpans.[2]

Guise's 6th Foot was the only regiment under Cope's command which could reasonably be described as a veteran unit and was said to have been nearly up to its full establishment of 780 rank and file. However as recently as May 1743 it had been able to muster only 674 men and after drafting was down to just 603 men by July in the following year. This means that if the regiment was indeed up to strength in the summer of 1745 then very nearly a quarter of the men in its ranks were relatively new recruits.[3] In any case by the time Cope was forced to take the field they had moved on from Aberdeen and the 'coast quarters' to take over responsibility for the Highland forts. They were not therefore available for operations and so need not be considered in the present equation.

As for the other regiments under Cope's command, all of them were newly raised, their Colonels having been granted their Letters of Service as recently as the summer of 1741 and thereafter they had spent all of their short existence in Scotland, whence they quite logically drew most of their recruits. Colonel John Lee's 55th Foot however had five of its companies in garrison at Berwick-upon-Tweed, in England and these were therefore outwith Cope's control. Happily the five remaining companies, led by Lieutenant-Colonel Peter Halkett, younger of Pitfirran, could probably muster something in the region of 291 rank and file at Prestonpans, so they must have been pretty well up to their established strength.[4]

Colonel Thomas Murray's 57th Foot on the other hand mustered about 580 men at Prestonpans,[5] but having until lately been scattered in a variety of forts and small posts across the length and breadth of the Highlands their battalion level training cannot have been of a very high order.

Colonel Peregrine Lascelles' 58th Foot, earlier dispersed on road-building, was now reasonably well concentrated at Edinburgh and therefore the best placed of all Cope's regiments to carry out some meaningful training, but it was judged expedient to place two companies into the castle in order to reinforce the garrison. Nevertheless Whitefoord records 593 rank and file present at Aberdeen plus another 100 officers, NCOs and drummers – although this total includes two companies of Guise's 6th.[6]

A fifth battalion, the Earl of Loudon's 64th Highlanders had, as Cope

13

remarks, only just commenced recruiting, and the first officers' commissions were signed in June. Its few men were virtually unarmed, almost certainly without uniforms and could by no stretch of the imagination be considered fit for anything, let alone active service.[7] In a similar state were the nine 'Additional Companies' scattered throughout Scotland. These were no more than depot units processing recruits for the British army's Scottish regiments. By Cope's testimony, they numbered about twenty-five wholly untrained men apiece:

> 'As to the Additional Companies of the Royal, Scotch Fuziliers and Semple's, by reason of the draughts made from them, and the difficulty the officers met with in getting men, I believe I may safely say, that upon the average they did not exceed 25 men per company, and those all new-raised men. The three Additional Companies of Lord John Murray's, I believe might be pretty near complete;'[8]

All in all, therefore, Cope could actually count on just two and a half weak battalions of infantry to form his marching army, none of whom had ever seen action before, and whose arms, described in 1744 as 'indifferent', were now 'consequently worse'.[9] And of course he also had two similarly untried dragoon regiments. The limitations of his little army were made all too apparent by the fate of the two Additional Companies of the Royals or 1st Foot.

Although the regiment is now firmly linked with the Lothians, throughout the 18th century the Royal Scots [as they became] actually found a fair proportion of their officers and recruits in the Highlands, and for that purpose therefore both of the Additional Companies were quartered in Perth at the beginning of July and had moved on to Fort Augustus a month later. Aware of the deteriorating situation, the governor of that place, Major Hu Wentworth of Guise's 6th, took it upon himself to order them south on the 16th of August, in order to reinforce the rather more exposed garrison at Fort William instead.

Given that the two companies under Captain John Scott and Captain James Thomson can have mustered no more than fifty wholly untrained men between them and were, as the Lord President sadly remarked, 'without anything Royal but the name' this was the height of folly. Nevertheless, and perhaps for that very reason, they almost got away with it, but were ambushed at High Bridge over the river Spean, just eight miles from safety. As it happens, at first the Royals were faced by only a dozen men under Donald MacDonnell of Tiendrish, but he kept them well concealed and unaware of this, Captain Scott attempted to withdraw. A running fight then ensued as more and more Highlanders arrived, in which two of the Royals were killed and Scott himself was slightly wounded. Hard pressed, Scott attempted to seek refuge in Invergarry, but was forestalled by yet more hostile Highlanders. By now surrounded, Scott formed a hollow square and tried to keep moving, but then MacDonnell of Keppoch arrived and called upon them to surrender. Exhausted and seeing no prospect of escape, Scott and his raw recruits finally laid down their arms.

Although the propaganda value was considerable, the Royals had in all the circumstances performed remarkably well and moreover stoutly refused all the blandishments offered to them both then and subsequently to change sides. Indeed as Colonel John Sullivan ruefully remarked; 'non of them wou'd take party, they were a great charge to us being obliged to escort them, and to see them every night into houses, whereas our men lay out in the open air,'[10]

It was an encouraging start though, and in the wake of this happy success, the Rebel standard was formally raised at Glenfinnan, on the 19th upon a rising piece of ground some distance from the present memorial:

'... the Prince parted from Kenloc-Moudiogh [Kinlochmoidart] wth about two hundred of Clenranold's men, to go to Glenfeenan wch was two days march ... Locheil arrived the day appointed, which was the 19th, with about 700 good men, but ill-armed; Kapock arrived the same day, with about 350 clivor fellows; yt Succour, tho' smale, made a very good appearance & began to raise every body's spirits.'[11]

Sir John Cope meanwhile had been assembling his meagre forces at Stirling. His original plan was simply to march straight into the Highlands and thus nip the affair in the bud. This was after all why old General Wade had set in train his famous road-building programme and he wrote in those terms to the Marquis of Tweeddale on the 10th of August:

'Upon a supposition, that the Persons mentioned in the last Account sent to your Lordship, would not venture to land without previously being encouraged by a Rising of some considerable Numbers of Highlanders in their Favour, the King's Servants, viz. the Lord President, the Lord Advocate, and the Solicitor General, have been of Opinion with me, that the most effectual Way of putting a Stop to wavering People joining with the Disaffected, so as to make a formidable body, was immediately to march to stop their Progress; ... This sudden March, with the Show only of some Artillery, &c. I am in Hopes and do believe with the rest of the King's Servants, will put a Stop to the Design some of his Majesty's Enemies may have to rise in Favour of the Pretender: And if it should not, small as my Force is, I will go to the first Body I can meet of them, and try to check their Proceedings ...'[12]

Resolute words indeed, but as further intelligence reports came in, all steadily inflating the Rebels' strength, it became apparent that it would

be extremely unwise to push only fifteen companies of Foot into the
Highlands. Finding sufficient men to do the job was far from easy. All
that he could actually muster fit to march were Murray's 57th, and
Lascelles' 58th Foot [less the two companies placed in Edinburgh Castle]
and the half battalion of Lee's 55th. Moreover should he march this whole
force northwards he was understandably apprehensive that Edinburgh
would be left exposed to a French landing in his absence. Consequently
Cope requested that the other five companies of Lee's should be marched
up from Berwick in order to secure the capital and had they done so
things might well have turned out very differently. As it was they never
stirred.[13]

The Additional Companies of Campbell's 21st and Sempill's 25th were
also left at Glasgow and at Stirling respectively,[14] but two of Lord John
Murray's Black Watch companies [neither of whom had broadswords],
commanded by Captains Aeneas MacIntosh of MacIntosh and Sir Peter
Murray of Ochtertyre, were added to his expeditionary force and the
third, under Captain Duncan Campbell of Inverawe, despatched to
Inveraray in order to 'assist the civil Magistrates in seizing the Boats, in
order to prevent the Rebels from coming in from the Western Islands
and in other services.'[15]

There was obviously going to be no point in taking his two dragoon
regiments into the hills, so Gardiner's 13th were concentrated at Perth
and Stirling, while Hamilton's 14th covered Leith and Edinburgh in his
absence. The brigade was left under the command of the senior officer,
Colonel James Gardiner, a 57 year old professional soldier, pending the
imminent arrival from England of Brigadier Thomas Fowke.

By way of an artillery train Cope had just four obsolete one and a half
pound curricle guns or gallopers[16] and four coehorn mortars, which might
well have been sufficient, were it not for the fact that he had only Major
Eaglesfield Griffith, the Master Gunner of Edinburgh Castle, and four
Invalids – one of whom had served in the old Scots Train before the
Union in 1707 – to man them.[17]

As for his staff, this comprised Colonel John Campbell, the Earl of
Loudon, serving as Adjutant General, Major William Caulfield, his
Quartermaster General, and Major James Mossman of the 55th, his principal Aide de Camp. In addition to looking after the guns, Major Griffith
also acted as Commissary General. One other officer who was to make
himself extremely useful to Cope was Lieutenant Colonel Charles
Whitefoord of Cochrane's 5th Marines. There being no requirement for
field officers of Marines to serve on board ships, he was on leave in
Scotland at the outbreak of the rising and immediately volunteered his
services. For some reason he declined a formal appointment either as
Adjutant General or Aide de Camp, preferring as he said to serve 'without

the emoluments attached to posts of official preferrment'. Instead he served as a transport officer, taking much of the burden off the aged Major Griffith's shoulders.

Although he was by now beginning to have considerable doubts about marching into the hills, Cope's orders from Tweeddale left him with no alternative but to march northwards on the 20th of August with the five companies of Lee's 55th, all ten companies of Murray's 57th and the two Black Watch companies. The eight companies of Lascelles' 58th had not yet got their camp equipage in order, so he pushed on to Crieff, leaving them to follow next day with a hundred horse-loads of bread and an additional 1,000 stand of arms [firelock and bayonet complete] in order to equip the expected loyalist volunteers.

In point of fact it became abundantly clear at Crieff that despite the promises which he had received from the Duke of Atholl and one of his younger brothers, Lord George Murray[18], and from Lord Glenorchy [representing his father, the Earl of Breadalbane] no-one was prepared to join him. Far from receiving and substantial reinforcements, all that came in were some unarmed and wholly untrained drafts for Loudon's 64th Highlanders. On the contrary, although desertion does not appear to have been a problem as far as his regulars were concerned, the two Black Watch companies 'mouldered away'.

Not surprisingly he was inclined to call the whole thing off, but then he received yet another peremptory letter from Tweeddale, ordering him to proceed northwards. Both Tweeddale and the Scottish law officers on the spot were evidently of the opinion that the rebellion had to be crushed before too many of their friends and neighbours were tempted to join the Prince's standard. Purely military considerations therefore had to give way to political expediency and Cope, 'a neat fussy little man' who owed his rank and position to wealth and influence rather than any outstanding military ability, gave way: 'My Orders in the Marquis's Letters of the 13th, 15th and 17th, the two first of which I received at Edinburgh and the last at Crieff were positive, and I was clearly of Opinion that I had nothing left to me but to Obey.' [19]

Sending 700 stand of arms back to Stirling, he reluctantly headed northwards. His initial objective was still Fort Augustus, the central position in what was known as the 'Chain' stretching along the strategically important Great Glen. The 'Chain' proper comprised three large firebases; Fort William at the southern end, Fort Augustus in the middle and Fort George [Inverness] at the northern end. There were in addition a number of smaller outposts such as the small barracks at Bernera overlooking the crossing to Skye, but the three firebases were originally planned to accommodate sufficient troops to move out and deal with any insurrection. Unfortunately the single infantry battalion assigned to look after all the

Highland forts was barely sufficient to defend them, let alone to undertake any offensive operations by itself. Fort Augustus in particular was considered to be especially vulnerable as it was split between two sites. Cope considered it imperative therefore that he should be able to throw 300 additional men into at least one of the firebases as soon as possible, and Fort Augustus was the obvious choice.

Meanwhile the rebels too were on the move now and spoiling for a fight. Since Glenfinnan they had been joined by young Glengarry and his MacDonnells so that they now numbered a fairly respectable 1,800 men. In order to reach Fort Augustus, Cope was going to have to lead his men over the seventeen traverses of the Corrieyairack Pass, and it was there that they elected to meet him, allegedly emplacing a number of swivel guns in 'sleeping batteries'[20] to enfilade the traverses.

Forewarned by Captain John Sweetenham, an officer of Guise's who had been captured by the rebels and subsequently released on parole, Cope halted at Dalwhinnie on the 26th of August and called a Council of War. Four options were open to him: he could either carry on with his original plan and attempt to force the Corrieyairack, he could stand fast at Dalwhinnie and offer battle there, he could retire to Stirling and hold the line of the Forth, or failing all of these, he could turn northwards and make for Inverness.

The first option was rejected unanimously; the Corrieyairack was a difficult enough climb at the best of times and certainly far too strong to be forced with the troops at hand. Nor for that matter was there much point in standing around at Dalwhinnie. There was no guarantee that the rebels would accept a battle at that particular spot and in any case Major Caulfield, the Quartermaster General, reported that there was insufficient food available locally to support the army while it waited to see if they would. The third course was similarly rejected. Cope and his officers quite properly recognised that a strategic withdrawal, however presented, would be seen as a defeat. Already the army had suffered considerable harassment and every night more pack-horses were stolen and bread-bags ripped open. A retreat now through increasingly hostile territory might well result in utter disaster.

The only realistic option open to them was to make for Fort George at Inverness, which, since it was one of the 'Chain' forts, would at least allow Cope to fulfil the letter if not the spirit of his orders, and to this resolution the officers composing the Council of War readily put their hands.[21]

Nevertheless Cope and his men were still not out of danger, and on the night of the 27th, while he was encamped at Ruthven Barracks, Cope received word both from one of his agents and also from Captain Ewen MacPherson of Cluny, an officer in the 64th Highlanders, that having been disappointed of fighting him at Corrieyairack, the rebels now hoped to ambush him in the steep and narrow Slochd Mor pass, between Carrbridge and Tomatin.[22] There was no time to lose. The Laird of Grant promised to secure the pass with his men, but then almost at once announced rather unconvincingly that he was himself in danger of attack and consequently quite unable to assist. If he was to avoid the trap Cope was going to have to march hard and march fast. On the following morning he added Captain George Holwell's company of Guise's 6th to his little army and raced northwards. Reluctant to abandon the fort entirely however he left behind in its place 'a very good Serjeant and twelve men, with a good quantity of Ammunition.' Evidently less than sanguine about their chances, his only orders to the sergeant were to tip the meal stored there into the well before surrendering.

Outpacing the rebels he then successfully crossed the Slochd Mor without interference and thankfully arrived in the comparative security of Inverness on the 29th. Unlike Tweeddale, the Lord President, Duncan Forbes of Culloden was not only on the spot but doing his utmost to contain the rebellion. Indeed he more than any other individual would be responsible for its ultimate failure and he had already made a famous start by dissuading MacDonald of Sleat and MacLeod of MacLeod from joining the rebels.[23] He was also a diligent recruiter and Cope was at last joined by his first substantial reinforcement since leaving Crieff; three incomplete companies of Loudon's 64th Highlanders and a 200-strong loyalist battalion raised by Captain George Monro of Culcairn.

While Cope was conferring with the Lord President and making arrangements to get safely back to Edinburgh as quickly as possible, a party of Camerons led by Locheil's brother Archy, and the rebel Adjutant General, an Irish professional soldier named Colonel John Sullivan, attacked the little garrison left behind in Ruthven Barracks. A stoutly built 45-year-old from County Kerry, Sullivan had held a French commission since 1721 and was a Captain on the General Staff when the Prince, desperately short of military advisors, invited him to join his side with the rank of Colonel. Much maligned by later historians, Sullivan was in fact a highly competent staff officer[24] and was by his own showing far from keen on this particular enterprise which actually seems to have been dreamed up by a veteran Jacobite, John Gordon of Glenbucket:

'It was determined the next day, yt the Prince wou'd not follow Cope, but wou'd make the best of his way to Blair, to raise the Athol men. The day the Prince was to decamp, Sullivan parted as usual to reconnoitre the Camp, & prepare the Prince's quarters, with Lochgarry & some other officers & about thirty men; John Murray was sent in all diligence after him with orders to take the road of Revin, where he'd

meet with Archy Cameron, & attack those Barracks, where there was
only a sergeant & sixteen men. Sullivan cou'd not but obey, but represented the difficulty of it, & yt there were no Barracks, without being
surrounded by walls & flanked, but one Gordon who was of yt neighbourhood, & was the man yt gave the project, assured it was an open
house only. Sullivan parted & met with Mr. Cameron about three mils
from Reven, continued his march as near as he cou'd to the Barracks
without being discover'd; he clad himself there in highland cloaths, &
went to reconnoitre, found this open house to be two buildings upon
a sugar loaf, joyned together by a very high rampart with a parapet,
wch formed a Square & flanked at every corner; there were stables
detached from the barracks & surrounded by a wall breast high, & the
ramp inaccessible in a manner.'

Sullivan's misgivings were well founded. Construction of the barracks
was begun in 1719 on the motte of a former castle, (Sullivan's 'sugarloaf')
and it comprised two three-storey accommodation blocks facing each
other within a square compound. The compound walls were 15 feet high
with a sentry walk carried on open ended vaults and on two (not four)
corners there is an angular bastion-like flanking tower. The main gate,
approached by two traverses (Sullivan's 'ramp') lies on the south side,
while to the north a small sally-port gave access to the quite separate
stable block. The barracks was not designed to withstand artillery, but
was well provided with musket loops. The outer wall of each of the
accommodation blocks is pierced with eight loops on the ground floor
and six more on each of the upper ones. The north and south compound
walls are similarly pierced with eight loopholes apiece and although the
outer walls of the two flanking towers are blank, the inner faces are
pierced with four loopholes apiece in order to allow enfilading fire across
the face of the compound walls.[25]

'Sullivan judged it to be unatackable with highlanders, & without
Cannon, but Gordon, who was, as I have already said, of the neighbourhood, had his raisons to get the Barricks distroyed, & represented yt the
quantity of meal & arms yt wou'd be found there wou'd be of great use.
In short Sullivan asked him whether there cou'd be ladders found, he
assured him there wou'd, then he desired Mr. Cameron & the other Gents
to consult their men if they wou'd attempt to scalled it, which they all
consented to, but when it came to get the laders, there cou'd but one
be found. In the meanwhile it was discovered yt there was a door of
communication from the Barracks to the Stables & yt we cou'd set fire
this door, upon wch an empty barrel was prepared with combustible
matters. The dispossition was made for the attack, thirty men Commanded by one Daniel Cameron at one side, was to plante his lader at

the first fire wch was to begin at the stable side, where Sullivan and Archy [Cameron] were to attack with thirty other men, & the other thirty, in reserve near the villedge. They got into the Stables without opposition, but not without difficulty, the fire was prepared, & set to the door, but there was three steps to mount to this door wch hindred the fire of makeing its effect, not a soul appear'd upon the ramparts, the sixteen men were divided in the flancks, where they were in safety, two men were sent to raise up the barrel and set the fire or flame towards the door, one of wch were killed & the other wounded. Sullivan had two men killed and three wounded at his attack & no sign of life from the other side, where it was not possible to bring up the lader, by the turnings & windings yt were in the ramp, so yt Sullivan after he sent off his dead & wounded made his retrait, & came off with his 'courte haute' & very sorry to have attempted it.'[26]

Inside the barracks, another Irishman, Sergeant Terry Molloy of Lee's 55th Foot sat down to pen his own very blunt and soldierlike account of the affair:

'Ruthven Redoubt, August 30th 1745
Honourable General, This goes to acquaint you, that Yesterday there apeared in the little Town of Ruthven above 300 Men of the Enemy, and sent Proposals to me to surrender this Redoubt, upon Condition that I should have Liberty to carry off Bag and Baggage. My answer was, that I was too old a Soldier to surrender a Garison of such strength. without bloody Noses. They threatened hanging me and my Men for Refusal. I told them I would take my Chance. This Morning they attacked me about twelve o'Clock, by my Information with about 150 Men: They attacked Fore-Gate and Sally-Port, and attempted to set the Sally-Port on Fire, with some old Barrels and other Combustibles, which took Blaze immediately; but the Attempter lost his life by it. They drew off about half an Hour after Three. About two Hours after they sent to me, that two of their Chiefs wanted to talk with me. I admitted and spoke to them from the Parapet. They offered Conditions: I refused. They desired Liberty to carry off their Dead men; I granted. There are two Men since dead of their Wounds in the Town and three more they took with them wounded as I am informed. They went off Westward, about eight o'clock this Morning. They did the like March Yesterday in the Afternoon, but came back at Night fall. They took all the Provisions the poor Inhabitants had in the Town; and Mrs McPherson, the Barrack-Wife and a Merchant of the Town who spoke to me this Moment, and who Advised me to write to your Honour: And told me there were above 3000 Men all lodged in the Cornfields West of the Town last Night, and their grand Camp is at Dalwhinny: They

have Cluny McPherson with them Prisoner, as I have it by the same Information. I lost one Man shot through the Head by foolishly holding his Head too high over the Parapet, contrary to orders. I prevented the Sally-Port taking Fire by pouring Water over the Parapet. I expect another Visit this Night, I am informed, with their Pateraroes [swivel guns] but I shall give them the warmest Reception my weak Party can afford. I shall hold out as long as possible. I conclude, Honourable General, with great Respect.

Your most obedient and humble Servant

MOLLOY, Sergeant[27]

Cope promptly forwarded this letter to Tweeddale with the generous recommendation that Molloy should be 'made an Officer for his gallant Behaviour'. In this matter at least the Secretary of State for Scotland acted promptly and on the 12th of September 1745 the Commission Registers record the promotion of 'Terence Molloy, Gent. Lieut to Company in Colonel Lee's Regiment of Foot.'[28]

The news about Cluny's capture was a bad blow though, and worse was to follow. He had met with Cope at Dalnacardoch a few days earlier, and on the 27th warned him of the intended ambush in the Slochd Mor. But now, like MacDonnell of Lochgarry, he defected to the rebels, not only taking his company of the 64th Highlanders with him, but also promising to raise the rest of his clan for the Prince.

In the meantime, Cope's abrupt departure from the scene momentarily left the Jacobites at something of a loose end. Far from immediately seizing the initiative by pushing southwards, they were initially extremely concerned at the prospect of proceeding southwards while leaving Cope loose in their rear. Some at first flatly refused to go, while as the Prince's secretary, John Murray of Broughton put it:

'The Consequences of going to the Low Country and leaving the Enemy intire behind him [the Prince] were to obvious to be overlooked.' [29]

The first reaction to the news of his marching towards Inverness was to pursue him northwards or at least to try to head him off at the Slochd Mor pass, although thanks to the speed of his march this particular idea did not in the end get beyond the abortive attack on Ruthven Barracks. Instead, an advance southwards into Perthshire was rather tentatively embarked upon and they reached Blair Castle on the 30th of August. Duke James had prudently taken himself off and an agreeable pause of two days was spent there while the army rested and potential supporters were sounded out.

Reinforced by the Stewarts of Appin under Charles Stewart of Ardshiel, the Rebels next marched into Perth on the 3rd of September. It was the first town of any size to fall to the insurgents and a considerable number of volunteers joined the Prince there, the most notable amongst them being the titular Duke of Perth and Lord George Murray.

Until now the army had more or less been run by committee with Colonel Sullivan looking after the details as Adjutant General. Now, however, three Lieutenant Generals were appointed. The first was Tullibardine, whom the Jacobites regarded as the rightful Duke of Atholl, and the second, the Duke of Perth, a long-time Jacobite plotter, once memorably dismissed as a 'silly horse-racing boy', who; 'though brave even to excess, every way honourable, and possessed of a mild and gentle disposition, was of very limited abilities and interfered with nothing.'[30] The third, and unquestionably the most able, was Lord George Murray.

The 51-year-old Murray had been 'out' in 1715 and 1719, but latterly his Jacobite credentials were badly compromised by the fact that a pardon was obtained for him by his loyalist brother, Duke James and that he had subsequently kept out of Jacobite circles. Indeed only a few weeks earlier he had accepted an appointment as a Sheriff Depute for Perthshire and in that capacity met Cope at Crieff and endeavoured, albeit without success, to raise men for King George.[31]

The urging of his Jacobite brother, Duke William, may have brought him 'out' again, but it is a measure of his initial uncertainty that he joined the Prince at Perth rather than Blair: 'tho'' as Sullivan remarks, 'his carracter was not of the best . . . his presence nevertheless was thought necessary, to determine the Athol men to joyn, as I don't doubt but it did, to' few or none of them had confidence in him in the beginning.'[32]

To make matters worse, although he soon proved in Sullivan's words to be a 'very active sturring man' he was not without considerable faults as even one of his own aide de camps, a bumptious Edinburgh snob named James Johnstone candidly admitted:

'Lord George was vigilant, active, and diligent; his plans were always judiciously formed, and he carried them promptly and vigorously into execution. However, with an infinity of good qualities, he was not without his defects: proud, haughty, blunt and imperious, he wished to have the exclusive disposal of everything and, feeling his superiority, would listen to no advice.'[33]

For the moment these faults, if apparent, were overlooked for Murray's support was considered essential if the Athollmen were to rise for the Prince. Before very long, however, he would be thoroughly distrusted by the Prince and many of his advisors, both Scots and Irish.

Encouraged by growing support, the rebels left Perth on the 11th of September and two days later crossed the Forth, eight miles above Stirling Castle, by the Fords of Frew. No attempt was made to stop them there by Colonel Gardiner and his 13th Dragoons, who instead fell back steadily on Edinburgh.

Sources

1. *The Report of the Proceedings and Opinion of the Board of General Officers on the examination into the conduct, behaviour and proceedings of Lieutenant General Sir John Cope, Col. Peregrine Lascelles, and Brig. Gen. Thomas Fowke from the time of the breaking out of the rebellion in North Britain in the year 1745 til the action at Preston-Pans.* (Cope), p. 5.
2. *Scots Magazine*, September 1745, VII, p. 440–1.
3. Atkinson, C.T. *Jenkins Ear, the Austrian Succession War and the Forty-five*, (Journal of the Society for Army Historical Research, vol. 22, 1943–4), p. 289, 290.
4. Whitefoord, p. 56
   'An Effective Return of the Honble Colonel Murray's Regiment' – including abstracts for the other regiments then with Cope, compiled at Aberdeen on 12th September 1745. Overall the total of rank and file dropped from 1699 at Aberdeen to 1467 at Dunbar.
5. Ibid.
6. Ibid. See also *Scots Magazine* op.cit. and 'Cope's Forces, August 1745' IN Jarvis, R *Collected Papers on the Jacobite Rising.*
7. One of the regiment's officers, Lieutenant Donald MacDonnell of Lochgarry had already defected to the rebels, taking his men with him.
8. Cope, p. 5.
9. Cope, p. 121 (Letter to Tweeddale of 11th August 1745).
10. Sullivan *1745 and After*, p. 61.
    The prisoners were eventually incarcerated in Doune Castle and guarded by a company of MacGregors.
11. Ibid., p. 59–60.
12. SP Scot, 25/58.
13. SP Scot, 25/29.
14. Cope, p. 16.
15. Cope, p. 173.
16. So called because the gun barrel was mounted directly on to the bed of a curricle or light cart, the shafts of which formed the trail.
17. Cope, p. 54.
18. Cope, p.16.
    Confusingly there were two Dukes of Atholl above ground at the same time. One, William Murray, Marquis of Tullibardine was an attainted Jacobite, while the other, his younger brother James adhered (not very actively) to the government The third brother, Lord George Murray, was soon to be appointed one of the rebel army's three Lieutenant Generals.
19. Cope, p.16.
20. There is in fact some doubt over this as Sullivan states that the guns were buried at Glenfinnan since they could not be carried over the mountains.
21. Cope, var. refs.
22. SP Scot, 25/106.
23. In 1740 the two of them had been caught red-handed in an attempt to sell a hundred of their people into slavery in North America. They escaped pros-

ecution however and it has been plausibly suggested that the price was their loyalty to the Government in 1745.

24. Usually referred to by others as O'Sullivan, he had been recommended by Colonel Sir John McDonnell: 'I therefore told him (Locheil) that the first thing to do was appoint a second in command to see to the details of guards, marks etc. and to avoid confusion; that I was sure Mr. Sulivan was as competent a man for this purpose as could be found anywhere, because I had known him in the Italian wars. Two or three days passed and nothing was done. I therefore took the liberty of suggesting to HRH to carry out the plan, otherwise his army would be all in confusion and disorder. The Prince approving I called upon Sulivan to write out an order for the detailing of guards as he thought fit, in order to instal himself as Adjutant-General, which was done . . .' McDonnell *IN* Sullivan, p. 60.

25. It was capable of housing two companies, but in practice only one was stationed there and the spare accommodation used as a transit block. The stables were sufficient to house thirty dragoon horses although no cavalry units were permanently stationed there.

26. Sullivan, p. 64–66.

27. Cope, p. 155. In addition to Terry Molloy and twelve other men of the 55th, there were evidently three or four Invalids; crippled or superannuated soldiers employed as a permanent staff.

28. WO25 Commission Registers.
    The conventional wording of the entry proves the old adage that all officers are gentlemen, if only by virtue of their holding the King's commission.

29. In Jarvis *Collected Papers* – 'Cope's March North', p. 19.

30. Johnstone, p. 33.

31. Cope, p. 16 & 132, (Atholl to Cope 14th August 1745) Sullivan, p. 67, 68.

32. Sullivan, p. 67–9.

33. Johnstone, op. cit.

CHAPTER 3

Hey Johnnie Cope

The Battle of Prestonpans

Not surprisingly the inhabitants of the capital viewed the impending approach of the rebels with some considerable concern. Although the town was still in part surrounded by a mediaeval wall, it was generally reckoned to be well-nigh indefensible. To make matters worse the Lord Provost, Archibald Stewart, was rightly suspected of being a Jacobite sympathiser but, in spite of his foot dragging considerable exertions were made to raise a sufficient body of men to defend Edinburgh against the approaching rebels.

In the first place there was the 126-strong Town Guard, an armed police force largely made up of old soldiers. Unwary strangers were apt to dismiss them as being old and decrepit, but those who knew better generally admitted them to be a pretty tough bunch indeed. Rather less impressive were the sixteen companies of part-time burgh militia, rejoicing in the archaic title of the Edinburgh Trained Bands. Although in theory 1,000 strong, their military value was negligible and two other units were therefore raised. One was the 'Edinburgh Regiment' a provincial corps for which Letters of Service were received as late as the 9th of September, notwithstanding which about 200 men were enlisted within a week. The other, and apparently slightly more genteel, unit was a body of some 400 middle-class volunteers. Unfortunately all four were, nominally at least, commanded by the pro-Jacobite Lord Provost.

On the 15th of September, Edinburgh's gallant defenders were mustered with the intention of marching out with the 14th Dragoons to join Colonel Gardiner, who was falling back to Corstorphine. Unfortunately their resolution barely sufficed to see most of them as far as the city's gates. For their part the Trained Bands flatly refused to march out at all and, encouraged by the Lord Provost's equivocation, the Volunteers too decided that their function was limited to defending the city instead of marching out of it. In the end only some 180 men drawn from the Town Guard and the Edinburgh Regiment could be persuaded to march out to Corstorphine and the rendezvous with Colonel Gardiner 'in order to Flank or File with the Dragoons for want of Military Foot.'

That evening, probably much to his relief since he was in poor health, Gardiner was superseded by Brigadier Thomas Fowke. A Dutch infantry regiment, although hourly expected to land at Leith, had not turned up however and nor was there any sign of Cope, who was now known to be hurrying south by sea. Recognising the importance of holding the capital Fowke at once conferred with Lieutenant General Joshua Guest, the governor of the castle, and his equally aged predecessor, Lieutenant General George Preston of Valleyfield. Both of them were safely esconced in the castle and intent on remaining there, but they agreed that Walter Grosset, an industrious customs-cum-intelligence officer, would go into the town with a proposal that the two Dragoon regiments should come within the walls to bolster its defences. To their astonishment and dismay the proposal was unaccountably rejected by the magistrates.[1] The best that could be done was to arrange for the Volunteers' arms to be secured in the castle and Fowke therefore had no option but to make a rather disorderly retreat eastwards to Dunbar, abandoning Edinburgh to its fate.

Meanwhile, having reached Inverness safely, Cope was only too well aware that he had somehow to get his army back to Edinburgh before the rebels simply walked in. Accordingly Captain Samuel Rogers of the 55th was hastily despatched to Edinburgh with instructions to arrange for transports to be sent north. Then, adding Captain Deane Pointz's company of the 6th Foot to his little command, and leaving behind in exchange all his sick and a company each of the 43rd and 64th Highlanders, commanded by Captain Aeneas MacIntosh and Major William MacKenzie respectively, he marched hard for Aberdeen. Reaching the port on the 11th of September he was then if necessary also prepared to march down the east coast, and Lieutenant Colonel Whitefoord, who was acting as a transport officer, was ordered to ensure that sufficient boats were available at Dundee to carry his army across the Tay.[2] Happily Captain Rogers had succeeeded in his mission and a small fleet of transports, escorted by HMS *Fox* turned up in time, but even so, precious hours were lost when Cope declined the magistrates' offer of fishing boats to ferry his men out to the transports. Consequently he had to wait while they nosed into the harbour by one tide and went out with another.

In the meantime yet another company of Loudon's 64th Highlanders, commanded by Captain Alexander MacKay, turned up just in time and, dismissing Culcairn's loyalists who were anxious to get the harvest in, he embarked all his regulars on the 15th and arrived off Dunbar on the 17th of September. Brigadier Fowke joined him there that evening with the now quite demoralised dragoons and the unwelcome news that Edinburgh had already been captured by the rebels.

Notwithstanding the imminence of Cope's arrival and the expectation of that promised Dutch battalion, the Edinburgh authorities had earlier opened tentative negotiations with the rebels. Despite the Lord Provost's alleged Jacobite leanings, these proceeded very slowly since Cope's transports had by now been sighted in the Firth of Forth, and suspecting that the magistrates were after all playing for time, the rebels decided on a surprise assault at the Netherbow Port.

A detachment of some 900 men was therefore chosen from amongst four of the clan regiments for the purpose: 'The detachment was drawn, and at the rendezvous wch was to be commanded by Ld George, but Locheil, Kapock, Clenranold & Glengarry out of whose regements the detachment were chossen & marched themselfs, desired to have Sullivan, wch was granted them; accordingly Sullivan who was preparing the detachment was sent for, recd his orders, & march'd. The Scheme for getting into the Town was yt a man cload in Lowland Cloaths, shou'd get the wikquet open'd, as if he was a servant belonging to an officer of the Dragoons, that forgot something belonging to his master in the town, at the same time yt the highlanders, yt were to be posted at both sides of the Geatte shou'd rush in, & seize upon the Guard. This being agreed upon, when Sullivan drew near the Geat, made his disposition accordingly, set twelve men at each side of the Porte, thirty just near them where they cou'd not be seen, & smal postes at the corners of every street, to hinder any body to passe & advertise & yt the detachment shou'd not be surpris'd. The servant went, but cou'd not get in, & was threttend to be shot if he did not retire; this set everybody to a stand.'[3]

Thus thwarted by the vigilant old soldiers of the Town Guard, the rebels were on the point of withdrawing when, at about five o'clock in the morning, the gate was unexpectedly opened after all in order to let a hackney coach pass out, apparently in order to return to its stable. Curiously enough it had just carried a party of magistrates back from their fruitless negotiations with the Prince at Gray's Mill, and in the light of the readiness with which the gate was now opened despite the earlier refusal of the Guard to be taken in by Colonel Sullivan's 'servant' ruse, there must inevitably be suspicions as to whether the opening was an accident, or whether it was 'arranged' by the pro-Jacobite element amongst the magistrates. Deliberate or not this was just what Sullivan was waiting for and his men immediately rushed in, disarmed the Guard and proceeded to quietly take possession of the sleeping city.

Undaunted by this unwelcome news, Cope set off on the morning of the 19th, with the intention of bringing the rebels to battle as soon as possible. Marching first to Haddington, he pushed on towards Prestonpans on the 20th, but then a reconnaissance party led by the Earl of Loudon discovered that the rebels were themselves approaching Musselburgh. At the time his men were standing on a flat and fairly featureless piece of stubble-covered ground, just to the north of the village of Tranent and considering it a suitable battlefield, Cope elected to stand and wait for the rebels there.[4] A useful description of the ground is provided by one of his volunteer ADCs, Captain James Forbes of Read's 9th Foot:

'The Field which the General Drew up in was about an English Mile Square, where Both Dragoons and Foot Could Act; and very well Secur'd on all Sides to prevent any Surprize; when we first Drew up the Front of the Army pointed South west, the village of Prestonpans and the Defiles Leading to it, and Colonel Gardiners House[5] in our Front; The Town of Tranent with a Great many Coal Pits, Hedges and Ditches on our Left Flank; Seaton House and a Narrow Defile Leading from Haddington in our Rear, and the Sea with the Village Cockenny (Cockenzie) on our Right Flank; And as Far as I can Remember our Army was Drawn up as follows; viz.: Two Squadrons of Colonel Gardners Dragoons on our Right, and two Squadrons of General Hamiltons on our Left; The Infantry was Dispos'd thus, five Companys of Col: Lee's Regiment on the Right, Col: Murray's Regtt on the Left; and Eight Companys of Col: Lascelle's and two of Genll Guises in the Center; The Corps De Reserve consisted of five Companys of Highlanders and two Squadrons of Dragoons, one of Each Regtt;'[6]

Lord George Murray, meanwhile, had impetuously decided to seize the high ground of Falside Hill, which overlooked Cope's position from the south, and without troubling himself to consult anybody promptly embarked on a brisk cross country march in order to reach it. This sudden move evidently took everybody by surprise and considerable straggling resulted, but in the end the effort turned out to have been quite in vain, for despite Murray's airy claim to know the area well, upon reaching the brow of the hill the Jacobites discovered to their dismay that it was quite impossible to charge down upon the enemy since a stretch of marshy ground, known as the Tranent meadows lay at the foot of it. As Murray's ADC James Johnstone ruefully commented:

'We arrived, about two o'clock in the afternoon, within musket shot of the enemy, where we halted behind an eminence, having a full view of the camp of General Cope, the position of which was chosen with a great deal of skill. The more we examined it, the more we were convinced of the impossibility of attacking it; and we were all thrown into consternation, and at quite a loss what course to take . . . The camp of the enemy was fortified by nature, and in the happiest position for so small an army. The General had on his right two enclosures surrounded by stone walls from six to seven feet high, between which there was a road about twenty feet broad, leading to the village of

Prestonpans. Before him was another enclosure, surrounded by a deep ditch filled with water and from ten to twelve feet broad, which served as a drain to the marshy ground. On his left was a marsh which terminated in a deep pond, and behind him was the sea, so that he was enclosed as in a fortification ... we spent the afternoon in reconnoitring this position; the more we examined it, the more our uneasiness and chagrin increased, as we saw no possibility of attacking it without exposing ourselves to be cut to pieces in a disgraceful manner.'[7]

To make matters worse the rebel leaders also spent the afternoon very much at odds with each other, and were quite unable to concert their activities. Sullivan properly placed an out-guard of fifty men from Locheil's regiment in and around the church at the north end of the village of Tranent; 'for what reason' commented Lord George Murray,'I could not understand.'[8] As events throughout the campaign were to demonstrate there was indeed much about soldiering which Murray did not understand. Sir John McDonnell on the other hand, commenting on his reluctance, pointed out that such outposts were 'the usual practice of infantry'[9] and indeed Cope for his part also covered his position with similar outposts.

At any rate, having posted this detachment Sullivan then also proceeded to have two battalions of the Atholl Brigade cover the roads leading to Musselburgh and Edinburgh, in case Cope should try to force his way through to the capital under cover of darkness. As soon as he heard of this however Murray was reported by Sullivan to have flown into a rage at not being consulted and ordered them back to their original position.[10] At the same time by his own admission, Murray took advantage of Sullivan's absence to withdraw the out-guard from Tranent since it was coming under fire, and begin marching the rest of the army round to the east of the village. Not surprisingly Sullivan thereupon 'came up and asked what I was doing.' To which Murray coolly replied 'it was not possible to attack the enemy on the west side of the village; that the men he had placed at the foot were exposed to no purpose; and that as there were exceeding good fields on the east side for the men to lie well and safe all that night, I should satisfy his Royal Highness how easy it would be to attack the enemy by the east side.'[11]

Of this there was no doubt, but it was hardly sensible of him to advertise such an intention to Cope by moving the army into position in broad daylight. Well aware that something was up (although not surprisingly a little puzzled by the to-ing and fro-ing), the General had already shifted his army round from its original westward-facing position to a southward-facing one in order to meet any attack from the direction of Tranent.

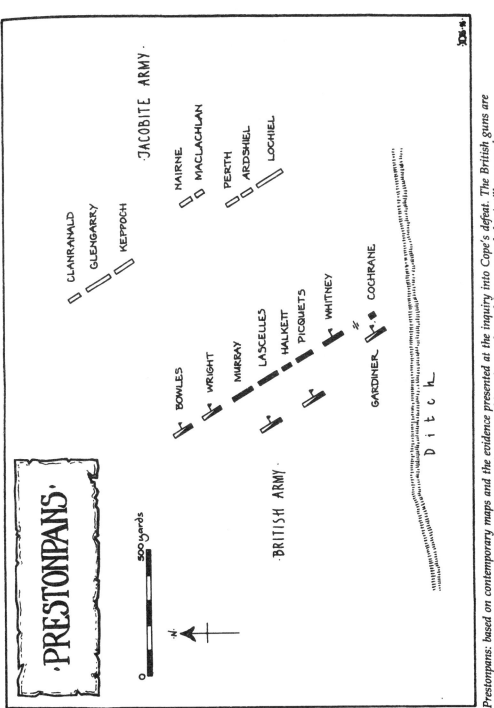

Prestonpans: based on contemporary maps and the evidence presented at the inquiry into Cope's defeat. The British guns are omitted for the sake of clarity but were positioned between Whitney's squadron of dragoons and the Artillery guard.

31

Map 1

Now, seeing the Atholl Brigade marching back in the direction of Mussel-burgh, he swung the army back through about 45 degrees into a position parallel with but a little forward of his original position. Then, finally, accepting that the move did not after all presage an attack from the west, he swung it around into its fourth position of the day, fronting the marshy ground with his right wing opposite Tranent.

Unabashed, Murray had meanwhile come up with yet another pro-posal, which involved swinging the army still further round to the east and crossing the marsh in order to attack Cope from the direction of Seton. Despite the fact that the proposed battlefield was even more flat and open than the one which he later vehemently criticised at Culloden, this plan was agreed to, and the chances of its success were considerably increased when a local volunteer, Robert Anderson of Whitburgh, pointed out a useful shortcut by way of a narrow footpath crossing the marsh near Riggonhead Farm.

Although it was thought best to make the final move under cover of darkness, any remaining hope of catching the British army unawares was scuppered when every dog in Tranent set up a furious barking at the movement, and then just before first light the head of the Rebel column was bumped by a dragoon picquet posted at Riggonhead[12]. Far from sleeping, Cope, who had already betrayed his nervousness by his frequent changes of position during the day before, spent the night waiting for just such an eventuality and;

'immediately order'd the Line to stand to their Arms, and wheel to the Left. The Dragoons by Squadrons and the Foot by Platoons, which they performed very Quickly and with great order; He at the Same time Sent orders to the out Guards and Picketts, to return to the Line; When the Artillery was posted, and the Line pretty near Form'd, the General rode from the Right, to the Left in the Front, Encouraging the Men, begging them to keep up their Fire, and keep their Ranks, and they would easily beat the Rebells;'[13]

The British army's morning states for the 21st September were appar-ently mislaid after the inquiry held into the debacle, but the *Scots Magazine* may have had sight of a copy at the time, for its September issue allowed Cope a total strength of 2,191 rank and file, exclusive of officers, sergeants and drums. This is probably a little on the high side, though not perhaps by very much, as Whitefoord states that Cope mustered only 1,467 rank and file at Dunbar, which if added to the 567 troopers of the two dragoon regiments quoted by the *Scots Magazine* will produce a total of 2,034 rank and file.[14]

On the left of the line stood Hamilton's 14th Dragoons under Lieutenant Colonel William Wright, with two squadrons up and one in reserve. As Cope was reliably informed that the rebels had no cavalry worth worrying about, he had already ordered both Hamilton's, and Gardiner's Dragoons on the right, to draw up in two ranks rather than the usual three in order to make the most of his superiority.[15]

Next came Murray's 57th Foot, commanded by Lieutenant Colonel Jaspar Clayton; and then a composite battalion led by Major John Severn comprising eight companies of Lascelles' 58th and two companies of Guise's 6th; then five companies of Lee's 55th under Lieutenant Colonel Peter Halkett. None of them were up to strength since 136 men, commanded by Captain Robert Blake of Murray's and Captains Thomas Collier and Adam Drummond of Lascelles' had been drawn from them to form the outward picquets and in the hurry to form the line it was thought expedient to fall them in as an ad hoc battalion on the right of Lee's instead of returning them to their parent units. In addition a further 100 men, commanded by Captain John Cochrane and Lieutenant George Cranstoun of Murray's 57th, were assigned as an artillery guard posted on the extreme right of the line, and a further 50 or so were with the baggage guard.[16]

On the immediate left of this detachment were placed four coehorn mortars, and the six one and a half pounders. Cope was afterwards criticised for keeping his guns together on the right, but although he requested that two of them be moved over to the left wing just as the battle was beginning, he actually had little option but to mass them together.[17] Both the civilian drivers and the nine sea gunners whom he had borrowed from HMS *Fox*, deserted before the battle started, leaving Lieutenant Colonel Whitefoord and Major Griffith with only their four Invalids to man all ten pieces.

It was originally planned that sufficient room should be left between the guns and the right flank of the infantry for two squadrons of Gardiner's 13th Dragoons to form up, but with the picquets rudely thrust into the line next to Lee's, there was only room for one of Gardiner's squadrons, commanded by Lieutenant Colonel Shugborough Whitney, to stand in the front line. Gardiner's own squadron was therefore ordered by Brigadier Fowke to post itself behind the guns. Between them, if the *Scots Magazine's* source was correct, the two dragoon regiments mustered 567 troopers, or say 650 including officers and NCOs.

In addition, Cope also had a company of the 43rd Highlanders, commanded by Captain Sir Peter Murray, and three and a half companies of Loudoun's 64th Highlanders, commanded by Captains Alexander Mackay, John Stuart and Henry Monro respectively, the remainder being part of his own company under Captain Lieutenant Archibald McNab. None of these companies were very strong and the *Scots Magazine* allowed a total of 183 rank and file in total. Moreover it is unlikely that they had yet received their uniforms, so at about nine o'clock the previous night they had very sensibly been posted well out of harm's way in an enclosure near Cockenzie to act as a baggage guard.[18]

The previous day Cope had also been joined by eighty loyalist volunteers, led by a Mr George Drummond, but although arms were issued to them by Major Griffith, they had been allowed to sleep in their own beds and consequently most of them missed the battle.[19]

Not surprisingly perhaps in the circumstances, the rebel deployment on the other side of the field went much less smoothly. In the race to form before Cope's men, the Duke of Perth, commanding the leading division, led his men too far northwards into the dawn mist. Under his immediate command he had the three MacDonald regiments under Clanranald, Glengarry and Keppoch; the first mustered about 200 men, the second as many as 400, including the Glen Urquhart and Glenmoriston men who had joined the army just the previous day, and the third some 250 or so, or perhaps more if the Glencoe Macdonalds are not included in that total. Sufficient room was to be left between this division and the marsh to allow room for the second division, commanded by Lord George Murray to form up beside them, but in the poor light Perth misjudged the distance so that a huge gap opened up between the two divisions.

Lord George Murray for his part also had three battalions under his command: the Duke of Perth's Regiment, seemingly commanded in his absence by Major James More Drummond, mustering about 200 men; the Stewarts of Appin, under Charles Stewart of Ardshiel also 200 strong; and slightly over 500 Camerons under Locheil.

By way of a reserve, under the Prince himself, there were three battalions of what was generally known as the Atholl Brigade led by Lord Nairne, probably mustering about 500 or 600 men between them. These men to some extent covered the huge gap in the front line, but so precipitate was the ensuing attack that they were quite unable to catch up and plug it properly. Finally there were also 36 horsemen commanded by Lord Strathallan and Sir John McDonnell posted over by Tranent, in order, as Lord Elcho charmingly put it; 'to take prisoners in case of a Victory.'[20]

The attack began as soon as Lord George Murray's division was formed up, or rather Murray went forward as soon as he was ready and then the others more or less followed in his wake as soon as they realised what he was doing. John Home, one of Mr Drummond's loyalist volunteers, heard rather than saw them coming:

'The ground between the two armies was an extensive corn field, plain and level, without a bush or tree. Harvest was just got in, and the ground was covered with a thick stubble, which rustled under the feet of the Highlanders as they ran on, speaking and muttering in a manner that expressed and heightened their fierceness and rage. When they set out the mist was very thick; but before they had got half-way, the sun rose, dispelled the mist, and showed the armies to each other.'[21]

As the Highlanders rushed towards them, the four Invalids still manning the guns took to their heels, but Lieutenant Colonel Whitefoord managed to fire five of the six cannon (one had already been fired as an alarm piece) and Major Griffith fired all four coehorns. Positioned on the extreme right they were able to partially enfilade the oncoming Highlanders and although there were some doubts as to whether the mortar bombs actually burst, they had the satisfaction of seeing the other artillery rounds take effect. Unfortunately, they could do no more. Major Griffith afterwards testified that he had provided forty rounds apiece for the guns, but when the Invalids bolted they took the powder horns with them so that he and Whitefoord were unable to prime let alone reload the guns after the initial discharge.[22]

Captain John Cochrane's artillery guard also 'gave a very irregular fire; and by falling back broke the Squadron of Colonel Gardiners that was in the rear;'[23] Then when Lieutenant Colonel Whitney tried to lead his squadron of dragoons forward, they first refused to follow him and instead, after he was wounded in the right arm, they too gave way, carrying both Gardiner's own men and the reserve squadron with them. Cope, seeing disaster looming, was on the spot almost at once:

'The General,' wrote Captain James Forbes, 'observing the Action begun on the Right, Gallop'd thither, and by the time he got to it, the Artillery Guard and Gardiner's Dragoons were in Confusion, We Endeavour'd to get them into order but it would not Do away they run;' [24]

Exactly what happened to Colonel Gardiner himself is uncertain. Only about fifteen troopers stood by him and a newspaper report current at the time claimed that he dismounted to place himself at the head of an infantry unit lacking officers, and that he was then killed while leading them:

'seeing the Officers who commanded the Foot, which his Regiment was appointed to guard, fall, the Colonel immediately quitted his Horse, snatch'd up a Half Pike, and took upon him the Command of the Foot, at whose Head he fought, until he was brought down by three Wounds, one in his Shoulder with a Ball, another in his Forehead by a Broad Sword, and the third, which was a mortal Stroke, in the hinder Part of his Head, by a Lochaber Axe: This Wound was given him by a Highlander, who came behind him, when he was fetching a Stroke at an Officer, with whom he was engag'd.'[25]

Which infantry unit this was is hard to say. At first sight, it may have been either the Artillery Guard or the picquets, both of which were posted in the vicinity, but none of the officers serving with these ad hoc units is known to have been killed or wounded, except Captain Blake. On the other hand Gardiner's Adjutant, Cornet John Ker testified to the inquiry that the Colonel fell off his horse after twice being shot in the side and was afterwards brought to the ground by half a dozen cuts in the head. These wounds he said were testified to him by those who treated him,[26] but the two versions are not incompatible and by a sad irony Gardiner afterwards lay dying on a mattress in the garden of his own home.[27]

On the left flank it was pretty much a similar story. Hamilton's Dragoons made no attempt to charge the MacDonald regiments to their front, but instead remained where they were until 'a few dropping shots' brought down a couple of men and horses. Unfortunately these included the commanding officer, Lieutenant Colonel Wright, and also Major Bowles who ended up trapped under his dead horse, whereupon their men, not surprisingly perhaps, also broke and ran. Captain Clark, commanding the reserve squadron, shouted to his men to stand fast, intending to charge the rebels as soon as the fugitives cleared his front, but to his consternation his men simply melted away with the rest.[28]

At this point, Lord Drummore, a judge who had been accompanying the army as an interested spectator, correctly 'concluded all was lost and that it was full time for a Pen-and-Ink Gentleman to provide for his Safety, which I did by riding off, but I hope with more Discretion and Deliberation than the Dragoons did.'[29]

Cope's infantry, commanded by Colonel Lascelles, held for a moment or two longer, but then a party of Locheil's Camerons and some other men belonging to Lord George Murray's division began rolling up their right flank. Major John Severn of Lascelles' afterwards testified that: 'A large Body of their Left rush'd on obliquely on our Right Flank, and broke the Foot as it were by Platoons, with so rapid a Motion, that the whole Line was broken in a few Minutes.'[30] Murray's 57th, overrun by the three MacDonald regiments, lost two officers killed and six others wounded, while Lee's and Guise's lost three officers killed and four wounded between them. Lascelles' on the other hand, facing the gap between the two Jacobite wings escaped comparatively lightly with only one officer killed and two wounded, who in any case may well have been with the picquets. They may also in consequence have stood their ground for longer than the rest of the infantry for Lord George Murray refers to pressing forward and suddenly finding that some regulars were still formed in his rear.

Colonel Lascelles himself, abandoned by his men, was suddenly confronted by a party of Highlanders who demanded he surrender, but no sooner had he handed over his sword than they rushed off, so that he; 'unexpectedly escaped to Seaton, between the Remainder of the left Column of the Rebels, and that next to it, which were at a considerable distance from one another' – an interesting comment which indicates that although the front rank men in the Jacobite regiments rushed on readily enough, there was some very considerable straggling amongst the rear ranks.[31]

Lieutenant Colonel Halkett of Lee's 55th, with five other officers and just fourteen men, made a brief stand within the ditched enclosure surrounding Bankton House, but seeing them, Lord George Murray brought up about a hundred men who still had loaded firelocks and politely invited Halkett to surrender.[32]

Meanwhile; 'Finding no good to be Done with the Foot; the General went again to Gardners Dragoons, who were stopt from Running Clear off the Field, by Mr. Erskine of Grange's Park walls and Did all he Could to prevail with them to Rally, but to no purpose; They stood Some Minutes with their Croops to the Enemy, and then broke away by the Defile that Leads by Col: Gardners House, The General Return'd a Second time, to Endeavour to Rally the Foot, but they were Intirely broke, and most of them he mett had thrown away their Arms;'[33]

Seeing Cope's line collapse, old Sir John McDonnell immediately tried to get Strathallan's cavalry to charge in amongst the fugitives, but to his astonishment Strathallan and his second in command, Oliphant of Gask, cried off claiming that their horses were not up to it. Nevertheless, Sir John, keeping to himself any private thoughts as to the real reason for their reluctance, spurred forward with a few volunteers and started snapping up straggling dragoons.[34]

Pushing their way through the lane between the Bankton and Preston Park walls, Cope and Forbes found the rest of the dragoons being rounded up by Loudon and by the Earl of Home, a Scots Guardsman who stood in the middle of the lane, pistol in hand, turning them into an adjacent field. According to Forbes about 450 troopers were rallied, but as they flatly refused to return to the fight it was in the end reluctantly decided to retire southwards to Lauder and Coldstream, and ultimately next day to Berwick.[35]

Behind them the Rebels were still mopping up. The Highland Companies at Cockenzie surrendered after firing a token volley and then the fighting, if not the killing was all over: 'As soon as the pursuit began,' wrote Lord Elcho, 'all the Principal Officers Mounted on horseback in order to Save and proteck Gen. Copes Officers as much as they Could, and had not they done it, Their would have been a great many of them kill'd, but as it happen'd their were very few.'[36] At any rate, the battle had lasted just seven or eight minutes in all and the official Jacobite account admitted to the loss of five officers and about thirty men killed, together with another seventy or eighty wounded. Four of the dead officers, Captain Malcolm Drummond (or MacGregor) of Perth's, Captain Robert Stuart of Ardshiel's, Lieutenant Allan Cameron of Lindevera and Ensign James Cameron, both of Locheil's, together with nine out of the eleven wounded men arrested when the rebel army evacuated Edinburgh, belonged to units in Murray's division.[37] The fifth officer to be killed was a Captain Archibald MacDonald of Keppoch's.

As to the British army, some Jacobite sources cheerfully put them as high as 500 dead, although John Murray of Broughton, the Prince's secretary, reckoned that 300 were killed. On the other hand, Andrew Henderson, a contemporary historian quoted a figure of 200 and the *Newcastle Journal*, employing 'the Utmost Care and Industry' arrived at the yet lower total of 150 dead. These included Colonel Gardiner of course, Captain John Steuart of Lascelles' 58th, Captains David Brymer and Samuel Rogers of Lee's 55th , Captain George Holwell of Guise's 6th and Captain Bishop and Ensign Forbes of Murray's 57th.[38]

Whitefoord says nothing as to the dead, but has a schedule enumerating the number of prisoners belonging to each battalion which produced a total of 844 unwounded NCOs, drums and privates, besides another 368 wounded men not broken down by unit; making 1,212 men in all – besides 114 captured dragoons.[39]

John Home later stated in his *History of the Rebellion* that only 170 of Cope's infantry escaped from the field, and if these men are added to Whitefoord's figures, then some 300 of Cope's infantry still remain to be accounted for. If all of them were to be numbered amongst the dead, that figure would accord with Murray of Broughton's, but it still seems rather too high. It is not clear of course whether those men who were subsequently persuaded to enlist in the rebel army were included in Whitefoord's figures, but the fact that only 155 NCOs, drums and privates from the Highland companies are recorded by him as being prisoners would certainly indicate that they were not. All in all therefore the *Newcastle Journal's* careful figure of 150 dead is still likely to be the most reliable.

Prisoners:

13th Dragoons –	Lieutenant	William Crofton	(wounded)
(Gardiner's)	Quartermaster	Henry Young	(wounded)
	Quartermaster	Ambrose Burroughs	(wounded)
	Quartermaster	John West	
	Privates: 52		

14th Dragoons –	Lt. Col.	William Wright	(wounded)
(Hamilton's)	Major	Richard Bowles	(wounded)
	Cornet	Jacob	(wounded)
	Cornet	Nash	
	Quartermaster	Nash	
	Privates: 62		
	Wounded: 5		
6th Foot	Captain	Deane Pointz	(wounded)
(Guise's)	Lieutenant	Cuming	
	Lieutenant	Henry Paton	
	Ensign	James Wakeman	
	Ensign	Irvine	
	Prisoners: 40		
43rd Foot	Captain	Sir Peter Murray	
(Black Watch)	Lieutenant	James Farquharson	
	Ensign	Allan Campbell	
55th Foot	Lt.Col.	Peter Halkett	
(Lee's)	Captain	Basil Cochrane	
	Captain	Russell Chapman	
	Captain	Charles Tatton	
	Lieutenant	James Sandilands	(wounded)
	Lieutenant	David Drummond	(wounded)
	Lieutenant	David Kennedy	
	Lieutenant	Leonard Hewitson	(wounded)
	Ensign	Hardwick	
	Ensign	John Archer	
	Ensign	William Dunbar	
	Prisoners: 157		
57th Foot	Lt.Col.	Jaspar Clayton	
(Murray's)	Major	Richard Talbot	
	Captain	Alexander Reid	
	Captain	John Cochrane	
	Captain	Edward Scott	
	Captain	Thomas Leslie	(wounded)
	Captain	Robert Blake	(wounded)
	Lieutenant	Thomas Hay	(wounded)
	Lieutenant	George Cranstoun	
	Lieutenant	Henry Disney	(wounded)
	Lieutenant	John Wale	
	Lieutenant	Chichester Wray	
	Lieutenant	Sims	(wounded)

57th Foot	Ensign	Andrew Sutherland	
(Murray's)	Ensign	Lucey	
	Ensign	Haldane	
	Ensign	James Birnie	
	Ensign	L'Estrange	
	Adjutant	Spencer	
	Prisoners: 226		
58th Foot	Major	John Severn	
(Lascelles')	Captain	Adam Drummond	
	Captain	Thomas Barlow	
	Captain	Cecil Forrester	
	Captain	Edmund Anderson	
	Captain	Richard Corbett	
	Captain	Thomas Collier	
	Lieutenant	Bladen Swiney	(wounded)
	Lieutenant	James Johnstone	
	Lieutenant	Edward Carrick	
	Lieutenant	Charles Dundas	
	Lieutenant	Henry Heron	(wounded)
	Ensign	William Stone	
	Ensign	Nicholas Cox	
	Ensign	John Bell	
	Ensign	David Gordon	
	Ensign	Goulton	
	Prisoners: 266		
64th Foot	Captain	Alexander MacKay	
(Loudon's)	Captain	Henry Monro	
	Captain	John Stuart	
	Capt.Lt.	Archibald McNab	
	Lieutenant	John Reid	
	Ensign	John Grant	
	Ensign	Malcolm Ross	
	Ensign	Alexander MacLaggan	

In addition both Major Eaglesfield Griffith and Lieutenant Colonel Charles Whitefoord were taken prisoner, the latter being wounded. On the other hand, although included in the rebels' official list of prisoners, Lieutenant Colonel Shugborough Whitney of Gardiner's Dragoons had in fact made his escape and was to be killed leading the regiment at

Falkirk. A total of 155 prisoners were taken from the Highland companies, but are not broken down by unit, and apart from 5 wounded men belonging to Hamilton's 14th Dragoons, the distribution of the 368 wounded is not known.[40]

Sources

1. Afterwards there was considerable confusion on this point as Stewart, the Provost, tried to shift the blame on to the military, but there seems no reason to doubt the evidence given by Fowke at Cope's inquiry.
2. Hence the 12th of September return. At first sight the two companies of Guise's 6th are not included, but in fact the *Scots Magazine* shows that they had temporarily joined Lascelles' 58th in order to replace the two companies left in Edinburgh Castle. This is also clear from a headcount of the officers belonging to both regiments who are known to have been present at Prestonpans; they add up to 25 which is precisely the figure quoted by Whitefoord for Lascelles'. Whitefoord p. 56.
3. Sullivan, p. 71–3.
4. Cope, p. 37–8.
5. Then called Olive Stob, but now better known as Bankton House.
6. Forbes IN Allardyce, *Historical Papers*, p. 279–80 (he had been in Inverness on leave and joined Cope there).
7. Johnstone, p. 35.
8. Murray, G. *Marches of the Highland Army*, p. 37.
9. McDonnell, IN Sullivan, p. 77.
10. Sullivan, p. 78.
11. Murray, p. 37–8; Sullivan, p. 78–9.
12. Cope, p. 66.
13. Allardyce, p. 280; Cope, p. 40, 54, 56, 57.
14. Whitefoord, p. 56.
15. Cope, p. 48.
16. Cope, p. 53.
17. Cope, p. 49.
18. Allardyce, p. 280.
19. Cope, p. 48.
20. Figures for the Jacobite regiments are taken from a variety of sources, but chiefly Elcho, p. 269–270.
21. Home, p. 113.
22. Cope, p. 54.
23. Cope, p. 57.
24. Allardyce, p. 281.
25. *Newcastle Courant*.
26. Cope, p. 96.
27. He was eventually carried to the manse in Tranent and subsequently buried in the churchyard there.
28. Cope, p. 58.
29. Cope, p. 147–8.
30. Cope, p. 57.
31. Cope, p. 69.

32. Murray, p. 40.
33. Allardyce, p. 281–282.
34. McDonnell *IN* Sullivan, p. 81.
35. Elcho, p. 272–3.
36. Allardyce, p. 282.
37. Elcho, p. 274, Seton & Arnot *Prisoners of the '45*, var.
38. Elcho, p. 274.
39. Whitefoord, p. 59.
40. Elcho, p. 275 – see also lists in contemporary newspapers, with corrections and Christian names taken from the commission registers in WO25. Interestingly at least 39 of the 80 odd officers killed or captured at Prestonpans were Scots. Whitefoord, p. 59.

CHAPTER 4
Raising the Stakes
More Preparations and Counter-preparations

Although Cope might easily have been forgiven for thinking otherwise, the Lords Justices, who were in charge of the country during the King's absence in Hanover, had been far from idle. But their defensive measures to date were in large part constrained by the army's reluctance to disengage itself from Flanders. After the defeat at Fontenoy in May, the Allies' position had grown increasingly difficult and King George's younger son, the 25 year old Duke of Cumberland, who was Captain General of H.M. Land Forces and Commander-in-Chief of the Allied army, initially considered it essential that his British troops should remain in theatre at least until such time as the French went into winter quarters. Therefore he resisted a call to send the Ostend garrison home on the 20th of August and the Lords Justices had perforce to look elsewhere for the necessary troops.[1]

On the 8th of September they accordingly ordered the various Additional Companies then recruiting in England to be formed into three provisional battalions, commanded by Lieutenant Colonels Frazer, Cotterell and Duncombe of the Marines.[2] Composed entirely of raw recruits they were of course quite unfit for operations in the field but were considered quite adequate as garrison troops. Frazer was ordered to concentrate his companies at Newcastle, and Cotterell his at Carlisle, while Duncombe was to relieve Houghton's 24th Foot from guarding French prisoners of war at Plymouth.

Better still, under a treaty signed as long ago as 1713, the States General of Holland were bound to despatch 6,000 men, when required, for the defence of the British Isles. A contingent had duly been requested and sent across during the invasion scare of the previous spring. Now they were summoned again and hard pressed as they were, the Dutch might now have found it more difficult to comply than before, but as it happened the former garrison of Tournai (which fell after the Allied defeat at Fontenoy)was providentially available. Having surrendered to the French on the 20th of June, the constituent regiments were parolled on condition of not bearing arms against France and her allies before January

1747. At this stage the rebels were not recognised as such and the Tournai regiments could therefore quite legitimately be deployed against them.

Thus the Earl of Stair, who was serving as Commander-in-Chief England, was able to report rather complacently in a memorandum drawn up early in September:

> 'There are now in England four battallions of guards, four other battallions besides three battallions to be formed of the additional companies: there are now actually embarkt at Williamstadt five battalions of Dutch troops, of which one is to go to Scotland, the four battallions which come into England are to be instantly followed by three more battallions; with these seven battallions of Dutch added to the eleven British battallions, with two regiments of horse and three regiments of dragoons Lord Stair thinks he can answer for the quelling of this rebellion.'[3]

His political colleagues and indeed the King himself, who returned to London from Hanover on the 31st of August, disagreed and a flurry of activity followed the unexpected news that the rebels had somehow contrived to get between Cope and Edinburgh and were reported to be at least three days march ahead of him. There was a lively possibility that in the circumstances even the Dutch battalions would not be enough to stabilise the situation and on the 4th of September positive orders were sent to a still reluctant Cumberland, requiring him to send home ten British battalions at once.

Next day the Lord Lieutenants of the four northernmost counties were ordered to muster their militias. It was generally agreed however that the militia were a pretty feeble lot and a number of associations sprang up throughout England pledging men and money for volunteer companies and regiments. These were invariably dressed in blue to distinguish them from the regulars. The volunteers raised in Devon were given blue coats lined and faced with red, hats edged with white worsted lace, and a pair of white gaiters to each man. Other 'Blues' included a company of Gentlemen Volunteers in London called the 'Loyal Blue Fusiliers', and Colonel Graham's 'Liverpool Blues' who were to do good service in breaking down the Mersey bridges ahead of the advancing rebels. The best known of these volunteer units were be the 'Yorkshire Blues'. Companies raised in the West Riding of Yorkshire had double-breasted coats of blue kersey faced with red kersey, baize lining and two dozen buttons to a coat. The clothing for the East Riding companies was also helpfully described as being 'exactly the same as the Swiss and Dutch troops are clothed, but with the linings considerably better.'

Historians (and indeed not a few contemporaries) have been quick to pour scorn on the apparently poor performance of both the militia and the blue-coated volunteers. However, while not denying a quite deplorable tendency on the part of all but a few to march not towards the sound of the guns, but away from them as rapidly as possible, their actual and exaggerated failings were in reality no more than a reflection of their circumstances.

Jacobite units were equally hastily raised, inadequately trained, poorly led and all too frequently worse clothed and equipped. But at least they were for the most part brought together to serve as a proper army and followed an admittedly rough and ready tactical doctrine – a headlong rush towards the enemy – which made the best of a raw material which at the end of the day was little different in quality and motivation from the loyalist volunteers.

With the best will in the world there was very little which these scattered little units could do, beyond serving as an armed police force, arresting 'suspected persons', and by their very presence calming the population at large and preventing any local uprisings. Neither this role nor the slightly more active one of breaking down bridges ahead of the advancing rebels might have been very glorious, but they saved the regulars from having to do it and thus ensured that they could concentrate on taking on the rebels in the field.

Finding enough real soldiers to do that job was of course the problem, but towards the end of the month they at last began to arrive.

A battalion of the Dutch regiment La Rocque was the first to embark from Flanders and was conveyed northwards by HMS *Glasgow*, but failing to reach Edinburgh in time to save the city was diverted instead to Berwick where it joined the defeated remnants of Cope's army. Meanwhile three battalions of the Swiss regiment Hirzler landed in the Thames and on the 19th of September received orders to prepare to march northwards. General Thomas Wentworth was to go to 'Lancashire, or any other county in England where he shall hear the rebels are', taking the Swiss, five companies of Blakeney's 27th Foot, and two regiments of cavalry. Four more Dutch battalions arrived next day, but only two were disembarked for it was decided to send the other two straight up to Newcastle-upon-Tyne.

Then, on the 23rd of September, the ten long-awaited British battalions under General Sir John Ligonier landed at Gravesend, Grays and Blackwall: Sowle's 11th, Pulteney's 13th, Howard's 19th, Bragg's 28th, Douglas' 32nd, Johnson's 33rd, Cholmondley's 34th and three battalions of Footguards. Ligonier was a 65-year-old professional soldier of considerable ability. All ten of his regiments had been brought well up to strength by drafting from those units left in theatre and in total they comprised 245 officers and 7269 ORs.[4] The arrival of these troops was timely, for the news of Prestonpans broke next day, and prompted a radical rethink of priorities.

Wentworth was ordered to stand fast for the time being and an ad hoc council of war comprising Lord Stair, Field Marshal George Wade, Ligonier and the Dutch commander, General Schwartzenberg, discussed how best to respond to the altered situation. Clearly the present emergency took precedence over the faltering campaign in Flanders and a further eight battalions were recalled immediately while the remainder of Cumberland's army was placed on notice to follow as soon as possible – all British troops were in fact recalled on the 1st of October.

The raising of no fewer than seventeen Provincial regiments was also sanctioned, largely on the King's personal say-so. One of them, the Edinburgh Regiment had as we have seen been authorised by the King as soon as he returned to London, but now thirteen infantry and two cavalry regiments were to be raised in England together with a single infantry regiment in Ireland. Initially a number of noblemen had offered to raise and maintain them at their own cost, but with the notable exception of Lord Kildare in Ireland, they soon got cold feet when the bills started to come in. Such was the need for men however that the army was persuaded to take over the English regiments once they were recruited up to at least half their establishments.

The army's reluctance to accept these units stemmed in large part from the fact that the noble founders were to have the sole nomination of the officers and that they would receive regular commissions, at once placing them on a par with men who had spent years working their way up to their present ranks. Moreover, this in turn meant that they were almost entirely captained by men with no previous military experience. Parliament was equally alive to the dangers of such blatant 'jobbery' and in the end it took the King's personal intervention to sanction their addition to the Army List.

Naturally it still took some time to get these provincial regiments off the ground, although one raised by the Duke of Bedford (who also happened to be the First Lord of the Admiralty) was reported half complete on the 10th of October and taken into the line as the 68th Foot, while the Duke of Kingston's 10th Horse was ready two days later. Unfortunately most of the others would not be ready until the end of the month or until early November. Even as late as the 30th of that month a rather jaundiced Cumberland inspected Bedford's 68th and wrote; 'I am sorry to speak my fears that they will rather be a hindrance than a service to me, for this regiment was represented to be the forward regiment of them, yet neither men nor officers know what they are about, so how they will do before an enemy God alone knows.'[5] Nevertheless, some of these regiments, most famously perhaps Kingston's 10th Horse, were in the end to make a vital contribution to the defence of the realm.

As it was gloomily anticipated that the rebels would soon follow up their victory by marching south through Northumberland, Wade was ordered north to Newcastle, taking all the Dutch troops and two of the newly arrived British battalions; Pulteney's 13th and Cholmondley's 34th. All but one of the battalions in the second lift, commanded by the Earl of Albemarle, were also ordered to sail directly to Newcastle and rendez-vous with him there,[6] while in addition two battalions (2/Royals and Battereau's 62nd) were recalled from Ireland after first being made up to 1,000 men apiece by drafts from the other battalions stationed there. Little however was at first available to Wade in the way of cavalry, indeed there were very few cavalrymen in England at all, but he was assigned three regiments of regulars; Montague's 3rd Horse (Bays), his own 4th Horse and St. George's 8th Dragoons. A fourth, newly raised regiment, Oglethorpe's Georgia Rangers was at that moment embarking for North America, but in the light of the emergency it was instead ordered north to Hull in order to join Wade.

Once these and any other locally raised troops were assembled, Wade ought to have more than sufficient men with which to confront the rebels, but recognising the possibility that they might well slip past him as easily as they had done Cope, Sir John Ligonier was ordered to the north west in Wentworth's stead.

Ligonier's orders initially were to cover a line from Chester to Notting-ham, blocking any incursion southwards or into Wales and later he was also to be allocated a series of fall-back positions, still with that same aim although he was also required to suppress any local insurrections which might flare up within his area of operations. While expected to operate independently of Wade, Ligonier was still to be subordinate to him and this subsiduary role was reflected in his comparatively meagre allocation of troops; just one regular cavalry regiment, Bland's 3rd Dragoons, and five infantry battalions, although once they were fully mobilised he would also be able to add two provincial cavalry regiments and four provincial infantry regiments.

Finally, London itself needed to be protected against the very real threat of a French landing on the south coast and the last of Cumberland's forces, which he grumblingly reported to be no more than thirteen 'broken' battalions and twenty squadrons, were, together with the Guards, earmarked for that task.

Unfortunately the process of assembling these forces received an unexpected setback when the convoy carrying Albemarle's battalions from Flanders to Newcastle sailed from Helvoetensluys on the 13th of October and five days later was scattered by a gale.[7] Some ships eventu-ally fetched up as far north as Berwick and as a result it was not until the 26th that they all managed to re-assemble on the Tyne, just three days ahead of those regiments which had marched up from London.

As far as Wade was concerned no harm was done, but the delay had a knock-on effect on Cumberland's forces. He had hoped to have the embarkation of his men completed by the 22nd of October, but the sudden demand for transports was already causing problems and now there was a shortage of shipping and in particular a lack of horse transports. As a result seven infantry battalions and the 1st (Royal) and Rich's 4th Dragoons, together with one squadron of Ligonier's 8th Horse had for the time being to be left behind.[8]

By the 1st of November Wade's army was more or less fully assembled at Newcastle and comprised no fewer than twenty battalions, half of them British; 2/Royals, Howard's 3rd, Barrell's 4th, Wolfe's 8th, Pulteney's 13th, Price's 14th, Blakeney's 27th Cholmondley's 34th, Fleming's 36th, Monro's 37th, Ligonier's 59th and Battereau's 62nd.[9] The other ten battalions were either Dutch, or Swiss in Dutch service, comprising the following regiments: Hirzel (three battalions), Villatre (two battalions), Holstein Gottorp (two battalions), Patot (two battalions), La Rocque (one battalion).[10]

Besides this more or less formidable array there were also four stray companies of the Dutch regiment Brackel, and a 100-strong Yorkshire volunteer company commanded by a Captain Jack Thornton.

Wade's cavalry however still comprised the three regiments which he had started out with, although the rather demoralised 13th and 14th Dragoons were still up at Berwick and two more weak regiments were on their way to join him. The first was the Georgia Rangers, with an establishment of only two troops, and the second a volunteer regiment variously known as the Royal Hunters or the Yorkshire Hunters. Confusingly both were commanded by Brigadier General James Oglethorpe and in many secondary sources are assumed to be one and the same unit. The first however was a green-jacketed mounted infantry regiment, while the second was composed of Yorkshire gentlemen and their servants, all clad in the customary blue coats turned up with red, and for some reason wearing green cockades in their hats.[11] While he would undoubtedly have liked more of them, they nevertheless considerably outnumbered anything which the rebels might put in the field.

Although both he and his men were somewhat worn out by the long march north, Wade and his second in command the Earl of Albemarle, agreed that they should tackle the rebels head on as soon as possible. Leaving Newcastle to be defended by Frazer's provisional battalion and the local militia they promptly set off for Scotland, but on the 3rd of November, before they had got the length of Morpeth, they received word that the rebels had themselves left Edinburgh and were moving south.

After the battle of Prestonpans the rebels returned to Edinburgh and to the unalloyed relief of the government stayed there for nearly six weeks. There were, it is true, suggestions in some quarters that they should march immediately upon Berwick, but this foolish notion was rightly rejected since there was no reasonable prospect of taking the well fortified town, garrisoned as it was by five companies of Lee's 55th, and at that moment by the Dutch battalion, La Rocque, together with Cope's runaway dragoons as well. The 2,500 odd clansmen who charged out of the early morning mist at Prestonpans had sufficed to chase off those dragoons and annihilate Cope's infantry, but they were quite inadequate to mount an invasion of England.

The army needed time to rest and to find new recruits, and so throughout October Edinburgh once more had a Stuart prince in residence. No-one however, from the Prince downwards, was under any illusions that their work was done, or that they would be left there undisturbed for very long. The question was what to do next.

Essentially there were just two options open to the rebels at that point: either they could continue to reassert Scotland's independence and with or without French assistance attempt to maintain it against all comers – even if that did mean temporarily abandoning Edinburgh and withdrawing into the hills; alternatively they could adopt the far bolder course of marching south in a bid to topple King George from the throne and thus end the struggle by a single decisive blow.

The 'Nationalist' case is baldly summed up in a later memorandum attributed to Locheil:

'Being . . . master of the field and of all Scotland, excepting only a few insignificant forts which could be blockaded by only a small force, the Prince had only to arm all the loyal Highlanders, summon the Estates of the realm and put together an army which could defend itself, or even help the English shake off the usurper's yoke. But the Prince allowed himself to be blinded by the ardour of his own courageous spirit. Sir Thomas Sheridan, puffed up with the success the Prince's enterprise had so far enjoyed, and believing that the situation in England was scarcely less favourable than in Scotland, was so rash as to maintain, against the near unanimous advice of the Scots, that the presence of H.R.H. at the head of 5,000 men would bring over a good part of the Government troops to his side and persuade the English nobility to declare themselves. Buoyed up with this hope . . . the Prince made a hasty march into that counry, and left Scotland without having taken the necessary measures to consolidate his authority there.'[12]

Attractive though this view may have seemed in the euphoria which followed that remarkable victory at Prestonpans, and even more so perhaps afterwards in bitter exile, it was in reality a complete non-starter. The plain fact of the matter was that notwithstanding their having destroyed

Cope's army, there was a very considerable difference between being 'master of the field' and 'all Scotland'. If Locheil was indeed the author of the memorandum, his claim that the army's garrisons might easily be blockaded is particularly ironic for it was his Camerons who were so ignominiously repulsed from Ruthven Barracks by a bare dozen men, and now his own blockade of Edinburgh Castle was destined to collapse after little more than a week.

After Prestonpans Locheil was appointed Governor of Edinburgh and with Sullivan's help established a series of checkpoints covering the various approaches to the castle. The castle's regular garrison of a handful of decrepit Invalids had progressively been reinforced that summer by the two companies of Lascelles' 58th left behind there by Cope, the remains of the Edinburgh Regiment, a variety of political refugees and even by some runaways from Prestonpans. Notwithstanding the rebel occupation of the city the garrison still continued to receive daily deliveries of fresh provisions by local tradesmen and, putting two and two together (and possibly getting five), the rebel leaders decided that the garrison must consequently be running short of food. The Camerons manning the main checkpoint, an old building called the Weigh-house which stood at the head of the Lawnmarket, accordingly received orders on the 1st of October to prevent any further deliveries.

Understandably irked by this, Generals Preston and Guest retaliated by opening fire on the Weigh-house, which lay only 400 yards from the castle's Half-Moon Battery. As their checkpoint quite literally collapsed about their ears, the rebels hastily withdrew, and thereafter every rebel who showed himself was shot at, regardless of collateral damage and civilian casualties. On the 3rd a party was let down on ropes from the castle wall, surprised an outpost in the West Kirk and captured Captain Robert Taylor of the Duke of Perth's Regiment.[13] Then on the 4th, Guest underlined his point by ordering a full scale sortie, gloomily described by the invariably impartial *Scots Magazine* in its October issue:

'On the 4th at noon, notice was sent to the inhabitants to remove from the North parts of James's court, and places adjacent, lest some balls might chance to come that way. A few hours after, a terrible cannonading began. When it became dark, a party sallied out from the castle, and set fire to a house, which was deserted by the inhabitants. This occasioned a great consternation. Mean time the salliers threw up a trench across the castle-hill; and, to prevent any interruption, scoured the street with cartridge-shot from some field-pieces placed on the castle-hill; by which a merchant's book-keeper and another person were killed, and severals wounded. Before their return, the soldiers pillaged some of the houses that had been deserted.

'The firing continued next day, and distressed the inhabitants exceedingly. Bullets did execution at the Flesh market close-head, so that no body was safe to stand on the street. Some houses were shattered. Those who lived exposed to the castle, removed; and carried out the aged and infirm at the imminent hazard of their lives. Great numbers that lived in places that were in no hazard, were likewise so frightened, that they ran out of town, not knowing whither. Several of the inhabitants sent off their valuable effects, and a good deal of them were lost in the confusion. It was a very affecting scene.'

It became even more affecting when HMS *Fox*, still sitting in the Forth, took to firing at any supposed rebels sighted in the port of Leith. Soon anxious deputations were begging the Prince to relax the blockade. At first he tried to stand firm, threatening General Preston that if the garrison did not give over firing on the town, the Jacobites would burn his own house at Valleyfield in Fife. Preston acidly replied that he would then return the compliment by ordering HMS *Fox* to burn Wemyss Castle (Lord Elcho's family home), and next day Guest continued his bombardment killing some more of the townspeople until on the afternoon of the 6th, the Jacobites capitulated and lifted the blockade.

Elsewhere in Scotland, far from meekly submitting to the embryonic Jacobite regime, substantial loyalist forces were already mustering in the north and west. Instead of 'consolidating his authority' the Prince was facing a full-blown civil war and this was made bleakly apparent on the 30th of October, King George's official birthday. At Dores, in Inverness-shire, the presbyterian minister, Archibald Bannatyne, had the mortification of seeing all his fuel seized and turned into a bonfire by some Jacobites, who then proceeded to drink the 'most shocking healths', but elsewhere it was a very different matter:

'At Perth the Mob rose, made bonfires and rung the bells, and obliged Mr Oliphant of Gask, the Deputy Governor, to retire into the councill house, where they besieged him with fire arms; and there was severall men kill'd on both Sides. Upon some highlandmen Coming from Athole next day to Mr Oliphants Assistance the quiet of the place was restablish'd. The mob rose likewise on the same day at Dundee and obliged Mr Fotheringham, the Governor, to quit the town.' [14]

The Prince's Council cannot have been aware of this when they met that day to decide upon the best course of action, but it would be surprising if they did not have a certain sense of foreboding, for Admiral Byng[15] had sailed into the Forth four days earlier, to join HMS *Fox*, bringing with him two men-of-war, another frigate, a sloop and some transports. Thus far they had done nothing beyond firing occasionally on the shore, but to guard against any raiding parties landing by boat, Lord Elcho's Lifeguards were ordered to patrol between Cramond and Musselburgh every night.

It was obvious that something constructive had to be done. The rebel council of war's decision on the 30th of October to march southwards was carried by only two votes – Elcho's and Perth's – but notwithstanding their legitimate misgivings the rebel leaders had little real choice. To remain in a divided Scotland would be fatal, only by provoking an English Jacobite uprising, or even a French invasion could they ensure their own survival and Scotland's independence.

During their ocupation of Edinburgh the rebels had received a considerable increase in their strength, but it was one which radically altered the character of the army. At Prestonpans all but a handful of the Jacobites were Highlanders, now, although the army was twice the size it had been in September, very few of the new recruits were Highland clansmen. Indeed with the exception of Cluny's MacPhersons (who only turned up just as the army was leaving Dalkeith) and small contingents from Skye and Glen Urquhart, none of the new regiments was raised in the Highlands.

Encouragingly though, help had also been received from France. On the 7th of October a ship arrived at Montrose, bringing £5,000 in gold and 2,500 stand of arms, and more significantly perhaps, Captain Alexandre de Boyer, Marquis d'Eguilles, the French King's unofficial ambassador to the Jacobite 'court'. Three more ships also arrived towards the end of the month, carrying artillery, small arms and a miscellaneous collection of military advisors. Apart from a dozen badly needed gunners there were as yet no French troops, but it was an encouraging sign and d'Eguilles assured the Prince that a full scale French invasion was imminent.

At this point the rebels were to need all the encouragement they could get, for in order to assemble an army capable of marching into England, they had to abandon Edinburgh and indeed all of Scotland south of the Tay estuary.

North of it, their position was anything but secure. After Prestonpans, Lord Strathallan and his second in command, Oliphant of Gask, were sent back to Perth. Ostensibly they were to take charge of a strategically important rendevous point for recruits, although if Sir John McDonnell's testimony is to be relied upon they had both been a little 'shy' in action and Strathallan at least was to prove quite ineffectual.[16] Further north, Aberdeenshire and Banffshire were entrusted to Lord Lewis Gordon, and in Forfarshire Sir James Kinloch was raising a second battalion for Lord Ogilvy's Regiment. Ominously however, the Highlands, which might otherwise have been expected to be the nursery of the Jacobite army were effectively abandoned to the Lord President and his loyalist levies.

The army which did march to Derby was divided into two divisions, besides the cavalry and artillery. Only the first division was wholly made up of Highland units, Glengarry (500), Keppoch (450), Clanranald (200), Cluny (300), Appin (150) and Locheil (500). The second division was something of a mixed bag, comprising the three battalions of the Atholl Brigade, viz: Lord George Murray (350), Menzies of Shian (300), and Lord Nairne (350), two battalions of the Duke of Perth's Regiment (750?), Gordon of Glenbucket's Regiment (200), John Roy Stuart's Regiment (200) and Lord Ogilvy's Regiment (200). Of the regiments in the second division, the three battalions of the Atholl Brigade, and Glenbucket's Regiment were Highlanders, though they were not clan regiments and by general consent were by no means as 'wild' as the western clans. A substantial part of Perth's original battalion was made up of MacGregors who were wild enough by anybody's standards, but the second was made up of men who had been raised in the lowlands of Aberdeenshire by John Hamilton and Moir of Stonywood and there were few if any Highlanders in the regiments raised by Lord Ogilvy and Colonel John Roy Stuart.[17]

As for the cavalry, there were four regiments: the blue-coated Lifeguards consisting of two troops commanded by Lord Elcho[18] and numbering about 150 officers and men, Lord Pitsligo's Horse (120), Lord Kilmarnock's Horse Grenadiers (100) and Murray of Broughton's Hussars – a 70-strong unit actually commanded by an Irishman, Major John Bagot.

The artillery, commanded by Colonel James Grant, a regular officer in the French Army, consisted of thirteen field-pieces: the six obsolescent one-and-a-half pounders captured from Cope at Prestonpans and six French pieces – brass four-pounders. The thirteenth gun, although certainly referred to from time to time, is a little obscure, but a report in the *Newcastle Gazette* detailing the men and equipment taken from the rebels at Carlisle includes under the heading of 'Ordnance', a 'Brass Octagon with a Carriage'.[19] In addition, they also dragged with them the four brass Coehorn and two Royal mortars taken at Prestonpans.

It was in all conscience a small enough army with which to encompass the restoration of the Stuarts to the crown of Great Britain.

Sources

1. Ironically Ostend was to fall to the French within the week and although the three battalions making up its garrison were allowed to march out with the 'honours of war', they were not available for service until the 11th of October.
2. Atkinson, p. 291, 295 *Newcastle Journal*. The Additional Companies were brigaded as follows:- Frazer's: 3rd, 19th, 31st, 33rd and 37th Foot; Cotterell's:

8th, 12th, 20th, 23rd, 36th and 59th Foot; Duncombe's: 4th, 11th, 13th, 28th, 32nd and 34th Foot. At least one of the Additional Companies belonging to Howard's 3rd (Buffs) was in South Shields on the 13th of September and Frazer himself arrived in Newcastle on the 28th.

3. *Culloden Papers* p. 218. Also quoted in Speck p30. Speck considers it to have been drawn up sometime in August, but the reference to the provisional battalions to be formed from Additional Companies, and the Dutch embarkation clearly places it some time in early September.

4. Atkinson, p. 292. *Newcastle Journal* provides the correct date.

5. Speck, p. 74.

6. The exception was a provisional battalion of Footguards made up of drafts from all three regiments, which had been trapped in Ostend when it fell. Its personnel were now to be reabsorbed into their parent units.

7. Atkinson, op. cit.

8. Atkinson, p. 293-4. In the end Rich's 4th Dragoons had to come across without their horses.

9. Actually there were only five companies of Blakeney's 27th, the other five, originally intended to form part of Wentworth's force had earlier been sent to Chester.

10. *Newcastle Journal*.

11. *Newcastle Journal*. It appears from contemporary newspaper reports that the Georgia Rangers were even accompanied by an 'Indian King' and his attendants.

12. Gibson, J.S., *Locheil*, p. 178-9.

13. Elcho, p. 292 and *Prisoners of the '45*, Vol. III, p. 368-9 (no. 3259). Although originally sentenced to death, Taylor was released in 1747.

14. Elcho, p. 306.

15. The same Admiral Byng who was to be shot for failing to relieve Minorca in 1756.

16. Strathallan's 'Perthshire Horse' were incorporated into Lord Kilmarnock's Regiment.

17. Largely taken from Lord Elcho's account, although he omits the Aberdeenshire battalion in the Duke of Perth's Regiment. Both the latter and John Roy Stuart's regiments contained substantial numbers of deserters from Cope's regiments at the outset of the campaign, but so many of them subsequently took the opportunity to get away that a composite battalion was subsequntly formed of escapers from Lee's, Murray's and Lascelles' at Newcastle.

18. Elcho had apparently been commissioned a Colonel of Dragoons by the Prince as early as 1744.

19. *Newcastle Gazette*, no.83 (January 15 1746).

CHAPTER 5

Invasion

The Jacobites March South

It is perhaps an indication of the pressure which the rebels were coming under that, although they had narrowly agreed to march into England, they set off from Edinburgh on the 31st of October with no very clear idea of exactly where they were going, and it was only when they reached Dalkeith that the final decision was taken.

Once again there were essentially two courses; the first and perhaps most obvious choice, warmly advocated by the Prince, was that they should continue upon their present road down through Lauder, Cold-stream and Wooler in order to fight Wade, who was known to be concentrating in the Newcastle area. Although they would thus by-pass Berwick and its garrison, there were very real fears that the roads were too bad for the artillery and wagons. Therefore the alternative proposal, urged by Lord George Murray and eventually accepted by the Prince, was to swing across to the west and enter England by way of Carlisle. Notwith-standing the unfortunate precedents for this route, there were persuasive arguments in its favour.

Murray once again claimed to know the country well and pointed out that the anticipated reinforcements could more easily join them by that route. More importantly, as that particular avenue was virtually undefen-ded by comparison with the eastern road, the rebels would be able to penetrate further and faster into England and thus increase their chances of triggering an uprising. What was more, in the event of Wade being able to intercept them after all, Murray also claimed that the mountainous terrain would favour the Highlanders.[1]

However, in order to lessen the chances of such an interception, a deception plan was agreed. While the first division, encumbered by the baggage and artillery, set off from Dalkeith on the 1st of November and proceeded by the more direct route through Peebles and Moffat, the more lightly equipped Highland division, commanded by the Prince and Lord George Murray, waited at Dalkeith until the 3rd and then took a more easterly road by way of Lauder and Kelso. Then, after a day's halt there, it abruptly swung westwards through Jedburgh and Liddesdale to rejoin the rest of the army under Perth and Atholl just north of Carlisle on the 9th of November.

This at least was staff work of the highest order and as Captain Johnstone remarked: 'This march was arranged and executed with such precision that there was not an interval of two hours between the arrival of the different columns at the place of rendezvous.'[2] The credit for this was undoubtedly down to the march tables drawn up by Colonel Sullivan but, admirably executed though it was, the stratagem merely confused rather than misled Wade, for although rebel cavalry patrols had penetrated as far as Wooler, he was evidently also aware that the rebel artillery was apparently heading for Dumfries.

Unable to make sense of these conflicting reports, Wade simply fell back from Morpeth to his base at Newcastle. On the face of it this was a sensible enough move as it placed him in a central position from which he could either move forward into Northumberland, or westwards to Carlisle as soon as he had more definite intelligence of the rebels' actual intentions. Unfortunately he appears to have done little or nothing to obtain that vital intelligence. As he had three regular cavalry regiments at his immediate disposal and two more at Berwick, it ought to have been easy enough to keep the rebels under some sort of surveillance, yet he did nothing – an omission which is all the more surprising in that he was himself a cavalryman. Consequently, by the time he did receive definite news that the rebels were marching on Carlisle, it was too late.

The only positive step which he could be persuaded to take was the despatch of Lieutenant General Roger Handasyde to Berwick with two regiments of foot, Price's 14th and Ligonier's 59th. There Handasyde added the 13th and 14th Dragoons to his little brigade and set off on the 12th to re-occupy Edinburgh. There was nothing particularly glorious about his feat, and indeed the castle garrison had already re-established control of the city, but it was a move which was to have far-reaching consequences.

Meanwhile, at Carlisle, a comic-opera siege was just beginning.

Although its importance as a border stronghold had long since diminished, its status as a military way station on the western route into Scotland still justified the castle's garrison of two companies of Invalids. Fearing the worst, the Government had prudently ordered Cotterell's provisional battalion to concentrate there, but neither he nor any of the companies allocated to it had turned up. Indeed, with the exception of a few fugitives from Cope's army, the only regular reinforcement received by the garrison was Lieutenant Colonel James Durand of the 1st Footguards.

Arriving at Carlisle on the 11th of October, Durand was met by Captain

John Bernard Gilpin, the senior Invalid officer actually on duty, and immediately proceeded to inspect his charge:

'. . . which I found in a very weak and defenceless condition; having no ditch, no out-works of any kind, no cover'd way, – the walls very thin in most places, and without proper flanks; but agreed with Captain Gilpin . . . not to mention our opinion of the weakness of the place for fear of discouraging the Militia and inhabitants; but on the contrary, to speak of it as a strong place and very tenable.'

That was bad enough, but when he then turned his attention to the garrison, the gout-stricken Guardsman's heart must have quailed, for it comprised only:

'. . . two companys of Invalids, making about eighty men, very old and infirm; two companys of Militia, about one hundred and fifty men; one troop of Militia Horse, about seventy; and the town's-people, whom the Deputy Mayor inform'd me he had divided into nine companys of about thirty men each; but whether they consisted of that number, or not, I cannot tell, – as I could never see them out, tho' often ask'd, in order to examine how they were armed, and to teach them a little discipline . . . Captain Gilpin had also appointed eighty town's men as gunners, for the service of the artillery in the Castle.

'These appearing to me to be too weak a garrison for town and castle (especially as they were only Militia) and being informed there were five companys more of Militia disposed in the open towns and villages, I sent that night an express to Lord Lonsdale . . . that I thought it would be more for His Majesty's service for those companys to march into Carlisle, and reinforce the garrison, than remain where they were; and accordingly his Lordship sent a letter to the Deputy Lieutenants who brought them in.' [3]

No sooner had they done so, however, than the Militiamen threatened to march out again as the County could only pay them for one month's service and that month was now up. Some of them did indeed try to return home but Durand sent the Militia Horse to round them up again and persuaded the reluctant civil authorities to find the money to pay them. Even so, he continued to have his doubts about them and when he inspected them at their morning exercise he discovered to his dismay that their 'arms were of different bores, so that it was impossible to fit them out of the stores, I desired every man would make a sufficient quantity of ball according to the size of his piece, and ordered lead to be delivered out for that purpose.'

As if this was not enough, he also had to arrange for some hasty renovations of the defences and carry out all the myriad other prudent precautions for a possible siege. The original plan to reinforce the garrison with Cotterell's provisional battalion had been abandoned and he was now concentrating it near Portsmouth instead.[4] Then two Additional Companies of Howard's 3rd Foot, who were already on Tyneside were promised, although in the event they never turned up either. This, naturally, was a considerable disappointment, but the Guardsman battled on. In addition to the castle's 20 six-pounders, Captain Gilpin had managed to borrow a further 10 ship's guns from Whitehaven to place on the town walls, but they turned up with only six rounds apiece and it was then discovered that there were no embrasures for them anyway. More ammunition therefore had to be sought and embrasures made, sandbags had to be run up and filled, hasty repairs carried out to the crumbling defences, food to be procured, fields of fire cleared (a very unpopular move and not wholly successful), but by the time the rebels turned up at the beginning of November, Durand was probably as ready as he was going to be.

Predictably, the Jacobites' approach was preceded by a number of false alarms, but when his usual sources of intelligence at Dumfries suddenly dried up, Durand correctly apprehended that the rebels had cut the road and ordered Colonel John Dacre, the commander of the Militia Horse, to send out some patrols in order to find out exactly what was going on. Enterprisingly, they not only found the rebel advance guard near Ecclefechan, but one of the patrols also managed to capture a stray Quartermaster named Robert Randall.[5] Suitably alerted, Durand bundled Randall off to be interrogated by Wade, and then tried to prepare his little garrison by dividing it into three 'reliefs' with the sensible intention that only one relief and a small picquet from the others should be on duty at any one time. Sir John Pennington, the commander of the Militia Foot readily assented to this proposal, but to Durand's astonishment his men refused to countenance the idea, insisting instead that all of them should man the walls every night and that the townspeople should do likewise. Only the stout old regulars in the Invalid Companies obeyed him.

Next day, the 9th of November, he was further shocked to find that notwithstanding the imminent arrival of the rebels, considerable numbers of people had been allowed to wander freely into town for the weekly market. No sooner had they been turned out again and the gates shut than a Jacobite cavalry patrol appeared two miles away and came forward to Stanwix Bank, a steep escarpment immediately to the north of the castle. From there they sent a countryman named Robinson in to the town with a note, demanding quarters for thirteen thousand foot and three thousand horse. To this Durand very properly replied by opening fire on the Hussars with the castle guns and had the satisfaction of seeing them retire.

It was obvious that the rest of the rebel army must be close behind, and Durand therefore sent an express to Wade acquainting him of the fact. The following morning, however, he awoke to find Carlisle and its environs blanketed in thick fog. Under cover of this fog, both sides proceeded to blunder around blindly, each trying to find out exactly where the other was and what he was doing. Dacre's Militia Horse went out and eventually managed to establish that several large bodies of rebels were on the move and closing in towards the town, while simultaneously, some rebel scouting parties were actually examining the town walls as best they could!

'There was such a fog that day,' wrote Sullivan, 'yt a man cou'd hardly see his horses Ears, some personnes pretended to have reconnoitred a proper place to establish a battery, from whence they cou'd batter the Irish Forte (the Irish or west gate) without any manner of risk, upon wch H.R.Hs. order'd yt the Cannons shou'd immediately be sent there. The Duc of Athol seeing yt the Princes intention was to beseege the Town, tho' we had no other artillery but our swedish pieces of four pounders[6], wch wou'd hardly beat down a barn, & Copes Cannons of one poundre, desired the Comand of the seege wch was granted him. Accordingly he marched wth his own men, & the Duc of Perths, for the highlanders are not fit for Seeges. Sullivan was sent with the Duc of Athol, who when he reconnoitred yt famiouse place for a Battery, found there was no possibility of undertakeing anything there, it was within a smal musquet shot of the Castle, not a picaxe, Shouvel or facine to raise a Battery, and if there were it wou'd signify nothing with our artillery. Sullivan represented this to the Duke of Athol, who retired.'[7]

That the earlier reconnaisance party failed to notice that the proposed battery position was overlooked by the castle may charitably be attributed to the thickness of the fog, but as a bare 50 yards separated the gate from the bridge over the river Cauda it is quite extraordinary that they pitched upon it in the first place. At any rate, at about noon, the fog started to lift and, seeing Atholl's men on the march towards the gate, Durand again opened fire and quickly persuaded them to retreat. Then another party was observed crossing the Carlisle fields and they too retired after being fired upon.

So far so good, and next day yet another rebel cavalry patrol was dislodged from Stanwix Bank, and was reported to have retired to Brampton. Nor were any rebels to be seen on Tuesday. But after sending out Dacre's scouts, Durand learned that they had indeed retired to Brampton, although a rearguard was covering Warwick Bridge. The withdrawal had been occasioned by a false report that Wade was on the march, and eager preparations were made to fight him there. His subsequent non-appearance caused a cavalry patrol to be pushed as far east as Haltwhistle (they may actually have gone even further for one of them was reported to have been captured at Hexham), but it returned to report neither sight nor sound of him. The Prince, enthusiastic as ever, immediately proposed that since Wade was obviously unwilling to face them, they should go and seek him out, but in the end the rebels decided to return to Carlisle.

This time the Duke of Perth was to conduct the siege, with the Atholl Brigade, Lord Ogilvy's Regiment, John Roy Stuart's Regiment, Glenbucket's Regiment and his own two battalions. The basic plan was simple enough; while Perth established a battery, Lord George Murray, who readily admitted he knew nothing of sieges, volunteered to cover the works and maintain a notional blockade of the town with what Sullivan rather grandly termed an army of observation.[8]

Their timing was particularly unfortunate, for shortly after Durand received ominous reports that the rebel detachment at Warwick Bridge was busy making scaling ladders, a messenger turned up, carrying Wade's reply to Durand's express. In it, Wade expressed scepticism that Carlisle was in any danger, declaring (rightly enough) that they did not have any siege guns and that it was much more likely that they would by-pass the town and make for Lancashire, where he (Wade) hoped to meet them 'and cause them to repent of their rashness.'[9] However, learning of the letter and its contents, the Militia officers concluded that since Wade was not coming to their aid, all was lost, and decided to escape from the town while they still could. At this point Durand, not surprisingly, lost his temper and sent them back to their posts, but his troubles with them were only just beginning.

On the night of the 13th, Perth proceeded to invest the town and under the direction of Colonel James Grant a battery was established about 300 yards from the East Curtain, a long straight stretch of town wall running on a north-south line between the Scotch and English Gates.[10] Unlike the position previously proposed outside the Irish Gate, this one was on the far side of the town from the castle and thus masked from its fire, but at a range of 300 yards the rebel 4lbrs were, as Sullivan acidly remarked, incapable of knocking down a barn let alone breaching the mediaeval walls.

Durand thought so too: 'At day break the Rebels were perceived throwing up a small entrenchment about three hundred yards from the Citadell; which being informed of, I immediately went to view it, and there found a great crowd of people, who seemed to be alarmed at it; upon which I said everything to encourage them to do their duty, assuring them that it was nothing but a poor paltry ditch, that did not deserve the name of

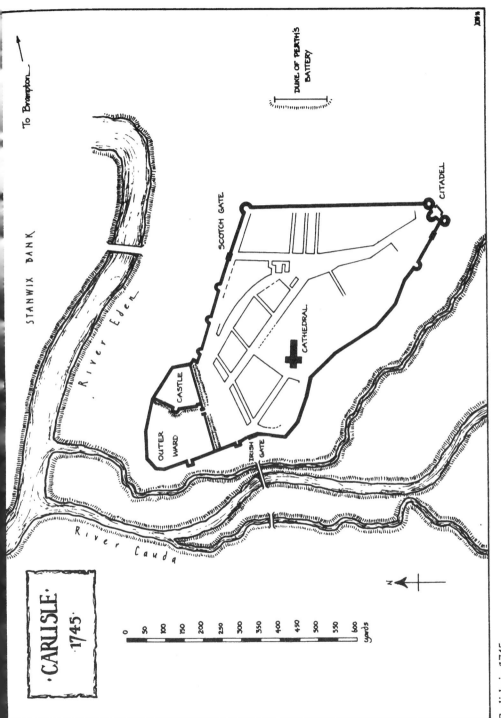

To Brampton

STANWIX BANK

River Eden

DUKE OF PERTH'S BATTERY

SCOTCH GATE

CASTLE

OUTER WARD

IRISH GATE

CATHEDRAL

CITADEL

River Cauda

N

·CARLISLE·
·1745·

0 50 100 150 200 250 300 350 400 450 500 550 600
yards

Carlisle in 1745.

61

Map 2

an intrenchment; that the Rebels had no cannon large enough to make a breach in our walls; . . . and gave orders to fire upon them.'[11]

His display of resolution was wasted, for on going next to the King's Arms, where the Militia officers were assembled, he was greeted by an announcement that neither they nor their men could defend the town any longer and they even presented him with a signed declaration to that effect. As a sop, they also added that Durand and Gilpin had 'well and faithfully done their duty', but the Guardsman was in no mood to be mollified and when the Deputy Mayor, Thomas Pattison, asked him what he intended to do, he snarled that he was; 'determined never to capitulate with Rebels, but would defend both Town and Castle as long as I could.'

Soon afterwards the townsmen decided to join with the Militia in surrendering, so after giving them all a piece of his mind Durand, who to add to his woes, was also lame with an attack of gout, retired into the castle with the Invalids. Soon afterwards he was joined there by most of the Militia officers and about 400 of their men, which restored some of his optimism. Unable to bring the guns in off the walls he ordered them spiked, recalled all the firelocks, ammunition and hand grenades issued to the town companies and gathered in all the provisions he could lay his hands on. Although evidence was later to be given at his court martial that the castle really required a garrison of 800 men, there was still no reason at this stage why he should not have been able to hold out indefinitely against the rebels.

Indeed had he but known it, the rebels had troubles enough of their own. Perth's men, having spent all night in the trenches, were now eager to be relieved, but Lord George Murray refused to release any of his blockading battalions for that purpose. On the contrary, having convinced himself that the detachments, which he had earlier placed to cover each of the town's gates, were so widely dispersed as to be vulnerable to a sally, he had in effect abandoned the blockade and recalled both Nairne's and Shian's battalions of the Atholl Brigade to his own headquarters at Harraby. He also wrote a querulous letter to his brother, expressing the opinion that Perth's battery was badly sited, and going on to say that he thought it:

'. . . my duty to tell you, so as you may represent it to his Royal Highness, that the men posted upon the blockade of Carlisle will not expose themselves, either in trenches, or all night in the open air, within cannon shot, or even musket shot, of the town, except it be their turn with the rest of the army, and that to be decided by lot who to mount that guard . . .'

As an opinion delivered beforehand in a council of war, the proposal may well have had some merit, but coming from an officer actually on duty, this refusal to relieve the men in the trenches was dangerously close to mutiny. Moreover, without pausing to draw breath or to acknowledge that not twenty-four hours before he had agreed to the Duke of Perth taking charge of the siege, he proceeded, without any reference to his supposed superior officer, to propose an entirely different plan for besieging the town:

> 'The way I would propose, if it be approved of by a council of war, is as follows: that fifty men be draughted out of each of the battalions that are at Brampton, with proper officers, and at least two majors out of the six battalions, and be sent to quarters at Butcherby, which, I believe, is within a mile of the battery; and, as I suppose one hundred and fifty men will mount guard at the battery, these six battalions will furnish two guards, your men [the Atholl Brigade] will furnish one, General Gordon and Lord Ogilvies, one, which in whole makes four Guards or reliefs; and I think, by that time, the town will either be taken, or the blockade removed. I don't mention the Duke of Perth's regiment, because they have more than their turn of duty already, besides furnishing workmen, &c.; and for Colonel John Roy Stewart's regiment, I suppose they have the guard of the equipage, &c. and they will perhaps be able to furnish some workmen. If anything be done of this nature, the sooner I hear of it the better.'[12]

In effect he was blandly attempting to usurp Perth's authority and gain overall control of the siege after all, but a council of war convened at Brampton to discuss his extraordinary letter decided in effect to ignore his proposals. The clan regiments would only relieve Perth's division after all Murray's regiments had taken their turn on guard, and 'no detachments can be sent from the different corps, nor do they think it fair to require them to do so, as they had all the fatigue and danger of the blockade in Edinburgh.'

Murray's immediate reaction to this rebuff is not recorded, for his proposal was in any case overtaken by events; at about five that evening, the white flag was hung out over the walls of Carlisle.

Perth, who was still in the trenches, refused however to accept the surrender of the town unless the castle was included in the capitulation and gave the magistrates until next morning to persuade Durand to follow suit. Durand makes no mention of such a proposal being put to him at that time, but at about one o'clock on the morning of the 15th, Captain Gilpin reported that none of the Militia were on the walls. Durand thereupon roused out Sir John Pennington who managed to persuade about thirty men to go on sentry, promising to relieve them within an hour. Unfortunately it was a dirty night and no sooner had the officers gone back to bed than they slunk off again. Worse still, they and the rest of the Militia then mutinied:

'A general confusion ensued, numbers went over the walls; others forced their way out the gates; upon which I earnestly entreated the Militia officers to go to their men and endeavour all their power to prevail upon them to stay and do their duty, which they promised they would, but without effect; for before eight o'clock in the morning, they had all left us to a man; and we remained with only our few Invalids, who from their great age and infirmities, and from the excesive fatigue they had undergone, occasioned by the frequent false alarms we had, which had kept them almost continually upon duty, were rendered in a manner of no use.'[13]

It was the begining of the end, and at ten o'clock he received a deputation from the town, informing him of the rebel threats that unless an immediate surrender was made the town would be set on fire and its inhabitants put to the sword. Defiant to the last Durand again refused and tried to persuade the Militia officers to bring their men back, but on their refusing he at last bowed to the inevitable.

The capitulation dictated by Perth provided that the castle garrison should march out with drums beating and lay down their arms, while the Militia were likewise to surrender both arms and horses. Both would then be allowed to depart after giving their paroles while Perth's Regiment received the reward of taking immediate possession of the castle, but for the Mayor and Aldermen further humiliation was to follow. They were to greet the Prince at the gates, hand over the keys and then proclaim King James at the market cross.

The triumph was, however, somewhat spoiled by Lord George Murray. Angered by the rejection of the proposals he had made the day before, and the fact that his rival, Perth (who had after all done the work) had been allowed to dictate the capitulation, Murray petulantly resigned his appointment as Lieutenant General that morning.[14] The Prince, who had no love for the arrogant Murray, accepted with alacrity, but first Atholl and then the other Colonels interceded on his behalf, urging a reconciliation and Murray's reinstatement. In the face of this vote of confidence in Murray, or rather lack of confidence in Perth and Atholl, the Prince reluctantly acquiesced and Perth generously relinquished his post in order to avoid any further clashes.

Unfortunately, it also meant that from now on operational command of the army was to be disputed between the Prince, whose optimism blinded him to the realities of the situation, and Lord George Murray, whose appreciation of those realities bordered upon insubordinate pessimism.

Meanwhile Wade was at last on the march. Convinced at last by the capture of the rebel scout at Hexham that the threat to Carlisle was real, but unprepared for the swiftness of its surrender, he ordered his army to move out of Newcastle on the 16th.

From the very start it all went badly wrong. The Swiss regiment Hirzler was to have the van, but refused to move until ten o'clock and then when they did move progress was painfully slow. The roads were a mass of frost-hardened ruts and the fields on either side were thickly carpeted with snow. Consequently they only got as far as Ovingham that night and were forced to bivouac on an open moor. Next day was no better and at Hexham, Wade learned that Carlisle had fallen, and the heart went out of his exhausted army.

Next day, Brigadier General James Cholmondley, the Colonel of the 34th, wrote from there to his brother about: '. . . miserable roads, terrible frost and snow. We did not get to our [camping] grounds till near 8 and as my quarters were five miles off I did not get there till 11, almost starved to death with cold and hunger, but revived by a pipe and a little good wine. Next morning we found some of the poor fellows frozen to death for they could get nothing to eat after marching 13 hours. The next day we marched to this place. Roads and weather the same. Got to camp about eight. Nothing for the men . . . it strikes me to the heart to see the distress of the poor fellows borne without murmuring. I do everything in my power to assist them, every morning I fill my pockets with sixpences which I give to the men and keep an open table for the subs: this is some relief although but a mite considering our numbers. Our men fall sick apace.'[15]

Disgusted by Wade's failure to provide adequate supplies for the expedition and dismayed by the sudden surrender of Carlisle, a council of war held at Hexham on the 19th unanimously agreed to retire to Newcastle. With Wade's army thus run into the ground and Sir John Ligonier no further north than Lichfield, England lay wide open to the rebels.

They, for their part, held a council of war of their own on the 18th. Once again the arguments put forward at Edinburgh were rehearsed and the question debated as to whether they should return to Scotland, hang around at Carlisle waiting either for reinforcements or for Wade to turn up, or else to push on southwards. The Prince was naturally in favour of 'Going Straight to London', but it was objected that the army was incapable of doing this without an English rising or a French landing. To this, the Prince replied that he was confident of both, and although sceptical, Murray agreed to go along with him. With a garrison in Carlisle to secure their retreat they had little to lose and everything to gain.

The heavy baggage had proved a serious impediment on the march from Edinburgh and indeed some wagons carrying the army's tents had been captured by Loyalist partisans near Dumfries. It was decided therefore that John Hamilton, who was to hold Carlisle with 300 men drafted out of the lowland regiments[16], would also be left in charge of the heavy baggage and a large proportion of the ammunition. The regimental women were to be left behind as well, though this particular prohibition seems to have been as little regarded as it was in the British army. Having lost their tents, the rebels also decided to march in two divisions, the first a day ahead of the second in order to ease the problem of finding sufficient accommodation.

Accordingly, on the 20th, Lord George Murray marched from Carlisle at the head of the Atholl Brigade, Glenbucket's, John Roy Stuart's and the Duke of Perth's Regiments. Ogilvy's Regiment was also supposed to form part of this division, but according to its orderly book it spent the day resting at Butcherby and therefore marched with the Prince's division on the 21st. The artillery was also attached to Murray's division, presumably on the principle that if it fell behind, the Prince's division would be able to pick it up. In the event it proved to be so much of an impediment that at Penrith, the first halt, all but a 'smale quantity' of ammunition for it was sent back to Carlisle.

On the 22nd both divisions joined at Kendal and rested there until the 25th when the Prince's division took the lead, and by the 29th they were at Manchester. The town had been captured by Sergeant John Dickson of the Duke of Perth's Regiment, his girlfriend, and a drummer.[17]

There, for the first time sufficient recruits were found to form a regiment. Two of the Irish officers, Francis Geohegan and Ignatious Browne had been given commissions by the Prince to raise men, but on second thoughts it was considered expedient to give the command instead to Francis Townley, a Lancashire gentleman who had previously served in the French army. Even so, the Manchester Regiment numbered little more than 200 men and barely sufficed to compensate for the men left behind at Carlisle.

Thus far the rebels had met no opposition since leaving Carlisle, but now that was to change.

Sources:

1. Elcho, p. 305.
2. Johnstone, p. 49.
3. *Proceedings of the General Court Martial held for the Trial of Lieutenant Colonel James Durand the 15th and 16th of September 1746*
4. They relieved Richbell's 39th as garrison of Portsmouth on the 14th of November, Atkinson, p. 293.

5. Randall, a former Customs officer, was sensible enough to co-operate with his interrogators and accompanied Handasyde to Scotland in order to 'make discoveries'. Consequently although sentenced to death, he was pardoned on condition of his enlisting in the army. *Prisoners*, no. 2782 – see also the *Newcastle Gazette*.

6. The 'Swedish' cannon were actually of French manufacture, having iron barrels which were shorter and much lighter in weight than their brass counterparts. With an effective range of 600 yards, the 'Swedish' gun was in theory reckoned to be capable of firing at the astonishing rate of eight rounds per minute in contrast to the three rounds per minute to be expected from more conventional 4 lbrs. However its low muzzle velocity made it much less effective when firing at stone walls.

7. Sullivan, p. 92.

8. Sullivan, p. 93; Elcho, p. 313.

9. Durand Court Martial.

10. Elcho, p. 313. The position of the battery is more precisely identified on a contemporary plan by G. Smith.

11. Durand Court Martial.

12. Murray, p. 49–50.

13. Durand Court Martial.

14. 'Sir, – I cannot but observe how little my advice as a general officer has any weight with your Royal Highness, ever since I had the honour of a commission from your hands. I therefore take leave to give up my commission. But as I ever had a firm atachment to the royal family, and in particular to the king, my master, I shall go on as a volunteer, and design to be this night in the trenches as such, with any others that will please to follow me, though I own there are full few on this post already. Your Royal Highness will please order whom you think fit to command on this post and the other parts of the blockade ... Lord Elcho has the command till you please appoint it otherwise.' Murray, p. 50–1.

15. Quoted in J. Black, *Culloden and the '45*, p. 105.

16. *The Orderly Book of Lord Ogilvy's Regiment* reveals that 6 officers, 2 Sergeants and 50 men were ordered to be drafted from the regiment on the 20th of November to join the garrison.

17. The story is to be found in Johnstone p. 54–6, and incredible though it may sound, it is confirmed by contemporary newspaper reports. For some reason he is identified by Livingston, Aikman and Hart (p. 68) as Thomas Dicks, but as Dicks was evidently unable to sign his own name, there is no reason to doubt that the enterprising Sergeant was in fact John Dickson (who *could* sign his name very clearly). Picked up at Prestonpans after Culloden, he was released in 1747.

CHAPTER 6

To Derby – And Back Again
The Campaign in England Concluded

Exhausted physically and mentally by his abortive excursion to Hexham, Wade did not get his army on the move again until the 26th of November. As we have already seen, Sir John Ligonier had been appointed to command an army placed to block any rebel force evading Wade, but unfortunately Ligonier fell ill before he could join it in its concentration area around Lichfield and would shortly be superceded by Cumberland. It is unlikely however that his absence actually made much difference at this early stage in the campaign, for as it happened he had in any case planned to keep his army in its concentration area for as long as possible, with a tripwire of Provincial troops and militia covering the Mersey crossings at Warrington and Stockport.

To that end Kingston's 10th Horse were ordered to assemble at Warrington, where they were reported 'half complete' and therefore fit to be accepted for service on the 12th of October, while Colonel William Graham's 'Liverpool Blues' were also ordered there on the 19th of November, armed with discretionary orders to fall back on Chester if it became necessary.[1]

Chester itself was intended to be well defended since it was regarded as strategically important, both as a gateway to Ireland, whence further reinforcements might be drawn, and more immediately perhaps to North Wales, which was widely seen as a possible Jacobite objective. Five companies of Blakeney's 27th Foot were therefore posted there in September, and Lord Cholmondley, disdaining even to try to muster the moribund militia, assembled his new 73rd Foot in the city. He was able to report it 'half complete' on the 4th of November[2], but the government, still concerned that they might not be sufficient, ordered up Lord Gower's newly raised 77th Foot from Birmingham, and Cumberland subsequently reinforced them with 220 men of Bligh's rather more reliable 20th Foot under Lieutenant-Colonel Edward Cornwallis.

The composition of the army assembling at Lichfield is at first sight unclear, for there are three extant lists, one published in contemporary newspapers, another, perhaps based on it which was passed on to the rebels by a captured British intelligence officer, Captain John Weir, and a third provided by Lieutenant Archibald Campbell which just covers the regular troops.

According to the first two, Cumberland had three battalions of Foot-guards, and seven other 'old' battalions: Howard's 3rd, Sowle's 11th, Skelton's 12th, Bligh's 20th, Sempill's 25th, Douglas's 32nd and Johnston's 33rd. In addition there were said to be six 'new' battalions: Bedford's 68th, Montague's 69th, Granby's 71st, Cholmondley's 73rd, Halifax's 74th and Gower's 77th. The cavalry element was reported to comprise four troops of Ligonier's 8th Horse, and three regiments of Dragoons: Bland's 3rd, Cobham's 10th and Ker's 11th, together with both Provincial cavalry regiments: Montague's 9th and Kingston's 10th Horse. In all, according to the newspaper reports they numbered some 13,900 men. Weir's very similar version, while listing the same regiments, quotes a total of only 8,250 infantry and 2,200 cavalry.

Neither list is accurate. In the first place both Cholmondley's 73rd and Gower's 77th were actually in Chester, while on the other hand, Lieutenant Campbell, serving as an ADC to General Bland, included Campbell's 21st and Handasyde's 31st.[3]

At any rate, by the time Cumberland took up his new comand on the 28th of November (the very day that Sergeant Dickson and his girlfriend were capturing Manchester), it was too late to think of holding the Mersey crossings. As early as the 23rd, Cholmondley had already ordered Graham to break two arches of the Warrington bridge and then retire into Chester. This should at least have blocked any rebel thrust towards Chester and North Wales, but some uncertainty on this point remained even after the rebels left Manchester on the 1st of December and crossed the Mersey at Stockport and Knutsford on their way to Macclesfield.

Anxious to find out just what was going on, Cumberland got his cavalry out, but unfortunately the only major contact was achieved at Congleton the next day, when Kingston's 10th Horse retreated hastily from the unexpected appearance of the Atholl Brigade and some cavalry under Lord George Murray. This was rather hastily interpreted by Cumberland's headquarters as the start of a move towards Wales after all, which was exactly what Murray had hoped to achieve, for the rest of the rebel army actually spent the day resting at Macclesfield before heading off south-eastwards to Leek on the 3rd. Consequently, while Cumberland halted at Stone in Staffordshire on the 2nd and occupied a suitable battle-field there on the following day, the rebels were able to press on unmolested to Derby, which their advance guard entered on the afternoon of the 4th.

So far so good, but the tables were about to be dramatically turned. Before leaving Congleton, Lord George Murray decided to send Lord

Kilmarnock's Horse on a reconnaisance towards Newcastle-under-Lyme. This time they surprised a party of dragoons at the Red Lion in Talke, just to the north of Newcastle. Once again a hasty retreat followed, this time so precipitately that in the confusion the dragoons managed to leave behind the very man they had been escorting – an intelligence officer named Captain John Weir. Disregarding enthusiastic proposals that he should be strung up on the spot, Murray decided that Weir was of more use alive and sent him straight back to be interrogated, with quite unforeseen results.

Having now arrived within striking distance of London, the Prince was confident of a glorious victory, and after a day's rest at Derby he proposed to press on towards London on the 6th. But to his astonishment he was suddenly told by Lord George Murray that it was the council's opinion that it was now time to retreat while they had the chance.

When Captain Weir was interrogated about Cumberland's forces, he had cheerfully handed over a copy of the newspaper report, which he no doubt reasoned the rebels would pick up for themselves sooner or later anyway. Even though he disarmingly reduced the printed figures for the infantry to allow for those units posted to Chester, and said nothing about the 21st and 31st, the totals were still vastly disquieting and probably far higher than anybody in the Jacobite camp had been expecting. Thoroughly alarmed Lord George Murray bluntly advised the Prince that the game was up:

> 'Lord George told him that it was the opinion of Every body present that the Scots had now done all that could be Expected of them. That they had marched into the heart of England ready to join with any party that would declare for him, that none had, and that the Counties through which the Army had pass'd had Seemed much more Enemies than friends to his Cause, that their was no French Landed in England, and that if there was any party in England for him, it was very odd that they had never so much as Either sent him money or intelligence or the least advice what to do...Suppose even the Army march'd on and beat the Duke of Cumberland yett in the Battle they must Lose some men, and they had after that the King's own army consisting of near 7000 men near London to deal with . . . that certainly 4500 Scots had never thought of putting a King upon the English Throne by themselves . . .' [5]

Only the Duke of Perth was prepared to support the Prince by voting in favour of continuing the march, and an immediate retreat was determined upon. Not surprisingly the highly strung Prince promptly fell into something of a 'passion' at this news. Indeed so violent was his tantrum that afterwards even Colonel Sullivan (who had not been present at the council, let alone supporting the Prince) for once let slip the professional staff officer's mask of loyalty:

'The Chiefs & others were sent for, who were the most part of them for the retraite, and really according to all the rules of War, & prudence, it was the only party to be taken (Sullivan propos'd it at Manchester finding yt not a man of any consequence appear'd;) but a Young Prince, yt sees himself within three days, or at utmost four days, march of the Capital, where if he was once arrived, wou'd in all appearance restor the King, cou'd not relish the word of retrait, & really he wou'd not hear yt word from the beginning, he had an avertion it self, but finding every body allmost of yt oppinion was obliged to consent. I never saw any body so concerned as he was for this disappointmt, nor never saw him take any thing after so much to heart as he did it.'[6]

The wisdom of their retreating at this point has always been a fruitful topic of debate amongst pro-Jacobite writers, and it is often claimed that had the rebel leaders but known it, a rising had actually begun in Wales under Sir Watkin Williams Wynn and that the insurgents were even then on the march. If the Prince and his followers continued southwards from Derby, it is argued that they would indeed have been joined by the supporters they sought and a Stuart restoration would thus have been assured. Although there were certainly rumours of such an uprising in contemporary newspapers, such an outcome is of course sheer wishful thinking. Even under vastly more favourable conditions in 1651, King Charles II had failed to raise more than a handful of English and Welsh reinforcements for the Scots army which he led to disaster at Worcester. A similar battle with Cumberland was perhaps no more than two days away, and even if the Welsh insurgents did exist they would be quite unable to affect the outcome of that encounter.

Moreover, if Cumberland's army was evaded or beaten there was still the army which the King himself was assembling at Finchley – and that was a good deal more formidable than Jacobite propaganda and Hogarth's infamous painting suggests.

The 5th of January return lists no fewer than eighteen regular infantry battalions in the London area, including the Footguards. Half of them appear to have been serving under Cumberland in December, but quite apart from a motley collection of volunteers, that still left nine battalions, besides two regiments of dragoons (one of them dismounted), the remaining two troops of Ligonier's 8th Horse, and the Horse Guards and Horse Grenadier Guards.[7]

Meanwhile, aware that the rebels had slipped past him, Cumberland had begun a forced march, intending to head them off at Northampton, which he reckoned to reach by the 8th. Thanks to their resting at Derby he was able to gain a whole day and by the 6th had most of his men on Meriden Heath, just north of Coventry, while his advance guard had actually reached the town. Consequently he did not receive word that the rebels had turned back until quite late in the day, but then once again he moved hard and fast. Recognising that they had a head start, he left most of his infantry behind under Ligonier and hurried on just with the cavalry and 1,000 volunteers who claimed to know how to ride mounted on country nags. This small force would not by itself be capable of taking on the Jacobites if they remained together in a body, but Cumberland was pinning his hopes on Wade's army being able to throw itself in their path.

Unfortunately Wade still lacked the sense of urgency and purpose being so forcefully demonstrated by the Duke and his men. By the 8th of December his cavalry had advanced no further south than Doncaster, while his infantry were still back at Ferrybridge. On receiving Cumberland's orders he duly turned westwards, but was no further forward than Wakefield on the 10th. As the Jacobites were then at Manchester there was clearly no prospect whatsoever of his being able to carry out Cumberland's wishes and at this point he simply gave up, turned around and headed back to Newcastle with his infantry and a single cavalry regiment, while a cavalry brigade commanded by Brigadier General James Oglethorpe made a gallant, if unsuccessful, attempt to get ahead of the rebels at Preston.

This brigade comprised Montague's 3rd Horse[8], St George's 8th Dragoons, Oglethorpe's own Georgia Rangers and the Yorkshire Hunters. In the event the rebels, by dint of a seventeen-mile march, arrived safely in Preston on the night of the 11th, while Oglethorpe's command was struggling into Huddersfield. Although the rebels had consistently shown themselves capable of marching further and faster than the regulars, these bursts of speed were bought at the cost of frequent rest days during which the army was totally immobilised. Thus, while they rested up at Preston on the 12th, Oglethorpe pushed on to Rochdale and a rendezvous with Kingston's 10th Horse, and the next day clattered into Preston just hours behind the rebel rearguard.

The rebels had considered making a stand at Preston, but after some discussion it was decided to continue the retreat while the Duke of Perth, escorted by Bagot's Hussars rode hard for Scotland to fetch reinforcements and in particular a French expeditionary force led by his younger brother, Lord John Drummond, which was now known to have landed in Scotland. At the same time, the Prince took it into his head to turn and fight, perhaps with the idea of defeating Oglethorpe before Cumberland could join him. To that end Lord George Murray and Colonel Sullivan were sent to reconnoitre a possible battlefield near Lancaster. Having provided themselves with a suitable escort they went back a couple of miles, where after some debate 'we found a very fine field, upon a rising ground, that could contain our whole army, and which, every way the enemy could come, we would be under cover of the rising ground till they were close upon us.'[9]

When they turned to rejoin the army, they discovered a dozen horsemen 'cload in green with leather caps'. Outnumbered by the rebels they at once attempted to escape, but being badly mounted one was shot and two taken prisoner. Under interrogation they revealed that they belonged to Oglethorpe's Georgia Rangers and that the rest of the Rangers were at Garstang, just a few miles away, while a great body of dragoons had just arrived at Preston.[10]

Cumberland had finally caught up, although he was already under pressure to slacken his pursuit. At Macclesfield a despatch caught up with him, in which he was instructed to stand fast and concentrate his army at Coventry, in readiness to deal with a threatened French landing. Unwilling to give up the chase at this juncture, and doubtless reflecting that as most of his infantry were still close enough to Coventry, he pressed on and linked up with Oglethorpe on the 13th. Then he received a yet more peremptory despatch containing the alarming (but false) news that the French had actually landed, and ordering an immediate return to London. Reluctantly he at once halted, but then the following day was delighted to have the orders countermanded. The chase was on again.

Realising that he had missed his chance to catch Oglethorpe unsupported, the Prince had ordered the retreat to continue and on the 15th, while Cumberland was still cooling his heels at Preston, the rebels marched to Kendal, where to their surprise they were rejoined by Perth and the Hussars. In marching south from Carlisle the rebels had met with no resistance, but now it was an altogether different matter, for the Militia had recovered their courage and had already tasted blood.

On the 28th of November, Hamilton, the rebel governor of Carlisle, had sent a party of 19 men southwards, seemingly with the intention of carrying news and despatches to the Prince. Arriving in Penrith, the rebels ordered supper, but intimidated by a gathering mob, they rode off to Lowther Hall instead. As the owner Lord Lonsdale was the Lord Lieutenant of the county they must have considered his house fair game, for they set about plundering his wine cellar. While they were thus agreeably engaged, a band of loyalist partisans turned up and launched a brisk attack at about eleven that night, which was graphically described by one of the participants:

'Mr Hermitage, Ld Lonsdales Steward, came to Penrith for Assistance, where 70 Men, 40 of them armed with Muskets, some of them with

Pistols, Swords, Pitchforks, &c. joined him. The Rebels had secured all the Gates and placed a strong Guard at the Porter's Lodge, nigh the great Iron Gate, where the first Attack began, but the Steward led us a private Way under their Noses; where we loudly huzzaing, the Guard fired upon us, which we returned with a constant running Fire for some Minutes; when the rest of them, from the Kitchen and Stables sallied out and flanked us. Then several of our men retreated and could never be brought up again; but about 18 of them having loaded, returned their Fire, and bravely drove them from the Lodge to the middle Area, among the Statues, where they fired from behind them; but were so warmly plied, and several of them wounded, that they were forced to retreat into close Quarters in the Kitchen and Stables; where after some Resistance, being surrounded, they begg'd Quarter. Ten of them were made Prisoners, four of whom were wounded.'[11]

Not surprisingly this skirmish produced threats of reprisal from Carlisle and by way of insurance a company of 60 loyalist volunteers was raised in Penrith. Thus when Perth turned up there en route back to Scotland he had an uncomfortably brisk reception, lost a couple of men wounded, and after unsuccessfully trying to get through or around the militia, retired back across Shap to Kendal.

There, Murray was vigorously arguing that the ammunition should be transferred from the big four-wheeled wagons into lighter two-wheeled carts which would be easier to get across Shap. He also claims to have advocated that the soldiers should be ordered to provide themselves with enough bread and cheese for the march, but that the Prince and Sullivan were too busy working their way through some 'mountain Malaga, which he seemed very fond of, and gave me a glass or two of it.' Moreover, continued Murray, the orders for the next day's march still had not been written when he left the convivial little gathering at eleven that night.[12] This particular incident is frequently quoted as an instance of Sullivan's incompetence but in actual fact the orders which he wrote for that day's march not only survive but are remarkably comprehensive and as usual eminently sensible. The order of march is detailed, and 'The Officers are to see that their men be provided with a day's Provision', while the artillery with its escort was to depart an hour before the rest of the army and march by way of Orton, presumably because it was reckoned easier going. Unspecified 'particular orders' were also to be given for the march of the artillery.[13]

These 'particular orders' presumably related to the substitution of carts for the heavy wagons, as Murray had asked, but it soon transpired that there were not enough of them to be had and the march was further delayed by soldiers straggling around Kendal trying to find the provisions which Murray had recommended that they be ordered to provide for themselves. After that bad start, things could only get worse. As Murray had predicted, the artillery wagons soon got bogged down and in the end it took two days for the rearguard and artillery to get up to Shap. The rest of the army by this time was at Penrith, and as Murray tried to regain contact, he became uneasily aware that the British army had once again caught up.

Oglethorpe had in fact caught up the night before. Encouraged by the happy sight of abandoned carts and ammunition, he and his men pressed forward through filthy weather only to find Shap still stuffed full of rebels. Since his men were too hungry and exhausted to mount an immediate attack in the gathering darkness, Oglethorpe turned aside to the tiny village of Orton and thus, to Cumberland's fury, lost contact with the rebels at a critical moment.

Later that night, the Duke, correctly deducing that there was only a rearguard in Shap, sent positive orders to Oglethorpe, requiring him to dismount his Dragoons and Rangers and throw in an immediate assault on the village. Unfortunately Oglethorpe neglected to inform the Duke's headquarters that he had left the road and moved to Orton and thus, by the time the messenger finally caught up with him, it was too late. Not only had the rebels got away, but next morning an enraged Cumberland actually reached Shap before Oglethorpe. The unhappy Brigadier was reprimanded in front of his men, and would later be court-martialled for his failure to pin the rebel rearguard, but for the moment the pursuit had to be maintained and at about noon the Georgia Rangers managed to get between Murray and the main body of the rebels at Penrith.

Realising the danger, the rebels attacked them at once:

'We stopped a moment at the foot of the hill, everybody believing it was the English army, from the great number of trumpets and kettle-drums. In this seemingly desperate conjuncture, we immediately adopted the opinion of Mr. Browne[14] and resolved to rush upon the enemy sword in hand and open a passage to our army at Penrith, or perish in the attempt. Thus, without informing Lord George of our resolution, we darted forward with great swiftness, running up the hill as fast as our legs could carry us. Lod George, who was in the rear, seeing our manoeuvre at the head of the column, and being unable to pass the wagons in the deep roads confined by hedges in which we then were, immediately ordered the Highlanders to proceed across the enclosure, and ascend the hill from another quarter. They ran so fast that they reached the summit of the hill almost as soon as those who were at the head of the column. We were agreeably surprised when we reached the top to find, instead of the English army, only three hundred light-horse and chasseurs, who immediately fled in disorder. We were only able to come up with one man who had been thrown from his horse and whom we wished to make prisoner . . . But it was impossible to save him from the fury of the Highlanders, who cut him to pieces in an instant.'[15]

Undeterred, the Rangers regrouped, and joined by part of Cumberland's personal Hussar escort (a small troop of Austrians and Germans, dressed in his livery of crimson and green) harassed the retreat of Murray's rearguard nearly all the way to Clifton. There Murray was joined by two cavalry units – Lord Pitsligo's Horse and Bagot's Hussars and encouraged by this evidence that he had not after all been forgotten, he secured the village with John Roy Stuart's Regiment and sent on the artillery escorted by Perth's Regiment, while he and the Glengarry men went looking for the Rangers at nearby Lowther Hall. Some were indeed there, though not as many as he expected. Nevertheless an officer was taken prisoner and with him one of the Duke of Cumberland's running footmen. A hasty interrogation then elicited the unwelcome news that Cumberland had indeed caught up and was less than a mile away. John Roy Stuart was immediately sent back to Penrith in order to alert the Prince, while Murray hurried back to Clifton.

In his absence, Cumberland himself had arrived before the village and in a brisk little skirmish drove off the rebel cavalry, as a gentleman styling himself a 'Volunteer Surgeon' related:

'On Wednesday Morning the Duke march'd out of Kendal at the Head of the Horse, the Foot did not come into Kendal till Three on Thursday Morning, having march'd that Day 43 Miles, which is the greatest March ever known; and next Day got to Penrith, which is 25 Miles more;[16] . . . As the Horse was coming off Clifton Moor into the Town, our Hussars and Rangers engag'd all the Rebel Hussars, who were headed by one Captain Hamilton, that was a Writer at Edinburgh, and had a paternal Estate of £500 a Year, a very bold Fellow; he was cut down and taken by one of the Duke's Hussars, after a stout Resistance; there is also a common Hussar taken by one of Oglethorpe's Rangers, who is a Manchester Man; but what he was he will not tell. This was at Three in the Afternoon;'[17]

Perth also turned up at about the same time as Murray, bringing with him Cluny's MacPhersons and the Appin men under Ardshiel, and airily informed Murray that he was only facing some militia. The sight of Cumberland's dragoons deploying on to the moor above the village was enough to disabuse him of this notion however, and he hastily galloped off to bring up the rest of the army for what was threatening to be a major battle.

In the meantime Murray prepared what few troops he had to hang on until they arrived. The Glengarry men were placed in the enclosures on the west side of the road, while Roy Stuart's Regiment was placed astride it in front of the village, and the two newly arrived battalions, led by Cluny and Ardshiel, went onto an enclosure on the east side. In all Murray reckoned he only had about 1,000 men, and so in order to conceal his weakness, he:

> '. . . caused roll up what colours we had, and made them pass half open to different places, bringing them back once or twice under cover; so that the enemy, seeing them as they were carried forward to different places, could not form any judgement of our numbers.'[18]

It was a forlorn hope, for Cumberland had a pretty good idea that he was only facing a rearguard, and as his mounted infantry had not yet caught up, he dismounted all his dragoons at about four o'clock and ordered them forward to take the village. At this critical juncture, John Roy Stuart turned up again with orders to fall back on Penrith. Murray at once pointed out the folly of trying to break contact just as an attack was coming in, especially as it was now dark. Instead, in the mistaken belief that there were only about 500 dragoons, he announced his intention of mounting an immediate counter-attack. According to his own account, both Stuart and Cluny MacPherson agreed that this 'was the only prudent and sure way;' but Cluny was actually far from keen on the idea, having correctly concluded that they were actually facing upwards of 1,000 dragoons. Nevertheless he reluctantly agreed to attack if ordered to do so. 'I do order it then,' replied Murray[19] and off they went.

'We advanced,' said Murray, who lost his wig and bonnet struggling through a hedge, 'and had a good deal of fire on both sides. After the Highlanders on that side had given most of their fire, they lay close at an open hedge, which was the second in these fields. We then received the whole fire of the dragoons that were at the bottom, upon which Cluny said 'What the devil is this?' Indeed the bullets were going thick enough. I told him we had nothing for it but going down upon them sword in hand, before they had time to charge again. I immediately drew my sword, and cried 'CLAYMORE!' Cluny did the same, and we ran down to the bottom ditch, clearing the diagonal hedges as we went. There were a good many of the enemy killed at the bottom ditch, and the rest took to their heels, but received the fire of the Glengarry regiment. Most of Ardshiel's men, being next the lane, did not meet with so much opposition. I had given orders that our men should not pass the bottom ditch, to go up to the muir, for they would have been exposed to the fire of the Glengarry regiment, that could not distinguish them from the enemy. We had no more firing after this; so we returned to our first post. We had now done what we proposed; and being sure of no more trouble from the enemy, I ordered the retreat, first Roy Stuart's, then Appin, Cluny, and the Glengarry men;'[20]

Naturally Cumberland's men saw the affair rather differently. Bland's 3rd Dragoons were on the right, facing Murray's attack, while both Cobham's 10th and Kerr's 11th Dragoons merely engaged in a firefight with the rest of the Jacobite infantry. Although Bland's men were undoubtedly driven back, their losses were nowhere near as high as those claimed by the rebels. The volunteer surgeon already quoted, who was probably best placed to know, reported; 'The kill'd on our Side were, six of Bland's, three of Cobham's, and one of Lord Mark Kerr's, all common Men, and four Officers of Bland's, viz. Col. Honeywood, wounded very much on his head; Capt East, a large Wound in his Neck, and some on his Head, both left for dead in the field, a Cornet, and a Volunteer almost cut to Pieces. On the Rebels Side, five left kill'd on the Spot;'[21]

That only ten British soldiers were killed is also confirmed by the Clifton parish register[22], though that did not prevent both sides from afterwards claiming to have disposed of about 50 or 60 of the opposition for little loss. Cumberland was of course left in possession of the field, which may have been small consolation for Murray's successfully breaking contact, but the fact of the matter was that he badly needed his mounted infantry, and was forced to wait for them in Penrith.

While he waited, the rebels reached Carlisle and took the fateful decision to leave their garrison there. The reasoning behind the Prince's insistence on doing so was quite straightforward. Once back in Scotland he intended to join Lord John Drummond's forces to his own and then mount a second invasion of England. In the meantime Carlisle would be held against his return, and the train of thirteen guns which had been so painfully dragged from Edinburgh to Derby and back again without firing a shot would also be left there.[23] John Hamilton was continued as governor, but his garrison this time seems to have chiefly comprised companies drawn from the second (Aberdeenshire) battalion of the Duke of Perth's Regiment, although there were also some officers and men from John Roy Stuart's Regiment and Lord Ogilvy's Regiment, probably attached to the artillery. There were also the 20 officers and 93 remaining soldiers of the short-lived Manchester Regiment. One man who was not left there however was Captain James Johnstone of the Duke of Perth's Regiment. He and his company were ordered to join the garrison, but he firmly refused, and to his credit refused to let any of his men be left there either.[24]

Having left these unfortunates behind, the Prince recrossed the border on the 20th, and next day Cumberland closed up on the town. Once again a rather curious siege began. Although the Duke had plenty of cavalry, he only had 1,000 mounted infantry and no guns. But nothing daunted, he set what infantry he had to blockade the three gates, borrowed some gunners from Wade, who by this time had trailed back into Newcastle, and ordered up six eighteen-pounders from Whitehaven.

A battery was then established on Primrose Bank, some 600 yards from the castle's west curtain. At first sight it appears an odd place to batter a breach as the curtain there is built on top of a steep escarpment and the presence of the river Cauda would have effectively prevented any assault from that direction. Cumberland however had no intention of launching an assault at all, even if the rest of his infantry, Campbell's 21st, Sempill's 25th and the 'new' 68th, 69th, 71st and 74th Foot, turned up in time.[25] By firing on the castle's west curtain he could be sure of battering the rebels into submission without inflicting unacceptable collateral damage on the town's civilian population and property.

And so it turned out. On the morning of the 30th of December the rebels hung out the white flag and asked for terms. Cumberland's reply was blunt and to the point:

'All the Terms his Royal Highness will or can grant to the Rebel Garrison of Carlisle, are, That they will not be put to the Sword, but be reserved for the King's Pleasure. If they consent to these Conditions, the Governor and principal Officers are to deliver themselves up immediately, and the Castle, Citadel, and all the Gates of the Town, are to be taken Possession of forthwith by the King's Troops. All the small Arms are to be lodged in the Town Guard Room, and the rest of the Garrison are to retire to the Cathedral, where a Guard is to be placed over them. No damage is to be done to the Artillery, Arms or Ammunition.'[26]

The rebels had been driven out of England and it was now time to clear them out of Scotland as well.

Sources:

1. Atkinson, p. 293, 294.
2. Ibid.
3. Elcho, p. 335 has the list passed on by Weir; the actual composition of Cumberland's forces may be gleaned from Atkinson p. 294–5 and Campbell's list in *Lyon in Mourning*, p. 94.
4. Speck, p. 88.
5. Elcho, p. 337–8.
6. Sullivan, p. 102–3. Neither Sullivan nor any of the other eyewitnesses and

participants record his presence at the council and indeed he is certainly known not to have taken part in earlier ones. This, however has not prevented some historians from representing him as a passionate supporter of marching on London.

7. Atkinson, p. 294–5.
8. Not to be confused of course with Montague's 9th Horse, who were with Cumberland.
9. Murray, p. 60–1.
10. Murray, p. 61; Sullivan p. 104; HMC Fitzherbert p. 174.
11. *Newcastle Courant*.
12. Murray, p. 61–2.
13. *Orderly Book of Lord Ogilvy's Regiment*.
14. Captain Ignatious Browne, of the Franco-Irish regiment Lally.
15. Johnstone, p. 67. As the Georgia Rangers comprised only two troops each with an establishment of four officers, four NCOs, two 'French Horns' and 60 privates, Johnstone is, as usual, exaggerating in claiming that there were two or three hundred of them. [WO.24/251]
16. They were of course still mounted on country nags.
17. *Newcastle Courant* 4th of January 1746. The surgeon may have been the Jervase Wright quoted in HMC Fitzherbert p. 172–3. Captain George Hamilton of Redhouse was executed at York in the following October. The 'Manchester Man' is unidentified.
18. Murray, p. 67.
19. Cluny's account is in the notes to the 1829 edition of Sir Walter Scott's *Waverly* and pp. 407–9 of the Oxford Paperback 1986 edition.
20. Murray, p. 70–1.
21. *Newcastle Courant*, op. cit.
22. 'The 19th of December, 1745, Ten Dragoons, to wit, six of Bland's, three of Cobham's, and one of Mark Kerr's Regiment buried, who was killed ye evening before by ye Rebells in ye skirmish between ye Duke of Cumberland's army and them at ye end of Clifton Moor next ye Town. Robert Akins, a private Dragoon of General Bland's Regiment, Buried ye 8th Day of Janry., 1745.'
23. Some accounts say that the six 'swedish' guns were taken back to Scotland but in fact all 13 guns were captured when Carlisle fell.
24. Johnstone, p. 224 – in which he remarks on the unsettling experience of seeing those officers he refused to join, being hanged at Kennington while he was on the run in London. He does not actually refer to his company being spared, but none of them appears amongst the prisoners.
25. Atkinson, p. 294 quotes a distribution return of the 24th of December which refers to 2 'old' battalions and 4 'new' battalions on the march north. Bligh's 20th appears to have been sent to reinforce Wade's army. All the other infantry with Cumberland's army had returned to London during the invasion scare.
26. *Newcastle Courant* January 15th 1746 – a very useful piece of reporting.

CHAPTER 7
Civil War
Containing the Rising in Scotland

When the rebels recrossed the river Esk they had been on English soil for little more than a month, but in that time the strategic position in Scotland had shifted in the government's favour. The decision by the rebel leaders to march south by the western route was largely influenced by the prospect of receiving reinforcements sent after them from Scotland, but those reinforcements had signally failed to materialise. Now it became all-too apparent that this failure proceeded not from any want of energy on the part of the admittedly ineffectual Lord Strathallan, or his more belligerent successor, Lord John Drummond, but rather was the direct result of some very prompt and effective action by loyalist and regular troops.

It was always to be expected that the Argyllshire Campbells would stand firmly behind King George and the Protestant Succession and, at the very outset of the rising, General Cope sent one of his Black Watch companies to Inverary in order to assist the local authorities there. Obviously a single company of raw recruits was not going to be able to accomplish much by itself, and at the end of October, Major General John Campbell of Mamore was very agreeably commissioned to go there and raise 'eight Independent Companies each of 100 men with the proper officers; and likewise to arm 16 such companies more, without the charge of commissioned officers, who are to serve without pay and are to be raised from the Duke of Argyll's and the Earl of Breadalbane's Contreys.'

Unfortunately Mamore was in London at the time and a mixture of administrative obstruction and bad weather conspired to delay his arrival in Inverary until the 22nd of December. In the meantime his son, Lieutenant-Colonel John Campbell of the 64th Highlanders was in charge, and although the Argyll Militia companies were probably to be the best known of the many loyalist units raised in Scotland, Mamore's rather tardy arrival on the scene effectively ensured that they would take no active part in the proceedings until late January of 1746. As far as the Jacobites were concerned, this was just as well for after quite a promising start, they soon found that they were having enough trouble simply keeping the other loyalist forces at bay.[1]

Starting on the 14th of November, two French frigates and six privateers employed as transports slipped out of Dunkirk and made for Montrose carrying Lord John Drummond with his own regiment: the *Royal
Ecossois*[2], six picquets or detachments drawn from the Irish regiments in
the French service and large quantities of artillery and ammunition. They
were taking a considerable risk of being intercepted by the Royal Navy,
but as chance would have it that night a severe storm swept down the
North Sea. HMS *Fox* was driven ashore at Dunbar with the loss of Captain
Beavor and all hands, and the rest of Admiral Byng's squadron was
scattered far and wide.

Fortunately, the French convoy was similarly dispersed and unknown
to Drummond, a naval sloop, HMS *Hazard* was lying in the large tidal
basin which formed Montrose harbour. Apparently seeking shelter from
the storm, Captain Hill took his sloop in on the 15th, and having satisfied
himself that there were no rebel troops in the town, he landed and seized
a number of guns from a fort at the harbour mouth. He also tried to
organise a loyalist militia company with the aid of Mr Cumming, the
local Excise Supervisor, but an attack which he contemplated on a Jacobite
outpost at Brechin, just five miles away, was thwarted when a rebel party
led by Sergeant Walter Young slipped into town and lifted Cumming
and two of his Gaugers.[3]

Suitably encouraged by this adventure, the rest of the rebels – two
companies of Lord Ogilvy's Regiment[4] led by Captains David Ferrier and
John Erskine – seized the town the following night. An attempt next
morning to ambush the *Hazard's* boat was only partially successful when
the rebels fired too soon, killing one seaman and shooting another in the
back. Hill naturally retaliated by firing on any rebel who showed himself
but the standard of marksmanship on both sides appears to have been
lamentably bad and no further casualties are recorded.

How long this might have gone on is anybody's guess, but Hill was still
sitting in the harbour when the first of the French ships, *La Renommeé*,
turned up on the morning of Saturday the 24th. In response to frantic sig-
nals from the shore, she came in without waiting for a pilot and promptly
ran aground. A scene of frantic activity then ensued as her passengers,
some 150 officers and men of the *Royal Ecossois* scrambled ashore and her
cargo of six heavy guns was landed. All six of her own guns were also
landed and two batteries established to fire on the *Hazard*. Hill's last chance
to escape came with high tide on the Sunday night, but unaware that the
Frenchman had been stripped of all her guns he was unwilling to run past
her. Next morning therefore he reluctantly surrendered.

That night a second French frigate, *La Fine*, arrived and, rather than
risk the narrow channel, landed her passengers, Lord John Drummond
and a further 300 of his men, on the open beach. Then at about midday on

Tuesday the 27th, HMS *Milford* appeared in the offing and the Frenchman's captain abruptly changed his mind. Cutting his cable he ran for the harbour and piled up hard on a shoal. Captain Hanway in the *Milford* tried to come in after him but also ran aground and only just managed to haul himself off before the tide fell. Balked of his prey Hanway simply dropped anchor, shot up the Frenchman's longboat, and had the immense satisfaction of seeing the stranded frigate 'hog' as her back broke on the ebb. As it was by now clear that a number of ships were making for the little port, he then stood out to sea again to see what else he could pick up.[5]

Sure enough, on the 28th he fell in with *Le Louis XV* off Montrose and captured her along with 8 officers, 5 NCOs, a drum and 46 men of Bulkeley's Irish regiment, 3 officers, 2 sergeants, a drum and 46 men of Clare's regiment, and 6 officers, 6 NCOs, a drum and 47 men of Berwick's.[6] Well pleased with his prize, Hanway bore off for Leith and as soon as he had gone the crew of *La Fine* crammed themselves aboard the *Hazard* (now renamed *Le Prince Charles*) and made their escape.

Three other French transports got safely ashore at Peterhead and Stonehaven, but the last one, *L'Esperance*, was taken off the Dogger Bank on the 25th while carrying about 60 men of the *Royal Ecossois* and a mixed bag of 20 officers.[7]

The loss of the three picquets and the men taken aboard *L'Esperance* was unfortunate, but the rest of the *Royal Ecossois* and three picquets from the regiments Dillon, Rooth and Lally landed safely, albeit scattered between Montrose, Stonehaven and Peterhead. On the whole therefore the operation was a success. The arrival of some 800 regular troops and half a dozen heavy guns – two 18-pounders, two 12-pounders and two 9-pounders – could reasonably be expected to do nothing but good for the Jacobite cause, especially as Drummond also had the French King's commission to raise a second battalion for his regiment in Scotland.

Moreover, as soon as his regiment was safely ashore, Drummond sent an envoy to Edinburgh pointing out that as French troops were now involved and that the Jacobites should legitimately be considered French auxiliaries, the Dutch troops should immediately stand down and take no further part in operations. Although happy enough to link the Jacobites with the French for propaganda purposes, the government had no intention whatever of formally or even tacitly recognising them as French auxiliaries. Drummond's own men however were a different matter and the Dutch thought so too. They were paroled prisoners of war and under the terms of their parole they were forbidden from serving against French troops.

Happily none of them were actually in Scotland at the time, so that the demand for their withdrawal did not prove critical. Instead they stood fast on Tyneside and awaited repatriation while the government arranged to replace them with Hessian mercenaries. In fact the only Dutch troops to be directly affected by the arrival of the French were a handful of gunners whom Wade sent to assist Cumberland's siege of Carlisle. The Jacobite garrison, as it happened, included two officers, a sergeant and three privates of the Irish regiment Lally, and Captain Sir John Arbuthnot of the *Royal Ecossois*[8] and, by way of trying it on, they demanded the withdrawal of any Dutch soldiers amongst the besiegers. Cumberland's reply was as brief as it was splenetic[9] but nevertheless he played by the rules and ordered the gunners back to Newcastle.

Meanwhile, any hopes which Drummond and Strathallan might have entertained of joining the Prince at the head of this valuable reinforcement, were dashed by Lieutenant-General Roger Handasyde.

Since his arrival in Edinburgh as Acting Commander-in-Chief Scotland on the 14th of November, Handasyde had overseen the raising of considerable numbers of loyalist troops. On the 20th of November, the Edinburgh Regiment was revived under his personal command. A small but enthusiastic battalion of about 180 men was raised in Paisley and Renfrew by another regular officer, Major William Cunningham the Earl of Glencairn, and Glasgow produced no fewer than fifteen companies totalling about 500 men who placed themselves under the Earl of Home's command. A fourth battalion of about 400 men was raised in Stirling and Linlithgow under the command, or rather patronage, of the castle's governor, General Blakeney. Added to his two regular battalions and two regiments of dragoons this gave Handasyde something in the region of 1,600–1,700 infantry and 500 cavalry, besides the castle garrisons and the Additional Companies of the 21st and 25th Foot.

As soon as word was received of the French landing, Walter Grossett, the enterprising customs officer cum intelligence agent, received orders from Handasyde to cross the Forth and seize every boat he could lay his hands on. No-one after all wanted a repetition of the rebel attempt on Edinburgh in 1715.[10] This could only be a temporary measure and on the 6th of December Price's 14th were sent to Stirling. Three days later Handasyde was ordered back to Berwick and superseded as acting Commander-in-Chief Scotland by General Guest. What lay at the back of this is not clear, but at any rate Guest was equally alive to the importance of holding the Forth crossings and promptly despatched Ligonier's 59th, the Glasgow and Paisley Regiments, and the 13th and 14th Dragoons as well. Only the Edinburgh Regiment, now commanded by Sir John Bruce Hope, remained behind to defend the capital.

There is no doubt that had Drummond mustered all the men available to him, he would have comfortably outnumbered Guest, both in regulars and in militia. However he had no cavalry. Inasmuch as Guest's two regiments of dragoons had run away from the Jacobite infantry at

Prestonpans, this might not have been an insuperable problem, but forcing a passage across the river against anything like a determined defence would be no easy matter at the best of times. As it was, Drummond also had to contend with a serious threat in his rear.

At the beginning of September General Cope had left two weak companies from the 43rd and 64th Highlanders respectively at Inverness and these now formed the nucleus of a loyalist army. Its notional commander was Cope's former Adjutant General, the Earl of Loudon, but it was actually raised by the Lord President, Duncan Forbes of Culloden. As early as the 13th of September he was authorised to issue commissions for no fewer than eighteen Independent Companies, and he bestowed them with considerable care. Some very properly went to known loyalists, such as Captain George Munro of Culcairn, while others were effectively used to bribe waverers undecided as to whether they should support King George or the Young Italian.[11]

The enthusiasm of some companies might therefore be questionable, but if nothing else it prevented them from joining the rebels and as ever success bred success and the growing strength of the loyalist forces at Inverness helped persuade the Laird of Grant, the Earl of Sutherland and the Skye chieftains Sir Alexander MacDonald of Sleat and Norman MacLeod of MacLeod to muster their clansmen in support of King George.

Useful though it undoubtedly was to corner the market in wild young men, there was a certain pressure to use them for something rather more positive. Unfortunately Loudon, although a competent enough administrator, was not the man to lead them. Indeed some years later as Commander-in-Chief North America he would be unkindly likened to the figure of St George on an inn sign – forever on horseback but going nowhere. Arriving in Inverness on the 14th of October, his command of the northern army got off to an unpromising start when an attempt was made to kidnap the Lord President himself.

About 150–200 rebels surrounded Culloden House on the night of the 27th of October and, having taken a number of ladders from an adjacent hay-yard, they crept towards the President's window at about two o'clock in the morning. Fortunately they were spotted by an alert sentry and saluted by a hail of small shot. A small paterero, or swivel gun, was also fired from a balcony and at that point the 'villains' fled, leaving behind a dead man, but consoling themselves by running off all the sheep and cattle they could find. Next morning a sweep through the adjacent woodland turned up another casualty, this time in the form of a wounded man who readily confessed that the party, commanded by James Fraser of Foyers, had been sent by the supposedly neutral Lord Lovat.[12]

After a lifetime of prevarication and double-dealing, the old fox had finally committed himself and, besides trying to snatch Forbes, had sent his son the Master to join Drummond at Perth. Although the kidnap attempt failed there was no question of letting such treachery go unpunished – otherwise, apart from anything else, there was a lively possibility that he or somebody else would try again. Therefore a punitive expedition was prepared, and on the 10th of December Loudon, who was never a man to take unnecessary chances, went looking for Lovat with no fewer than 500 men at his back, comprising about a hundred men of his own 64th Highlanders, and seven of the Independent Companies.[13] Lovat was evidently not expecting so swift or so robust a response and for once in his life he was caught napping and carried off a prisoner to Inverness, although he managed to escape on the night of the 19th of December.

Notwithstanding its unfortunate sequel, the expedition might therefore have been adjudged a success were it not for the fact that it served to divert both men and attention away from a much more important venture, the recapture of Aberdeen.

Ever since Cope's departure the otherwise loyal burgh had been in Jacobite hands. At first the rebels had been content to pass through on their way to Edinburgh, though there had been a humiliating episode when the Pretender was proclaimed at the Cross and the Provost had a glass of wine poured over him when he failed to join in the spirit of the occasion. Then however a local laird named James Moir of Stonywood turned up 'supported by a couple of broken merchants and York Street Cadys all in white cockades.'[14] and eventually raised a battalion in and around the burgh for Lord Lewis Gordon's Regiment.

A younger son of the Duke of Gordon, Lord Lewis was a renegade naval officer – formerly Third Lieutenant in HMS *Dunkirk* – and as his family had been pre-eminent in the North-East for generations, the Prince appointed him Lord Lieutenant of Aberdeenshire and Banffshire. Active and peremptory to the point of being highly strung, he organised the raising not only of Stonywood's Aberdeen battalion, but also another in Strathbogie, and notionally at least he also took a Highland battalion raised in Mar by Francis Farquharson of Monaltrie under his wing as well. In addition a company was raised largely around Old Meldrum by James Crichton of Auchengoul. The area was in short regarded as a dangerous nest of Jacobitism and one which needed to be dealt with as quickly as possible. Inexplicably Loudon himself remained at his headquarters in Inverness and gave the job to the Laird of MacLeod who had no discernible qualification for it beyond the fact that he had raised four of the five Independent Companies assigned to the expedition. They left Inverness shortly after the 10th of December and the first obstacle which faced them was the crossing of the Spey at Fochabers, where the rebel Lieutenant-Colonel John Gordon of Avochie and his men were quartered. Belatedly reflecting that five companies were perhaps a little inadequate for the task in hand, Loudon accordingly sent Munro of Culcairn hurrying after him with just two more companies.[15]

As it happened the otherwise circumspect Laird of Grant had for once bestirred himself, raised some 400 of his men and created a sufficiently convincing threat to send Avochie hurrying back to Aberdeen. As a result MacLeod passed across the river unopposed on the 15th and looked forward to a rendezvous with Grant's men at Keith next day. This happy conjunction did indeed take place, but unfortunately Grant then received a singularly ill-timed letter from Loudon advising him that as he had not authorised him to raise his men, neither pay nor arms could be provided for them. Hardly surprisingly, Grant then turned around and went home again.[16] This brought the expedition to a complete standstill, but reassured by a letter from the Lord President which advised him, *inter alia* that Loudon would be 'quickly up to sustain him,' he lurched forward again on the 20th and this time got the length of Old Meldrum, within striking distance of Aberdeen.

There he got word of the arrival of French regulars in Aberdeen and, taking counsel of his fears yet again, turned aside for Inverurie and finally linked up with Culcairn's two companies. As neither he nor Culcairn had any intention of going anywhere near Aberdeen until Loudon turned up, they settled down to wait for him, blissfully unaware that he had in fact gone off in pursuit of the fugitive Lord Lovat. To make matters worse they also dispersed their 700 men far too widely:

> '400 of those under McLeod were quartered in the town of Inverury, the rest of that name and Culkairn's two companies were cantonned in farmers' houses along the Ury to the north west of the town, many of them more than a mile and a half's distance though there was no worldly necessity for this, as the town of Inverury contained two regiments of the Duke's army for some weeks without a man of them going a stone cast from it.'[17]

This was bad enough, but Culcairn, who as a professional soldier should have known better, refused to send out any scouts on the grounds that the countryside was hostile! Naturally the Jacobites had no such inhibitions and soon gained a pretty good idea of how many Loyalists they were facing and where they were lying. They were also pulling in all the reinforcements they could lay their hands on, and on the morning of the 23rd of December, they marched out of Aberdeen spoiling for a fight.

All in all they appear to have been able to muster something in the region of 1,200 men with which to face MacLeod and Culcairn, made up of all three battalions of Lord Lewis Gordon's Regiment, two small units commanded by James Crichton of Auchengoul and Sir Alexander Bannerman of Elsick respectively, a detachment of Lord Ogilvy's Regiment and perhaps most important of all two companies of Lord John Drummond's *Royal Ecossois*. With the exception of the French regulars the military value of these units was not particularly high[18], but at least they had surprise on their side, and although Lord Lewis Gordon was notionally in charge, he was also sensible enough to defer to Major Lancelot Cuthbert of the *Royal Ecossois*.

The rebels divided their forces into two columns one of which, led by Gordon of Avochie and a Major Gordon in the French service[19], proceeded straight along the main road through Kintore, while the other crossed the river Don and swung around to the north. Cuthbert, who accompanied the latter column, was taking a risk in splitting his forces but in view of the Loyalists' inactivity it was worth it, for they were occupying an awkward position to attack.

Inverurie at this time comprised just the usual string of houses and back yards, lining either side of the main road, which ran more or less north-south just above a ford across the river Don. About 500 yards to the east of this ford was another, crossing the rather smaller river Urie and Cuthbert's plan was to attack across both simultaneously. What followed was a complete shambles.

Cuthbert's column, comprising Stonywood's and Monaltrie's battalions, Auchingoul's and Elsick's companies, together with the French regulars, arrived at their jumping-off point early and had to hang about in and around the church at Kinellar while they waited for Avochie to turn up. Discipline was poor and basic security consequently bad. Instead of staying put many of the rebels insisted on sneaking up to the fir plantation around Keith Hall to have a look at the town, and inevitably after a while they were seen and pointed out to MacLeod and Culcairn. Incredible as it may seem neither took any notice and made no attempt to find out what was going on. Nor did they even take the elementary step of calling in their outlying companies, far less ordering them to stand to.

Their complacency was therefore rudely shaken when at about four in the afternoon the lone sentry at the southern end of the town saw a body of men with the white colours of Gordon's Regiment come marching down the hill towards the Urie ford: 'upon which he fir'd his piece to give the alarm, whereupon as the townsmen say they turned out in great confusion.'[20]

There was still time though to intercept the rebels at the fords and as it happened the Urie ford was still dominated by a long abandoned 12th-century motte, known as the Bass of Inverurie. Had some of the Loyalists been posted on top of it and in the adjacent walled churchyard they could have made life very difficult for Cuthbert and his men. Instead, coming under attack from two directions, MacLeod and Culcairn made the mistake of drawing their men up equidistant between the two fords and out of effective range of either. Afterwards it was claimed that their men were greatly disadvantaged by being armed only with firelocks and bayonets, rather than with; 'their darling weapon, the Broadsword,' but that was neither here nor there – none of the Jacobites had any either. The real problem was the total want of commonsense, let alone ability displayed by their officers, for as the anonymous author of 'Memoirs of the Rebellion in Aberdeen and Banff' makes clear in his very lucid account of the affair, the rebels had very little to congratulate themselves on either:

'The van of the Rebels' main body consisted of the French and some picked men and was lead only by Major Cuthbert, these with all the gentlemen, the volunteers, and some of the common men crossed the Ury, very alertly, and as they passed, drew up behind the Bass, and the Churchyard. But many of their common men ran off and skulked by dyke-sides till the action was over and could neither be brought out by threats nor entreaties till then. Major Gordon and Avachy with about 50 or 60 of their men crossed the Don very briskly, and behaved well, but the rest of the Corps took shelter among the Broom, till they saw the event.

'The action began near an hour after sunset with a clear moonshine, by some passing shots from some ten or twelve of the McLeods who advanced so far, some to one Foord and some to the other, and fired on the enemy as they were passing and killed two or three men in the water, and immediately retired. The Body that crossed the Ury moved up first to attack, but were received with two or three fires from the McLeods, which they returned indeed two for one, but both were at too great a distance to do great execution. But as the party from Don was by this time coming to attack them in flanks, and as the French were advancing with a close regular fire and like to bear very hard on them, the McLeods found themselves unable to stand this shock, and accordingly gave way; yet not so that a party of them loaded their pieces retiring, and finding some of their men, especially the wounded, like to fall in the enemy's hands, they wheeled about before they were halfway up the town, and made another fire, but immediately ran off. On this the French advanced through the town with an incessant street fire[21] and the rest divided themselves and went firing up each side of it, being too by this time joined by most of their skulking companions. After this, as some of the McLeods were running off on the stubble ground on the North end of the town, some person gave a cry that McLeod was taken, on which they turned about again and made another fire but immediately marched off. The Rebels meanwhile being at a considerable distance and not observing them so exactly going off, but seeing a ridge with a few furrows in it, amidst a great deal of unploughed stubble ground, and taking it by the moonlight for a row of men, they fired once or twice into it very succesfully. And thus in whole the firing continued for more than twenty minutes. The companies of McLeods and Monroes that were cantonn'd out of the town, had unluckily no Officers with them; these happened to be with McLeod in Inverury, and went out to engage along with the men that were there (which by the bye as there were thirty of them on guard, and many straggling through the country seeking provisions did not much exceed three hundred), these therefore having no body to draw them together, ran up different ways on hearing the firing till they met some of their friends flying, or were informed of the event, and then they ran off.'[22]

Having started running they do not appear to have stopped until they were safely on the other side of the Spey. Behind them they left five dead and two more who subsequently died of their wounds. Despite the amount of firing, as John Daunie commented: 'night coming on apace; they could not be supposed to see to levell their pieces.'[23] and Jacobite losses were also light. One account reckoned ten or twelve killed; 'several of these French, but all common men'[24], but Daunie stated that there were 14 killed and 20 wounded on both sides. If the five dead MacLeods are removed from this figure that leaves nine Jacobite dead, but as to the wounded it is hard to say much beyond the fact that Daunie says two rebels were hurt crossing the Urie ford, and that it is likely Daunie's figure does not include those wounded Loyalists who were able to get away.

Notwithstanding the fact that most of their men had kept their heads down throughout the battle, it was a neat little victory for the Jacobites, but they were in no position to exploit it. Instead, leaving Aberdeen garrisoned by Elsick's men and a predatory band of MacGregors, they headed south to join Lord John Drummond, who was at last preparing to march on Stirling.

Sources:

1. See the very useful essay on the Independent Companies by A MacLean IN Scott-Moncrieff The '45; to gather an image whole, pp. 123–139.
2. The 'Royal Scots' – this is the contemporary spelling. The regiment was raised in France in 1744 around a cadre of men drawn from the red-coated Irish regiments. Unlike them the Royal Ecossois wore a very distinctive uniform of short blue jackets turned up with red, and blue bonnets.
3. Young later fought at Inverurie, Falkirk and Culloden, but was arrested after the rising. The 26-year-old sailor then turned King's Evidence and was ultimately released. Seton & Arnot no. 3468.
4. They belonged of course to the regiment's second battalion, raised by Sir James Kinloch.

90

5. Erskine's account is to be found in *The Lyon in Mourning*, Vol. III, p. 18–21.
6. *Newcastle Courant*. Picquets were the standard form of provisional unit in the French Army at this time. The 1750 *Regulations* laid down that they were to comprise a captain, Lieutenant, two sergeants, a drummer and 47 men, all drawn from the fusilier or battalion companies. To judge by the numbers captured on the *Louis XV* this regulation reflected established practice.
7. Confusingly she had previously been known as the *Soleil* and is sometimes referred to by that name.
8. *Newcastle Gazette* of January 15 1746 lists Captain Sir Francis Geogean, Sergeant Pierre La Locke, and Privates Pierre Bourgogne, Francis Carpentier, Jeon Poussin and Pierre Vickman of Lally's Regiment, amongst the prisoners, to which should be added Captain Ignatious Michael Browne, who had earlier escaped over the wall.
9. Ibid.: 'To let the French officer know, if there is one in the Town, that there are no Dutch Troops here, but enough of the King's to chastise the Rebels, and those who dare to give them any Assistance.'
10. *Origins* pp. 345–6, 7 and 379–80. In 1715 a considerable body of rebels led by MacIntosh of Borlum rowed across the Forth, seized Leith and were all set to have a go at Edinburgh when Argyll arrived just in time. Afterwards they marched south to link up with the English Jacobites and eventually surrendered at Preston.
11. *Origins* p. 104 enumerates 19 companies, of which only 17 actually turned up at Inverness. Stewart of Garth Vol. II p. 293–4 refers to 20 companies but only lists the officers for 18 companies.
12. *Origins*, p. 106.
13. *Origins*, (op.cit.) assigns him 800 men, which would certainly be in keeping with his cautious attitude to military campaigns, but it is rather unlikely that all the Independent Companies were able to muster 100 men apiece.
14. *Origins*, p. 117 Cadys were messenger porters – the term still survives in golf.
15. One was Culcairn's own Independent Company, the other was the Inverness Burgh Company commanded by Captain William MacIntosh.
16. *Origins*, pp. 292–5.
17. *Origins*, p. 137.
18. An intelligence report sent to the Laird of Grant on the 11th of December declared that Avochie had only 300 men, 'and of these only 100 have joined; mostly herds and hiremen from about Strathbogie and unacquainted with the use of arms; many of them are pressed and intend to desert; 100 or 150 men would drive them to the devil.' *Origins* p. 287.
19. This Major Gordon is unidentified, although most of the French officers serving with the Jacobites seem to have had brevet promotions. He may have been a volunteer but it seems likely that like Cuthbert he was really only a Captain and the commander of one of the two *Royal Ecossois* companies which took part in the action.
20. *Lyon in Mourning*, Vol.II, p. 344: John Daunie's account.
21. In 'street firing' a company formed up in a column slightly narrower than the width of the street or other narrow passage it was negotiating. It then moved forward, firing by ranks.
22. *Origins*, p. 143–4.
23. *Lyon in Mourning*, op. cit.
24. *Origins*, p. 144.

CHAPTER 8

The Most Despicable Enemy
The Battle of Falkirk

The reappearance of the main Jacobite field army in southern Scotland naturally led to a considerable flurry of activity. It did not help that they had come the length of Moffat before anyone realised the danger, but then General Guest hastily recalled the regulars from Stirling to Edinburgh and to general approbation the Glasgow and Paisley regiments chose to accompany them.

Cumberland for his part had been called south again to face the continued threat of a French invasion, but Lieutenant General Henry Hawley superseded the fumbling Wade at Newcastle and immediately began moving his troops northwards. Now in his mid-60s, Hawley had been a soldier since he was 15. Too often dismissed simply as a boorish and vicious martinet, he was actually nobody's fool and passionately interested in the theoretical as well as the practical aspects of his profession. He was undoubtedly irascible and possessed of a black sense of humour, but if the soldiers now under his command considered him harsh, that undoubtedly reflected the crying need to take them in hand and restore discipline in what was a badly demoralised army.

Indeed as events would show, Hawley's preoccupation with the needs of his regiments, allied to the fact that all he had so far seen of the rebels was their retreating backs, seems to have blinded him somewhat to the true nature of the task facing him. It is not uncommon for commanders to underestimate their enemy, but he appears to have been too busy nursing his own men to pay very much attention to just what the rebels were up to.

To make matters worse, the prevailing bad weather and a lack of suitable quarters meant that no more than two battalions could move together and each pair therefore marched a day apart. As a result the first two battalions only arrived in Edinburgh on the 2nd of January, and it was the 10th of January by the time the last of them closed up. In theory, until that date Edinburgh might have been vulnerable to a rebel offensive. Fortunately, the decision to retreat from Derby, justified and sensible though it was, seems to have deprived the rebel leaders of their

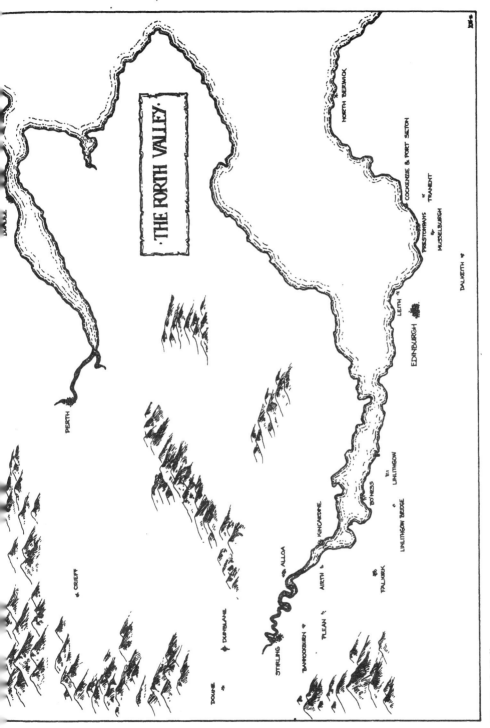

The Forth Valley

93

Map 3

earlier sense of purpose and far from seeking to regain the initiative, they occupied Glasgow instead and on the 4th of January moved northwards to rendezvous with Lord John Drummond's forces at Bannockburn. The greater part of the army was then temporarily cantoned in the surrounding area, while Lord George Murray took the clan regiments across to Falkirk and cavalry outposts were established at Elphinstone, Airth and Callendar.[1]

Far from marching on Edinburgh, they had decided to besiege Stirling Castle, not through any pressing strategic necessity, but rather it seemed for lack of anything more positive to do. First though they had to capture the burgh itself and even this apparently simple operation went less than smoothly. It was, according to a contemporary journal, defended by: 'The inhabitants, to the number of three hundred, joyned with two hundred military forces[2], with eight companeys of militia, extending to three hundred and twenty, all well armyd from the castle;'[3]

Notwithstanding this relatively sizeable force, on the 7th of January, the town council arranged to surrender at 10 o'clock the following morning, and that evening the loyalists and the militia gloomily deposited their arms in the castle with the governor, General Blakeney. Some of them also joined the garrison, but not everybody was willing to surrender so easily:

'Notwithstanding whereof the tounsmen took to their arms, elected new officers in place of such as desarted [ie, had taken refuge in the castle] and placed their guards as uswall, though the cannon from the ribles battries firing closs upon the toun, from seven att neight till ten, having discharged nine rounds without the least execution. The Generall, observing the bravery of the inhabitants, gave orders that whosoever of the militia inclined to go out to their assistance, should have allowance; whereupon one Mr McKillop, one of the captains of the tounsmen, came out with some of the militia, about twelve o'clock at neight, who all keept their posts that neight.'[4]

Next morning however, receiving renewed assurances from the rebels that they would not be plundered or have contributions levied on them, their leaders Walter Stephenson and William Wright agreed to surrender after all, and once their arms were safely deposited back in the castle, the gates were finally opened to the rebels.

Like its Edinburgh counterpart, Stirling Castle is perched on the summit of an outcrop of volcanic rock, rising sharply from the surrounding alluvial plain, and the biggest challenge to any besieging force without the time or patience to starve the garrison into submission was to find a suitable position on which to raise a battery. First they had to get Drummond's big guns down from Montrose. Two of them were dragged with some difficulty across the Forth at the Fords of Frew, but then somebody had the bright idea of loading the others on to a ship at Alloa and floating them upriver to Stirling.

With this object in mind a brig was seized at Airth and carried up to Alloa. Two others however had been beached in the tidal harbour and, before they could be got off, Captain Faulkener of the *Vulture* sloop sent in his longboats and successfully burnt them. After this promising start the operation nearly went badly wrong when the longboats grounded and came under fire from a three-gun battery on the shore, but Faulkener ran in and extricated them after a brief exchange of fire. He had missed the brig of course, but now the indefatigable Walter Grossett turned up. In an attempt to intercept it, the customs officer got 300 men of the 27th Foot, led by Lieutenant Colonel Francis Leighton, embarked on the night of the 8th of January and set off in pursuit. Unfortunately the wind dropped before they could reach their objective and the attempt had to be postponed until the following night.

By that time the Jacobites were thoroughly alerted to the danger and had erected a battery of four field pieces at Elphinstone Pans, where the river was quite narrow, and thus they thought could easily be blocked. Grossett however was equal to the occasion and shipped a detachment of just fifty men in longboats and quietly rowed past the battery. The intention was to lie in wait for the brig, but to Grossett's disgust, 'the commander of the largest Boat being seized with an unreasonable Pannick, could not be prevailed with to stay at the place appointed tho' there was much less Danger in remaining there than in returning:' [5]

Sure enough, as they tried to run past the rebel battery for the second time one of the boats ran aground and woke the rebels up. Happily Grossett had the foresight to line the sides of his boats with flax mats so that only one man was killed and another wounded. This setback only appears to have made him more determined for, after a landing at Kincardine was aborted as being too dangerous, he enterprisingly managed to arrange for the rebels' pilot to run the ship aground and followed up this happy stroke with a full-blown assault on the rebel battery at Elphinstone.

This was attacked by two sloops, the *Vulture* and the *Pearl*, an armed vessel, *Pretty Janet* and an armed sloop called the *Jean*. According to Grossett the three hour battle, fought out within 'less than Musquet Shot of the Battery', ended with all but one of the rebel guns being silenced, but both Maxwell of Kirconnell and Lord Elcho record no damage at all. [6] As to casualties, Grossett admitted to four dead and eleven wounded while the rebels claimed to have lost no men at all. Grossett however also claimed to have killed their chief engineer – a claim later repeated in a number of newspaper reports. [7] The engineer, Colonel James Grant, was in fact very much alive, but although no Jacobite source mentions him having even been wounded, his being temporarily rendered *hors de combat* at this point might well explain why he was not employed in the subsequent siege of Stirling Castle.

By that time General Hawley was on the move. Orders were given to set up a depot of bread and forage at Linlithgow and, getting word of this, Lord George Murray set out from Falkirk at four o'clock on the morning of the 13th and, joined on the road by Elcho's and Pitsligo's Horse, took possession of Linlithgow at dawn.[8] Cavalry patrols were then sent out along the roads to Edinburgh and soon returned with the alarming news that the enemy was approaching.

Major General John Huske had been ordered to Linlithgow with a division comprising four regular infantry battalions, the loyalist Glasgow Volunteers, and the 13th and 14th Dragoons. Although he too had five infantry battalions, Murray had no intention of fighting, and very smartly withdrew across the bridge at the western end of the burgh much to the disappointment of Huske who had hoped to take him by surprise. Feeling himself secure, Murray then organised an ambush, hoping to tempt Huske's dragoons across the bridge, but they were having none of it and the affair petered out in what Elcho called 'very abusive language.'[9]

With a major battle impending, Hawley was determined to feel his way forward as carefully as possible. His artillery train was still delayed at Newcastle, but ten assorted pieces were assembled by Captain Archibald Cunningham and manned by an equally miscellaneous collection of Royal Artillerymen, civilian haulage contractors and even some seagunners rounded up in Bo'ness by Grossett. The guns and the rest of the infantry were pushed forward to Linlithgow on the 15th and next day Hawley himself came up with the newly arrived Cobham's 10th Dragoons and pressed on to Falkirk. The army marched through the town, which had been evacuated by Murray, and pitched camp in a fairly strong position: 'having on our Front a Deep hollow, Morassy Ground, and on our right Flank, some Inclosures with large wet ditches.'[10]

The defeat at Inverurie provided Loudon with sufficient excuse to remain inactive at Inverness, but young Mamore marched his Highlanders across from Dumbarton to join Hawley at Falkirk early on the morning of the 17th. His arrival was timely, for the rebels had decided that they had no alternative but to go over on to the offensive. Three battalions, John Roy Stuart's and the Duke of Perth's Regiments, together with the greater part of Drummond's *Royal Ecossois* were left in Stirling, but the rest of the army was mustered on Plean Muir, about six miles from Falkirk:

'The Prince employed the 15th in chusing a field of battle, and the 16th in reviewing his army. That evening he got advice that Hawley had

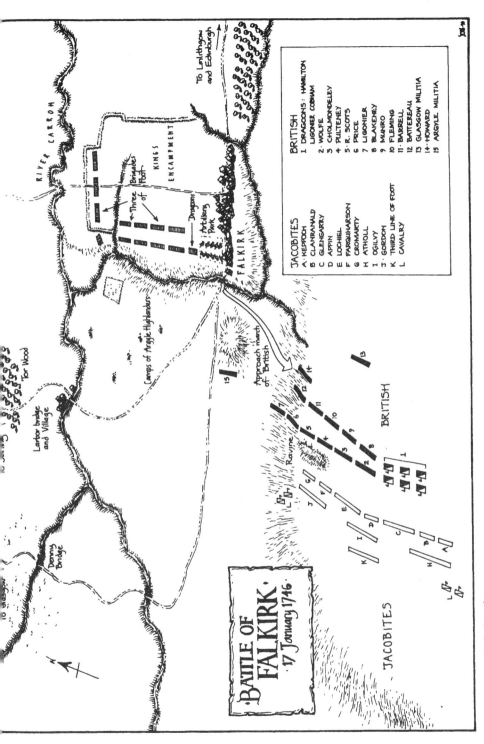

The battle of Falkirk, based on a contemporary map.

JACOBITES
A. KEPPOCH
B. CLANRANALD
C. GLENGARRY
D. APPIN
E. LOCHIEL
F. FARQUHARSON
G. CROMARTY
H. ATHOLL
I. OGILVY
J. GORDON
K. THIRD LINE OF FOOT
L. CAVALRY

BRITISH
1. DRAGOONS: HAMILTON
    LIGONIER COBHAM
2. WOLFE
3. CHOLMONDELEY
4. PULTENEY
5. R. SCOTS
6. PRICE
7. LIGONIER
8. BLAKENEY
9. MUNRO
10. FLEMING
11. BARRELL
12. BATTEREAU
13. GLASGOW MILITIA
14. HOWARD
15. ARGYLE MILITIA

BATTLE OF FALKIRK
·17 January 1746·

97   Map 4

advanced to Falkirk, and had encamped his whole army on the plain betwixt that town and the river Carron: upon which he called a Council, and it was unanimously resolved to march next day and attack the enemy. The field that had been pitched upon was of no use now that Hawley was within six miles. As the Prince had no tents he could not keep his men together above four-and-twenty hours, and if Hawley did not come up in that time they must be sent back to their cantonments; in that case Hawley might beat up the quarters, one after another, and destroy the whole army without a battle.'[11]

Lord George Murray proposed that they should begin by seizing the Hill of Falkirk, a bare open ridge on the south-west of the town which overlooked Hawley's camp. As usual a deception plan was also arranged and Lord John Drummond ostentatiously headed off down the main road in the opposite direction with the cavalry and some of the French regulars, while Murray swung southwards covered by the thick Torwood. Drummond's force was seen, as it was intended to be, and orders were given to Hawley's regiments to be ready to turn out at a moment's notice. No-one however, least of all Hawley who had taken himself off to dine at Callendar House, thought to take the elementary step of sending out a few cavalry patrols to find out exactly what was going on.

This indeed was Hawley's biggest mistake. He had an overwhelming superiority in mounted troops – no less than three regiments of dragoons – and as an experienced cavalryman he should have known how to use them. Admittedly Hamilton's 14th Dragoons were generally allowed to be in a deplorable state and Ligonier's 13th not much better, but both regiments were familiar enough with the roads in the area, and there was absolutely nothing wrong with Cobham's 10th. In short there was no reason at all why they should not have been allowed to build up their confidence through aggressive patrolling, and at the same time keeping their commander fully informed as to where the rebels were and what they were doing. Instead he was plainly reluctant to let them out of his sight and kept them close to his infantry with the result that he was effectively blind.

At any rate the troops in the camp at Falkirk remained oblivious of the danger until a loyalist scout rode in at about one o'clock with the news that the rebels were coming on fast. 'Daddy' Huske promptly formed the army again and sent word to Hawley at Callendar House. The General thereupon just as promptly galloped to the top of the hill with one of his aides-de-camp, James MacKenzie, and, 'sent me to order the Cavalry to move that way immediately and the Infantry and Artillery to follow them as fast as possible, he being afraid the rebels might get by us on the left, and perhaps cut off our communication with Edinburgh, or, at least, get away from us, which was the thing we were most afraid of.'[12]

Unable to see what was happening, a rather bewildered Brigadier James Cholmondley described the subsequent race to gain the summit of the hill.

'The Army was immediately order'd to stand to their Arms, and form, in the front of their incampment, All the Cavalry were order'd to march to the Left, to take post there, and the two Lines of Infantry were order'd to face to the Left, and in this Position, we march'd to the Left near half a mile, but as we had hollow roads, and very uneven Ground, to pass, we were in great Confusion. Here we formed again, in my Opinion a very good Situation, but we were no sooner form'd but order'd a second time, to take Ground to the Left, and as we march'd, all the way up hill, and Over very uneven Ground, our men were greatly blown.'[13]

Deployed from left to right in the rebel front line were Locheil's Regiment (800), the Stewarts of Appin (300), the Master of Lovat's Regiment (300), Lady MacIntosh's Regiment (200), Farquharson of Monaltrie's Battalion (150), Lord Cromartie's Regiment (200), Cluny's MacPhersons (300), and the three MacDonald regiments, Clanranald (350), Glengarry (800) and Keppoch (400).

The second line comprised only three bodies covering the left, right and centre – the two remaining battalions of Lord Lewis Gordon's Regiment (400), two battalions of Lord Ogilvy's Regiment (500) and the three-battalion Atholl Brigade (600).

Finally, a third line was formed comprising the cavalry under Sir John McDonnell, and some French regulars led by Lord John Drummond. The former, according to Lord Elcho, numbered about 360 men in total, though this is probably on the optimistic side. The French regulars comprised the three Irish picquets, another picquet from the *Royal Ecossois* and the grenadier company of that regiment. They probably totalled no more than 250 officers and men but, although this provisional battalion was not particularly strong, it was made up of picked men and certainly behaved like an elite unit.[14] In all, the Jacobite army appears to have numbered something in the region of 5,800 infantry and 360 cavalry – something rather less than they are usually credited with.

Facing them, again from left to right, were three dragoon regiments – Ligonier's 13th, Cobham's 10th and Hamilton's 14th. Then came Wolfe's 8th Foot, Cholmondley's 34th, Pulteney's 13th, 2/Royals, Price's 14th and Ligonier's 59th.

The second line was made up of Blakeney's 27th, Monro's 37th, Fleming's 36th, Barrell's 4th and Battereau's 62nd, while Howard's 3rd, lagging behind, formed a reserve. All in all, according to his official returns Hawley mustered 5,488 infantry and 519 Dragoons on the 13th of January, to which should be added a further 300 odd Dragoons of Cobham's 10th who joined the army some days later.[15]

Hawley also had a fair number of Loyalist troops with him – the Glasgow and Paisley Regiments, forming a little brigade under the Earl of Home, mustered about 650 men between them, although an Edinburgh company and some of the Stirling volunteers were also present which might have raised the total to something over 700 men. This brigade was posted amongst some houses and walls at the foot of the hill behind the dragoons.

Lieutenant-Colonel John Campbell of Mamore's contingent, comprising one company of the 43rd and three of the 64th Highlanders, together with twelve companies of the loyalist Argyll Militia, mustering about 800 men in total, similarly formed in the rear of Hawley's left wing, but unlike Home's loyalists they played very little part in the battle.

Falkirk was a confused, scrambling affair which began before the second line of either army had deployed properly and was latterly conducted in pitch darkness and a wild storm. It is hardly surprising therefore that both sides afterwards claimed victory and while there is no doubt that a substantial part of both armies fled from the field, other units stood fast.

The battle began at about four o'clock in the afternoon when the three dragoon regiments launched an unsuccessful frontal assault on the Mac-Donald brigade. Afterwards the Jacobites thought this was simply a last attempt to hold on to the crest, but James Mackenzie relates that 'as the General imagined the enemy was more afraid of horse than foot, he ordered the dragoons to begin the attack'[16] At any rate, Lord George Murray, who was standing in front of the MacDonald regiments, ordered the Jacobites to kneel and directed a well disciplined volley which stopped most of the dragoons dead in their tracks. How many were actually killed is not certain. A loyalist volunteer named Corse claimed to have seen 'daylight' appear in their ranks but only three officers are actually known to have been killed – all of them belonging to Ligonier's 13th Dragoons – which would suggest that the overall casualties were not very high. At any rate it was enough to halt the charge and the few troopers who actually reached the Jacobite lines were beaten off with some loss after a brief struggle. Most of Ligonier's and Cobham's galloped off towards the right, passing between the two armies and being fired upon by the rest of the rebel front line, but Hamilton's went straight down the hill and rode over the Glasgow Volunteers. They, understandably enough, 'were so provoked that they gave them a Volley, and unsaddled several of them.'[17]

Suitably elated by their success, the MacDonalds ignored Murray's orders to stand still and instead set off down the hill in pursuit of the fleeing dragoons and got in amongst Home's loyalist battalions as well.

The rest of the rebel front line immediately followed their example under the cover of a heavy rainstorm driven by a strong wind blowing in the faces of the British infantry. Most of them, already breathless and disordered by their hurried march up the hill, panicked and fled back down it again, but over on the right wing others, Barrell's 4th and Ligonier's 59th, led by Brigadier General James Cholmondley, stood fast behind a ravine and fired into the rebels' flank.

'We then formed our Front where our Left Flank was before,' wrote a Sergeant of Barrell's, 'and forced the Hill against the whole Body of the Rebels with our little Regiment, and advanced towards them in the greatest Order, tho' above 3000 of them were marching towards us. We put them to a Stand by our Front Rank's kneeling, and the Center and Rear Ranks firing continually upon them.'[17]

John Roy Stuart immediately called out to stop, fearing some kind of ambush. Some of the rebels did just that and others in the second line immediately turned tail and ran. '. . . the cursed hollow square came up,' said Sullivan, referring to Cholmondley's brigade, 'took our left in flanc & obligded them to retire in disorder. There was no remedy nor succor to be given them. The second ligne, yt H.R.Hs. counted upon, went off, past the river & some of them even went to Bannocburn, & Sterling, where they gave out yt we lost the day.' In actual fact it only appears to have been the second-line units on the Jacobite left who ran away, while the Athollmen followed after the MacDonalds. Nevertheless things were suddenly looking desperate and Sir John McDonnell, having 'quitted the cavalry which would not listen to orders' helped Colonel Sullivan to rally some of the runaways and lead them back to the field.[18]

This also gave time for Cholmondley to get together about a hundred of Cobham's and Ligonier's Dragoons. Encouraged by the rebels' obvious confusion, he then attempted a local counter-attack and, 'got them to the top of the hill, where I saw the Highlanders formed behind some houses and a barn (I was forced to fire a pistol amongst them, before I could get them to do this), I then returned to the two battalions to march them up, here General Huske joined me, and I told him, that if we could get some more battalions to join us, we might drive them'.[19]

All the while Howard's 3rd Foot had also been standing fast and 'Daddy' Huske for his part rallied at least two other battalions, Price's 14th and Fleming's 36th, on them, while somewhere to his rear Brigadier-General John Mordaunt was trying to round up the others. Huske however was much less keen than Cholmondley on counter-attacking in the failing light. Indeed one problem by this time was finding any formed bodies of the rebels to fight.

Eventually Colonel Sullivan managed to bring up the French Picquets and at this Cobham's Dragoons sullenly retired and Huske fell back with his infantry as well. On the way back to their camp they were surprised to find the artillery train, which had been abandoned at the bottom of the hill by Captain Cunningham (not surprisingly he was subsequently cashiered) and the grenadiers of Barrell's succeeded in dragging one gun away with them while two others were recovered later.

The storm by now was at its height and as one correspondent wrote, 'The weather was so severe that he (Hawley) chose rather to abandon his camp, and retire to Linlithgow, than to destroy the Men by lying on their Arms all Night, wet to the Skin, subject to continuall Alarms.'[20] This withdrawal, and the subsequent ocupation of Falkirk by the French Picquets, gave the rebels sufficient excuse to claim a famous victory, but too many of their own men had also run away, and their true feelings are apparent both from their failure to pursue Hawley to Edinburgh, and from their subsequent retreat northwards rather than face another battle.

Casualties on both sides were light. The Jacobites afterwards admitted to 50 killed and 60–80 wounded, while Hawley initially returned 12 officers and 55 men killed and 280 others missing. In actual fact there were 20 officers killed in just five regiments:

Ligonier's 13th Dragoons:	Lieutenant-Colonel Shugborough Whitney
	Cornet Monk
	Cornet Thomas Crow
Wolfe's 8th Foot:	Captain John Dalton
	Captain Peter Guerin
	Captain Malcolm Hamilton
	Captain Thomas Launders
	Captain Hale
	Lieutenant William Rickson
Blakeney's 27th Foot:	Captain Edward Todd
	Captain Richard Kellett
	Captain Robert Dalrymple
	Captain William Edmonstone
	Lieutenant Supprige Fairfield
Cholmondley's 34th Foot:	Lieutenant-Colonel Maurice Powell
Monro's 37th Foot:	Colonel Sir Robert Monro of Foulis
	Lieutenant-Colonel James Biggar
	Captain John Hill
	Captain Thomas Fitzgerald
	Captain Henry Wheterall[20]

All of the dead infantry officers belonged to regiments on the left which had obviously been cut up as they fled. Indeed afterwards Hawley's officers were quite candid in admitting that so few men were lost simply because they had run away so quickly and that in those regiments a relatively high proportion of officers were killed because they had been abandoned by their men. This was particularly true of Monro's 37th – a fact which they were to remember three months later, especially since there was an ugly rumour that Monro himself, whose body was particularly mangled, had first been wounded and then murdered along with his brother, Doctor Monro, while his injuries were being treated.

At Linlithgow it was soon found that all the ammunition remaining in the men's cartridge boxes was soaked, and as the burgh was overcrowded anyway it was then decided to continue the retreat to Edinburgh in order to reorganise and resupply them in some security. For their part the rebels, in no very good humour, rejected any notion of following up their dubious success with an advance on Edinburgh and instead returned to their rather futile siege of Stirling Castle.

With Colonel James Grant temporarily out of action for whatever reason, the conduct of the siege was placed in the hands of another French engineer named Gordon[21] who soon proved to be an incompetent alcoholic. After an attempt to establish a battery in an old house called Mar's Wark was abandoned as being too exposed, another was constructed on top of the Gowan Hill with considerable difficulty. This work was done largely by the *Royal Ecossois* since the Highlanders considered it beneath their dignity and the lowland troops were considered 'too lazy'. As there was insufficient depth of soil on the rock the gun emplacements eventually had to be built up with wool-packs, but no sooner did the battery open fire than it was quickly knocked out by the castle's guns and newspaper reports gleefully recorded the subsequent arrival in Edinburgh of deserters from the French regiments, who were no doubt fed up with doing all the hard and dangerous work of the siege.

At any rate the rebels were still half-heartedly persevering with the siege on the 30th of January, when the Duke of Cumberland arrived in Edinburgh to supersede Hawley. He found the army in surprisingly good heart, for with the dismal exception of Hamilton's Dragoons, it did not consider itself beaten. Nevertheless the arrival of Cumberland was in itself a considerable boost to their morale, for not surprisingly the cavalry in particular had lost confidence in Hawley. After Culloden a trooper in Cobham's 10th named Enoch Bradshaw referred *inter alia* to, 'General Hawley, who does not love us because our regiment spoke truth about Falkirk job.'[22]

Although Hawley at first wrote ferociously of his intentions to hang or shoot dozens of the runaways, his bark as usual proved to be much worse than his bite. Only four men were actually executed after the battle, three – Francis Forbes of the Royals, John Irvine of Ligonier's 59th and

David Welsh of Pulteney's 13th – were deserters who had joined the French service after Fontenoy only to be retaken aboard the *Louis XV*, and the fourth, Henry Macmannus of Hamilton's 14th Dragoons, had enlisted with the rebels after Prestonpans.[23]

The gallant stand made by Cholmondley's and Huske's battalions lay at the bottom of this mood, but another boost to morale was provided by the indefatigable Walter Grossett, who launched a daring raid on Glamis Castle deep in rebel-held territory, only the day after the battle. With the aid of loyalist partisans and a covering force provided by the Argyll Militia, he succeeded in rescuing thirty-one of the officers who had been captured at Prestonpans and conveyed them safely back to Edinburgh.[24]

At the same time substantial reinforcements were coming in almost daily. Sempill's 25th Foot marched into Edinburgh on the 17th and Campbell's 21st Fusiliers followed the next day, together with the long awaited Royal Artillery detachment. As a result the Glasgow Volunteers were rather belatedly presented with their colours and graciously dismissed, while the arrival of Lord Mark Kerr's 11th Dragoons on the 25th meant that there was no longer any need to rely on the quite useless 13th and 14th Dragoons.

There was no reason therefore for Cumberland to linger in Edinburgh, particularly as provisions were running short in Stirling Castle, and he marched for Linlithgow on the 31st of January. In the face of this advance, the Prince was once again faced with what he regarded as a mutiny staged by Lord George Murray and his supporters. Rightly judging their depleted and demoralised regiments to be incapable of fighting a second battle, they announced their decision to retire northwards, sugaring the pill with the confident assertion that they could spend the winter in reducing the various loyalist-held posts before taking the field again, 10,000 strong in the spring.

On the 1st of February Falkirk was evacuated, only hours ahead of the British army and with Stirling Bridge still broken down, they streamed away next morning to the Fords of Frew, abandoning their wounded prisoners as well as a number of their own sick, their heavy guns and other equipment and blowing up a magazine established in St Ninian's church.

On the 3rd the lowland units and French regulars reached Perth, while the clans straggled into Crieff. An extremely heated council of war was held there that night, fuelled by the realisation that the scale of desertion was not as bad as had been supposed. There was still no question however of making a stand and, having agreed to make for Inverness, next day the two divisions parted. The clans set off to march directly over the hills, while Lord George Murray took the rest round the coast by Aberdeen.

1. Colonel Gardiner's house, Prestonpans

2. Robert Gordon's College, Aberdeen. Surrounded by a palisade, this was occupied as a fort by Captain John Crosbie's company of the 21st Foot during the latter part of the rising.

3. Arthur Elphinstone, Lord Balmerino. Colonel of a troop of the
Prince's Lifeguards he surrendered after Culloden and was executed on
the 18th of August 1746. He appears to be wearing the uniform of the
troop – a blue coat turned up with red.

EARL of KILMARNOCK

4. William Boyd, Lord Kilmarnock. Colonel first of a troop of Horse-Grenadiers and then a regiment of Footguards. Taken prisoner at Culloden he was executed together with Lord Balmerino on the 18th of August 1746.

5. Ruthven Barracks

6. Culloden Moor.

7. Culloden Moor – the Atholl Brigade charged towards camera across this area. Now properly cultivated it would still have been plashy and heather-covered in 1746.

8. Old Leanach Cottage, Culloden, as viewed from the position occupied at the start of the battle by Ligonier's 59th Foot. During Huske's counter-attack they were forced to divide into two wings in order to clear this building and an adjacent barn.

9. The remains of the Culwhiniac Park walls at the point where Ballimore's Highlanders broke through.

10. Culchunaig Farm, Culloden Moor, as seen from the point where Ballimore's Highlanders broke through the park walls.

11. Culchunaig Farm today.

12. The re-entrant, Culloden Moor. This is taken from the viewpoint of General Hawley, looking towards the battlefield. Culchunaig Farm is in the trees on the right of the skyline. The crest and the rebel infantry lined along the top of it prevented Hawley from seeing what was happening up on the moor.

Having occupied Perth on the 6th of February and seeing little profit in pushing his men on through the snow which was now falling, Cumberland halted and waited to see whether or not the rebels now intended to disperse as their predecessors had done in very similar circumstances in 1716. In the meantime up to six battalions of Hessians accompanied by a detachment of hussars and a small train of artillery landed at Leith on the 8th[25], and at a conference held in Edinburgh on the 16th of February Cumberland decided to march his men northwards only as far as Aberdeen, while his line of communications was covered by Hessian units posted at Stirling and Perth, by St George's 8th Dragoons at Bridge of Earn and the remnants of the 13th and 14th Dragoons at Bannockburn. Edinburgh itself was to be held by its loyalist battalion, and five companies of Lee's 55th called up from Berwick. The final destruction of the rebels would wait until the spring.

Sources:

1. Maxwell, p.94. Lord Kilmarnock was agreeably quartered at his own home in Callendar.
2. This reference is to Blakeney's Loyalist Volunteer Battalion, rather than to the regulars in the castle.
3. Chambers: *Jacobite Memoirs*, pp. 96–99.
4. Ibid.
5. *Origins*, p. 355–6.
6. *Origins*, Ibid., Maxwell, p. 95; Elcho, p. 367–8. The Lifeguards were present, covering the battery against a possible landing by the troops carried in the two smaller vessels.
7. The *London Gazette* for January 18th reckoned him killed in the earlier attack on Airth, but otherwise there is a fair consistency in the story.
8. Maxwell, p. 96. A number of loyalist militia were taken prisoner – presumably belonging to the Linlithgow company of Blakeney's volunteers.
9. Murray, p. 78; Elcho, p. 369–70.
10. Brigadier Cholmondley *IN* HMC Rep.10, App. 1, p. 440.
11. Maxwell, p. 98–9.
12. HMC Trevor, Mss. p. 139.
13. Cholmondley, op. cit.
14. These figures are largely taken from Elcho, though Kirkconnel p. 100 is very helpful in describing the composition of the French regulars. Picquets were to all intents and purposes second grenadier companies.
15. Home, p. 392.
16. Maxwell, p. 101–2; HMC Trevor Mss. p. 139.
17. *Newcastle Courant*.
18. Johnstone p. 88; Sullivan p. 118; McDonnell *IN* Sullivan p. 115. Ogilvy's Regiment ran away so fast that Ensign James Stormonth threw away the colour he was carrying.
19. Cholmondley, op.cit.
20. *Newcastle Courant*, with corrections and christian names taken from the Com-

mission registers in WO25. To this list should perhaps be added Major Browne of Fleming's, who died in Edinburgh on the 30th of January from unspecified causes and Colonel Francis Ligonier of the 13th Dragoons and 59th Foot who died of pleurisy on the 27th.

21. He is usually referred to as Mirabelle de Gordon, but at least one account refers to Mirabelle being a *nom de guerre*.
22. *Lyon in Mourning*, p. 381.
23. *Newcastle Gazette* – the report rather obscurely added that they were Irish.
24. *Origins*, p. 363–4; Whitefoord p. 68–9.
25. There were six battalions, made up of a battalion of grenadiers, the Prince Maximilian Regiment, Lieutenant General Ansbach's Regiment, each of two battalions, and six companies of Guards.

CHAPTER 9
St. George on Horseback
Loudon and the Highland War

Although free from pursuit, the rebel withdrawal was not without incident, and on the 10th of February old John Gordon of Glenbucket
attended to some unfinished business by taking his regiment up to
Ruthven Barracks and demanding its surrender. Lieutenant Molloy,
defiant as ever, answered: 'That it was not consistent with his Honour
to do so, and that he would not give up his Garrison until he was besieged
in Form, and that he could not see yet but he was able to make a good
Defence.'

The phrasing might be a little more elegant than his robust response
to the last summons in August, but Glenbucket had come prepared this
time and halfway through the afternoon Colonel James Grant turned up
with three cannon, emplaced them in the village and announced the fact
by firing three rounds in quick succession. To the rebels' chagrin however
the expected white flag failed to appear and after a while Grant and
the Deputy Barrackmaster, John MacPherson[1], went up to the gate and
delivered a more formal summons:

> 'These are by his R.H. Order. I send you this to desire you will surren-
> der, without Loss of Time, to give up the Barrack, and so render your-
> selves Prisoners at Discretion; or these are to certify, you are to expect
> no Mercy. GORDON'

These were of course pretty much the same terms so recently offered by
Cumberland to the unfortunate garrison of Carlisle, but it was no way
to try to intimidate a man who had previously responded to such threats
with the dry comment that he would take his chances. Nevertheless,
recognising that he could not now hold out against artillery, Molloy
offered his own terms:

> 'Sir, I don't see but I am in a Condition to make a good Defence in my
> Garrison. Still I know I cannot stand a long and regular Siege, especially
> against Cannon; yet I am resolved to the last Extremity, in every respect,
> to sustain the Character of a Gentleman, and to answer the Expectation

and Confidence of my Royal Master, with Regard to what he has committed to my Trust. To be brief, I will not surrender until your Prince's Approach to this place, and then upon the following Conditions only: 1st. That my Men and I be humanely treated, as I am inform'd of the Revenge and Threats denounced against us by the Clans who attacked this Garrison last August. 2ndly, That we shall not be rifled or pillaged; and that your Prince grant me my Parole of Honour, and set my men at Liberty as he has done other Prisoners hitherto, considering the Difference betwixt Prisoners of this Kind, and those taken in the Field of Battle – Gen. Gordon, an experienced humane Officer, can't deny this reasonable Intreaty; and upon Performance thereof, I will deliver the Keys of the Garrison to your Prince, upon giving a Guarantee to fulfill the above Conditions. Further I permit Gen. Gordon to send his Horses and Grooms to my Stables this night, without Arms: All I require for my Honour and Security on this Head, is, that Col. Grant may be permitted to stay as a Hostage in my House until the Prince's Arrival. MOLLOY'

Not surprisingly Glenbucket retorted that Molloy was coming on 'too high', but perhaps embarrassed by the fact of his being defied by only a dozen men ('whereof three were useless'), he assured him of good treatment providing he allowed twenty or thirty men to occupy the barracks until the Prince arrived. He also made it clear that this was his final offer, but an hour later Molloy agreed to accept sixteen men and surrendered at noon next day.[2] According to an intelligence report forwarded to Loudon by the Laird of Grant, the barracks was burned on the 14th and the stables next day although the damage cannot have been too great, for it was used intermittently afterwards.

On the night of the 16th Loudon, displaying uncharacteristic energy, riposted with an enterprising attempt to kidnap the Prince from his quarters at Moy Hall, eight miles south of Inverness. Intelligence reports suggested that the rebels were widely dispersed, but employing his usual caution Loudon took about 1,200 men with him after throwing a security cordon around Inverness itself. Unfortunately word of the expedition still managed to precede him[3], and while his quarry bolted in his nightshirt, the local blacksmith and four other men were sent out to delay any pursuit.

Loudon meanwhile had halted three miles short of the house in the early hours of the morning and sent thirty men to seal off the approaches. In the darkness they stumbled over the blacksmith and his mates and briefly exchanged fire. Not surprisingly nobody managed to hit anything, but a mile further back the noise of the exchange threw the main body of the loyalists into confusion. They were still formed up in a column on

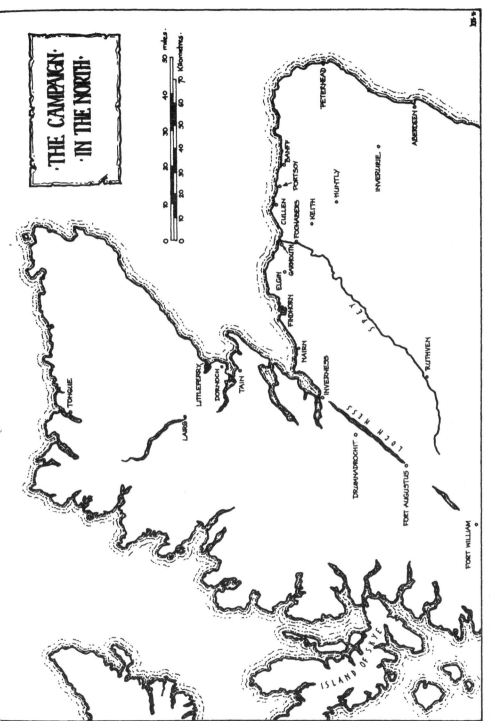

The campaign in the north.

109

Map 5

the road by companies, and as soon as the shooting was heard, the fifth company from the end of the line promptly turned tail and ran, carrying away with it the four companies standing behind – including one commanded by Munro of Culcairn. Somehow or other Loudon managed to hold on to the rest and formed them into some kind of a firing line, but in the confusion there were a number of negligent discharges, one of which killed the piper standing by his side. Unwilling to go forward into the unknown, but equally reluctant to retreat, he then hung around for the best part of an hour before finally coming to the obvious conclusion that surprise must have been lost and ordering his men back to Inverness.[4]

As it turned out the Prince's nocturnal excursion was to bring him down with something akin to pneumonia, but this can have been scant comfort to Loudon, who continued his headlong retreat through Inverness and straight across Kessock Ferry into the Black Isle on the 18th. Roused by the attempt on the Prince, the Rebels were close enough behind him to plant a field gun on the shore, which fired several times on his boats to no effect. Then, having seen him off the premises, they turned their attention to the small garrison left in Fort George – the northernmost barracks in the 'Chain'.

At first sight it appeared strong enough, having been built on the old castle-hill and incorporating the original tower-house. The garrison, commanded by Major George Grant of the 43rd Highlanders, was also adequate enough and well supplied with food and ammunition. It comprised some 80 regulars of Guise's 6th[5] and two Independent Companies, the Laird of Grant's and one commanded by the Master of Ross[6], and afterwards was reported to have had sixteen guns – probably swivels.

At this stage the rebels had only one field gun with them, which was clearly not going to accomplish very much by itself, so Sullivan and the Jacobite Colonel Grant decided instead to sink a mine into the gravel beneath the wall. Unable to depress their swivel-guns far enough to fire on the works, the garrison resorted to showering them with hand-grenades, but when this failed to stop the digging, Major Grant agreed to surrender for which he was afterwards court-martialled and dismissed the service. Elcho refers to two or three men being killed on either side during the short siege but the only recorded casualty was a French artilleryman, Sergeant L'Epine, who contrived to blow himself up when the fort was being demolished *after* the surrender.[7]

Having so easily taken the Highland capital, the rebels then set about securing their position. One fort in the 'Chain' had fallen and it would obviously be advantageous to take the other two, Forts Augustus and William, as well. Loudon's army was also a distraction which needed to be dealt with, and at the same time it was also important to retain control of as much of the east coast as possible in order to facilitate the landing of fresh supplies and reinforcements from France.

The first priority was Loudon, and the Earl of Cromartie and Lord Kilmarnock were sent off in pursuit of him. Fortunately however Loudon had managed to secure all the available boats in the immediate area which meant that the Jacobites were forced to march the long way round, and Kirkconnell explains the problems which resulted with rueful clarity:

'As the former (Cromartie) was obliged to go round the head of the first frith, (the Cromarty Firth) the latter had abundance of time to retire across the frith that divides Ross-shire from Sutherland (the Dornoch Firth); he took up his quarters at Dornoch, where he seemed to be perfectly secure, as Lord Cromarty had no boats. It was not so easy to go round the head of this frith, which reaches a great way into a mountainous country; and when Lord Cromarty attempted it, Lord Loudon sent some of his men back by water to Ross-shire, which determined Lord Cromarty to return to Tain, but Lord Loudon had already brought back his men to Dornoch.'[8]

This fruitless dodging about was to continue for some time and Lord George Murray was ordered north to take charge of operations. But he too, for all his bluster, could make no headway and soon returned to Inverness in disgust. However an attempt to take Fort Augustus was much more successful. Originally it had been no more than a simple barracks constructed to pretty much the same design as Ruthven (although larger) on a low hillock at the southern end of Loch Ness, but Wade considered it both too small and situated too far away from the loch. A new fort was therefore built and completed as recently as 1742, consisting of four large, sharply-pointed bastions, linked by substantial barrack blocks and protected by the customary ditch, covered way and sloping glacis. Its erection on a level 'greenfield site' by the shore allowed the engineer, Captain John Romer, to design a perfectly symmetrical structure unhampered by any need to take account of existing structures or awkward terrain features, but unfortunately he made a fundamental (if understandable) error in assuming that it would not be exposed to artillery fire.

Permanent fortifications of this period normally took the form of massively thick earthen ramparts faced with stone, it having been long recognised that stonework alone was too brittle to withstand artillery fire. This was indeed the case with the four large bastions at Fort Augustus, but the curtain wall which linked them was a different matter altogether. Instead of constructing the barrack blocks within the curtain walls, Romer actually designed them so as to form a part of it, which had an undeniable elegance but also meant that the Fort's walls were utterly incapable of resisting artillery fire – a defect compounded by the fact that at the time of the siege the barrack blocks still had their temporary thatched roofs. In itself this was bad enough, but Romer had gone on to build in a second defect in his design, which made the breaching of the curtain quite unnecessary. This was the siting of a circular pavilion in the centre of each bastion. One was a girnel or oatmeal store, another contained the well, the third was the fort's 'necessary house', and the fourth was the magazine. Being well dug in to the earthen core of each bastion they were safe from any direct fire, but were easily identified by their high conical roofs, and horribly vulnerable to mortar fire.[9]

Yet another drawback, although of considerably less importance, was that the original barracks had not yet been demolished and the governor, Major Hu Wentworth of Guise's 6th Foot, felt obliged to occupy them with one of his three companies. The vulnerability of this outpost then became starkly apparent when the Jacobites turned up in the form of the *Royal Ecossois* and the three Irish picquets led by Lieutenant Colonel Walter Stapleton of the Regiment Berwick. Disdaining to wait for his artillery, the Irishman formed up his men and assaulted the old barracks there and then. Suitably impressed, the garrison just as promptly beat a hasty retreat back to the Fort and waited for his next move.

On the 3rd of March Colonel Grant opened his first trench, thus formally beginning the siege, and started dropping some mortar shells on to the bastions. The effect was startling, for the easily identified magazine turned out not to be bombproof and demonstrated this defect in the clearest possible fashion by exploding and taking enough of the bastion with it to create a practicable breach two days after the siege began. With rather more excuse than Major Grant, Wentworth surrendered, but like him he would shortly be court-martialled and cashiered for doing so. In the meantime, the Jacobites moved south to deal with the last remaining link in the 'Chain' – Fort William.

The oldest of the forts, it occupied a rather cramped position with its back to Loch Linnhe and although apparently more solidly constructed than the newer Fort Augustus, it had the great misfortune to be overlooked by some high ground just a hundred yards to the east. More fortunately its garrison – four companies of regulars, two of them from the ubiquitous 6th Foot, and one of the Argyleshire companies – was commanded by the very capable Captain Carolina Frederick Scott and he soon turned out to be as resolute as Terry Molloy.

The Fort had been blockaded and sniped at by the local clan regiments under Locheil[10] since the 24th of February, but on the 20th of March Colonel Grant began raising his first batteries about 800 yards south-east of the Fort, and that night fired off eighteen rounds from his mortars. According to Elcho's account they all fell short, though the journal of the siege says they, 'threw in a great many Cohorn Shells six Inches Diameter, and Inch thick in the Shell.'[11] Either way, Grant was dissatisfied with his performance and next day pushed the mortars a hundred yards closer and also established a three-gun battery – one four-pounder and two six-pounders – as well. That night 60 or 70 shells were dumped on the garrison and the following morning a French drummer was belatedly sent to demand its surrender. Scott however flatly refused to admit him, let alone look at his 'Credentials'.

'On his Return,' wrote the unknown diarist, 'they ply'd us hard all that Day with their Cannon; and betwixt Three in the Morning and Ten at Night, they threw in, from a Battery of five and another of four Cohorn Mortars, 194 large Shells: These Batteries are about 200 Yards distant from the Walls.'

On the 23rd another battery was opened at the foot of the Cow Hill but it proved to be too exposed and for the next three days the bombardment was carried on from the original battery. Then on the 27th another one – comprising four six-pounders – was unmasked above the Governor's Garden, 200 yards from the Fort. Despite a quite prodigious expenditure of ammunition it was becoming steadily more apparent that Grant's guns were incapable of breaching the walls, so he changed his approach and planted his fourth battery on the Craig:

> '29th, At Break of Day they unmask'd a new Battery at the Craig of three Brass four Pounders, within 100 Yards of the Wall and cannonaded us from this and the other three. As they carried a Furnace with them, they threw in a great many hot Bullets, and some bearded Pieces of Iron, Foot long and Inch thick, which they design'd should stick in our Timberwork and set us on Fire. They fir'd Grape and Partridge Shot and ply'd us hard from all Hands with Small Arms but did little Damage.'

Unable to batter down the walls, Grant now hoped at least to render it untenable; and a letter from one of the garrison admitted that 'the Roofs of the Fort are exceedingly damaged, the old Pile of Barracks almost quite beat down, both Roof and Walls. There are not six Panes of Glass in all the Windows.'[12] The mortar shells, according to the journal, were sufficiently heavy as to come crashing down all the way from the roof to the ground before exploding. Recognising the danger, Scott riposted by launching a sally. About 11 o'clock on the morning of the 31st one party, led by Captains Foster and McLauchlane, suddenly marched out, fired a volley and stormed the battery on the Craig at the point of the bayonet. Inside they found three brass four-pounders, the two Royal mortars and the shot furnace. There was no question of carrying off the mortars, so they were spiked together with two of the four-pounders although the third (and an unfortunate French gunner) was carried off in triumph, for the loss of two men killed and three wounded. The second party, led by Captains Paton and Whitway, was less fortunate. Attacking the Cow Hill battery they were beaten off with the loss of five killed, although they too managed to take a couple of prisoners.

Under interrogation the prisoners admitted to running short of ammunition and indeed the journal records that next day 'they cannonaded us, but not very hotly.'[13] More rounds were fired into the Fort on the 2nd, and that night a last 17 rounds apiece of roundshot and mortar shells, but next morning the defenders woke to find the siege lines empty and the rebels in full retreat towards Inverness.[14]

Meanwhile, having had no success in chasing Loudon, Murray took on a much more agreeable project, generally referred to as the Atholl Raid. A number of loyalist outposts had been established in Atholl, covering the approaches to the Hessian base at Perth. These were for the most part rather slackly occupied by detachments of the Argyll Militia and judged to be vulnerable to surprise.[15] Accordingly between three and five in the morning on the 10th of March, Murray's Athollmen and Cluny's MacPhersons attacked them more or less simultaneously and carried all of them with the exception of Blair Castle.

Although the castle was admitted by Murray to be his primary objective, the attack here failed because its garrison comprised regulars belonging to Campbell's 21st, led by Lieutenant Colonel Sir Andrew Agnew.[16] Instead Murray was forced to besiege it, but as he grumblingly admitted he only had two four-pounders which were quite incapable of penetrating the castle's seven foot thick walls – and to make matters worse: 'The cannon were not only small, but bad. One of them seldom hit the Castle, though not half-musket shot from it.'[17] The fruitless siege continued for nearly three weeks, increasingly harassed by the cautious but nevertheless persistent attentions of the Hessians and St George's 8th Dragoons under Lord Crawford.

Murray originally planted an outpost of his own at Dunkeld, but under pressure from Crawford he pulled it back to Pitlochry just below the Pass of Killiecrankie. The Hessians were, understandably enough, reluctant to make any attempt to force the narrow Pass but they and the dragoons could and did constantly skirmish with the rebels on a daily basis – 'picqueering' Murray called it, which is a polite way of saying that both sides blazed away without hitting anything.

On the 30th of March Crawford eventually succeeded in forcing the rebels to evacuate Pitlochry and retire into the security of the Pass itself. But by that time too Murray was receiving ever more peremptory orders to return to Inverness, and on the 31st he raised the siege and retired northwards – dropping off Cluny's men in Badenoch to guard the southern approaches to Inverness.

In Murray's absence, a renewed attempt was made to destroy Loudon and his loyalist army. As Cromartie was plainly not up to the job, the Duke of Perth was assigned to command the expedition this time, with Colonel Sullivan as his military adviser. Thus far Loudon had been able to outmanoeuvre his pursuers by exercising a monopoly on the boats which were so essential for passing the Dornoch Firth. But now the rebels had scoured the coast of the Moray Firth for all the fishing boats they could lay their hands on and assembled them at Findhorn. On the night of the 18th of March, Lieutenant-Colonel James Moir of Stonywood took charge of the flotilla and under cover of darkness successfully slipped past the naval patrols in the firth to reach Tain by dawn. The next stage of the exercise did not go so well. The following night about 800 men of the first wave were crammed into the boats, but then got lost in thick fog and turned up back on the same beach they had embarked from. However, setting off a second time they successfully effected a landing on the other side early on the morning of the 20th.

This amphibious assault took Loudon completely by surprise. His forces were strung out in a long, over-extended cordon all the way from Dornoch itself along the north shore of the Firth and up the river Shin to Lairg, and he himself had just set off that morning to inspect the quarters along the Shin. Consequently, when the rebels came ashore on Dornoch Sands, the only troops actually in the area were 120 men of the 64th Highlanders led by Major William MacKenzie. Sending word to the MacKay Independent Companies three miles away at Muckle Ferry, he immediately beat to arms and hurried down to the beach only to find 800 rebels already there and the second wave actually in the process of landing. Discretion at this point was obviously the better part of valour, and so MacKenzie promptly faced about and hastily retired back to Dornoch, dumped his reserve ammunition and then headed northwards to the Little Ferry.

What happened next is not entirely clear. Loudon had three store-ships there guarded by another thirty or so men of his regiment, but they had already exercised their initiative by executing a swift retreat northwards. Unable to get everybody across the ferry before the rebels arrived, Mac-Kenzie then decided to surrender, after giving time for those officers who had earlier been taken prisoner at Prestonpans to make their escape.[18] Loudon himself meanwhile had tried to regain contact with his regiment, but could only find scattered fugitives from the MacKay companies. Realising that nothing could be done in the fog, he turned around again and retreated westwards, gathering up his Independent Companies as he went. Not surprisingly they were thoroughly demoralised and deserting fast so, abandoning any thoughts of making a stand, he carried on retreating all the way to the Isle of Skye.

Without so much as a single shot being fired on either side the loyalist army, assembled with such pains by the Lord President, had virtually ceased to exist. Nevertheless, some of the loyalists who had retreated northwards remained in arms and in a curious reversal of fortunes contributed not a little to the final defeat of the rebels.

Although plans for a full-scale invasion were called off early in the year, the French Government had not yet abandoned the rebels. On the 10th of February three privateers, *Le Bourbon, Le Charite* and *La Sophie* slipped out of Ostend carrying the whole of Fitzjames's Horse, an Irish regiment in the French service, but ran into the Royal Navy. The first two, carrying 359 officers and men, including the Comte de Fitzjames himself, turned back and sailed again on the 20th only to be captured by HMS *Hastings* the next day. As a result only *La Sophie* reached Scotland, dropping into Aberdeen harbour on the 22nd. There she landed 130 officers and men, together with saddles, horse-furniture, breastplates and arms.[19] There were however no horses and in consequence both Lord Pitsligo's and Lord Kilmarnock's Regiments were ordered to turn their's over to the new arrivals.[20]

In the meantime two more troop lifts were planned, one from Dunkirk carrying 650 men of the regiments Berwick and Clare, and another from Ostend carrying the Regiment Rooth. In the event the latter never sailed, but the Dunkirk convoy got out on the 18th and most of the ships arrived safely off Aberdeen on the 27th, only to be told by 'a man with a gun accompanied by a dog', that the rebel army had evacuated the town and that the British army was just about to march in. In the face of this gloomy news the French decided to return to Dunkirk without landing their troops, although *L'Aventurier* had managed to land forty-two men of the Regiment Berwick at Peterhead two days before.[21]

This was the last attempt to transport a substantial number of troops for it was clear that the North Sea was becoming far too dangerous. Nevertheless a number of small blockade runners still attempted it on their own and in mid-March *Le Prince Charles* (formerly HMS *Hazard*) sailed for Scotland with £12,000 in gold, the usual miscellaneous collection of officers in both the French and the Spanish service, and a picquet of the Regiment Berwick.

Knowing that Aberdeen was in government hands, the plan was to put them ashore at Portsoy in Banffshire, but instead on the 24th she was intercepted by four naval vessels and chased northwards to the Pentland Firth. Realising that escape was impossible, her Irish commander Captain Richard Talbot tried to take refuge in the Kyle of Tongue, but although he had provided himself with two involuntary pilots snatched up from a fishing boat, he still managed to run her aground. Nothing daunted, Captain Lucius O'Brien brought HMS *Sheerness* into the mouth of the

Kyle and in a three-hour battle battered the crew of the *Prince Charles* into submission.

Talbot himself was in no mood to surrender, however, and quite literally nailed the colours to the mast before abandoning his ship under cover of darkness. More resolute than the crew, the Irish soldiers brought the gold ashore and, led by Colonel Ignatious Browne of the Regiment Lally, rather optimistically set off to march to Inverness.[22] By sheer chance, later that night they managed to stumble across William MacKay of Melness, who 'seemed very much for us', and he not only sold them two horses to carry the gold, but also considerately provided his son as a guide. Whether he also sent word across to a couple of loyalist companies quartered at nearby Tongue House is less certain, for they must already have been alerted by the naval action, but word about the gold does seem to have got about remarkably quickly.

At any rate the loyalists – a company of the 64th Highlanders led by Captain John MacLeod, and an Independent Company commanded by Captain Alexander Mackay,[23] – hurried up shortly after first light on the 26th of March and began a running fight which ended beside Loch Hacoin, not far from the head of the Kyle. Recognising that the game was up Browne and his men – 21 officers and 110 soldiers and sailors – surrendered, allegedly after dumping the gold into the loch, although local tradition holds that a substantial proportion of it was actually pocketed by the victorious loyalists. No doubt much of it was, but there was also a more official share-out ordered by Cumberland himself: £500 each to Captain Mackay and Captain O'Brien of the *Sheerness* 'and in proportion to the other Officers', while the ordinary seamen and loyalist soldiers got five guineas a man.

This was not however the end of the affair, for although the Duke of Perth had decided to return to Inverness after his bloodless victory at Dornoch, and Sullivan was recalled shortly afterwards, Cromartie remained behind to try and recover the gold and some other money raised for the Prince in Orkney by Sir James Stewart of Burray. Exactly how many men he had with him is a little uncertain, but apart from his own regiment and John MacKinnon's little company from Skye, he also had the distinctly dubious support of a contingent under old Coll Mac-Donald of Barisdale and an equally wild gang of MacGregors. Had Cromartie succeeded in recapturing the gold it is perhaps questionable whether very much of it would have escaped the sticky-fingered Barisdale and Robert MacGregor of Glencarnock, but as it was they were still hunting for it when Cromartie received positive orders to return to Inverness on the 13th of April.

Two days later the Mackenzies were ambushed at Embo, just outside Dunrobin. Cromartie and his officers had gone to pay their respects to the loyalist Lady Sutherland at the castle, and had not yet caught up with their men, when three companies of loyalist militia led by William Sutherland of Sibberscross[24] caught his regiment strung out on the march. Seeing that the rebel officers were trailing in the rear, Sutherland despatched 26 men under Ensign John Mackay to get between them and their men, while he attacked the main body in flank.

Taken completely by surprise, the Jacobites broke and ran without putting up any resistance worth mentioning. Sutherland afterwards reported six men wounded, but none killed, while claiming 50 of the rebels killed or drowned trying to get over the Little Ferry, and another 165 prisoners besides the officers.

As for the latter, Mackay had succeeded in chasing them northwards, away from their men and into Dunrobin Castle. There they at first refused to surrender, but admitted Mackay to discuss terms. This, as it turned out, was a big mistake for when Cromartie asked for half an hour to think it over, the enterprising young officer agreed, went downstairs and cheerfully assured the rebel sentries that their officers had just surrendered and that they should therefore hand over their arms. All unsuspecting, they did just that and let the Ensign's men come in, whereupon he went back upstairs and informed his Lordship that the game was up.[25]

The only fly in the ointment was that insufficient men were within reach to go after Barisdale as well, but it was a creditable enough little victory for all that and the prisoners were handed over to Captain Dove of the *Hound* sloop, who brought them into Inverness the day after Culloden. This is, however, to anticipate matters a little and it is now necessary to look at what was happening elsewhere.

Sources:

1. MacPherson was evidently playing a somewhat equivocal role in the proceedings. Although his wife provided Molloy with intelligence during the first siege, he now assisted the rebels and after Molloy and his men had gone continued to act as Barrack-Master in the rebel service.

2. The complete exchange of correspondence is to be found in the *Newcastle Gazette*. Molloy and his men were duly set at liberty by the Prince and arrived in Perth on the 27th. Although a promoted ranker, Molloy was evidently well educated and afterwards did well for himself. By 1753 he was his regiment's senior Lieutenant and two years later the tough old soldier fought his way out of Braddock's disaster on the Monongahela. Indeed he not only survived but prospered and was promoted to Captain-Lieutenant. At that point however he obviously decided to quit while he was ahead and on the 5th of November 1755 he sold out to Lieutenant William Littler and thereafter vanishes from history.

3. According to one account he was betrayed by Captain Aeneas Macintosh of the 43rd Highlanders, whose wife had raised a rebel regiment and was now

entertaining the Prince at Moy. In some versions of the story she is represented as organising the Prince's escape, but Sullivan, who was present paints an altogether different picture of her rushing around in a state of panic, dressed only in her shift.

4. Sullivan, p. 129–131; MacLean *IN* Scott Moncrieff, p. 130.
5. *Origins*, p. 108; Sullivan, p. 133.
6. *Origins* op.cit., Grant was himself the younger brother of the Laird of Grant.
7. Sullivan, p. 133–5; Johnstone, p. 104.
8. Maxwell of Kirkconnell, p. 128.
9. Tabraham & Grove: *Fortress Scotland and the Jacobites* , pp. 78–81.
10. A contemporary journal of the siege enumerates Locheil's Camerons, the MacDonalds of Keppoch and Glencoe, and the Stewarts of Appin amongst the attackers.
11. Elcho, p. 411, *Newcastle Courant*. Although the unknown author of the journal invariably refers to mortars as Coehorns, the shells described here were evidently fired from the slightly larger *Royal* mortar – two of which had been captured from Cope at Prestonpans.
12. *Newcastle Courant*.
13. A letter written from Fort William on the night of the 1st April also refers to the landing of a reinforcement of 70 men from Johnson's 33rd Foot, but no mention of them is made in the journal.
14. This account of the siege is very largely based on the anonymous journal. Although Elcho adds some useful detail, his version of events corresponds so closely to the journal as to indicate that he himself made use of it. He concludes with the statement that thirty were killed or wounded on either side – the journal notes that in the course of the siege the garrison buried six men and had another twenty-four wounded. One of the Jacobite wounded was Colonel Grant. Scott had his reward in November when he succeeded Hu Wentworth as Major of Guise's 6th.
15. By all appearances these were the companies serving without pay and hardly therefore the pick of the bunch.
16. Murray (p. 107) claims that the garrison was 300 strong, but although there were no doubt some of the Argyll Militia with Agnew, this is a palpable exaggeration.
17. Murray, p. 108.
18. Sullivan, pp. 137–141. These were officers who had been rescued by Grossett and his loyalist partisans after Falkirk. There was some uncertainty as to their status since they had given their paroles to the rebels after Prestonpans. In consequence they were not actually under lock and key when rescued and it was therefore a fine point whether they could legitimately take up arms again. One or two affected scruples on this point, including the most senior, Lieutenant-Colonel Whitefoord, but in the end most returned to duty and Whitefoord himself was present at Culloden as a volunteer.
19. Gibson, *Ships of the '45*, p. 23, *Newcastle Courant*.
20. Sullivan states that about 60 dragoon horses were found for them, but as these had been turned over to the artillery after Prestonpans, they must by now have been in poor condition.
21. *Origins* (p. 151) has a footnote reference to their landing on the 21st, but this is clearly a mistake for the 25th. No sooner had these men been landed than the *L'Aventurier* was intercepted by the Royal Navy and driven ashore.
22. Browne was the same officer who had earlier escaped from Carlisle just before

the surrender. His promotion was a brevet one granted by the Prince and courteously confirmed by the French government.

23. These were men who had succeeded in escaping across the Little Ferry before the surrender. At least one of the 64th officers, Lieutenant John Reid, had been captured at Prestonpans.

24. The other company commanders were Robert Gray and Robert Mackallaster.

25. *Newcastle Courant.*

CHAPTER 10

Over the Spey

Cumberland Closes In

Untroubled by the retreating Lowland division, Cumberland advanced up the east coast as far as Aberdeen, which he entered late on the 27th of February. He was joined there by Bligh's 20th Foot who had been transported north by sea. The weather by now had turned very bad indeed and, while the rebels continued their retreat into the teeth of a ferocious blizzard, the British army settled into its winter cantonments. Most of the infantry battalions were quartered in Aberdeen itself, and a number of security outposts were established around the burgh. Some of these were only small cavalry picquets, but Major General Humphrey Bland was pushed forward with a rather more substantial force of four battalions and two regiments of cavalry. Initially he took his infantry no further out than the small towns of Inverurie and Old Meldrum, but Cobham's 10th Dragoons were quartered in the parish of Udny, and fifty of Kingston's 10th Horse went the length of Fyvie. No reference is made in the quartering returns as to the whereabouts of the Argyll Militia, but to judge from subsequent events, at least some of them must have been attached to Bland's force and a company sent with the detachment of Kingston's Horse at Fyvie.[1]

On the 17th of March, Bland pushed forward as far as Huntly. As it happened a fairly large rebel detachment led by Colonel John Roy Stuart was also in the area, intending to attack the Laird of Grant's men at Clatt. Failing to make contact with the loyalists, the rebels returned to Huntly and ordered dinner, only to receive the unwelcome news that Bland was approaching fast. A hasty retreat then followed, covered by the Hussars and some of the Prince's Lifeguards.

As he was very much in unknown territory, Bland decided to let them go, and thereupon lodged 2/Royals in the castle and his other three regular battalions – Barrel's 4th, Price's 14th and Cholmondley's 34th Foot – in the town. Naturally, he also considered it prudent to establish a system of patrols, but on the night of the 20th of March, one of them came to grief at Keith, a small town some six miles west of Huntly and lying halfway between that town and the rebel base at Fochabers.

The commander of this detachment, Lieutenant Alexander Campbell of Loudon's Highlanders, had earlier shown some aptitude for outpost work, but unfortunately he now came up against one of the rebel army's more professional officers, Nicholas Glasgoe, Lieutenant in Dillon's Irish regiment, and Major of Lord Ogilvie's rebel one.

According to Bland's subsequent report, Campbell's 70 Argyllshire Militia and 30 troopers of Kingston's Horse were merely supposed to make a reconnaissance, but: 'Being determined to do something that should transmit his name to future ages, he took upon himself to act quite contrary to my orders. He formed a wild project of his own to surprise Fochabers and lay all night at Keith, where he was surprised.'

A rebel officer, Captain Robert Stewart of Colonel John Roy Stuart's Regiment, subsequently wrote a detailed and remarkably honest account of the affair which reveals that such operations have changed little if at all over the years:

'... the Colonel gave orders for five men of a company to be turned out, the whole fifty to be commanded by Captain Robert Stewart, younger ... and, upon his examining the men's arms and ammunition, and finding them in very indifferent order, was obliged to disperse the most of all his own powder and shot ... Then, throwing away his plaid, he desired that every one might do the like, &c.; then ordered by the Colonel to march his men to the Cross of Fochabers, there to wait for farther orders from Major Glasgoe, who was to command the whole party in chief. Upon his marching back to the Cross again, the inhabitants seemed a little surprised; but, to prevent further conjectures, Captain Stewart called out, pretty loud, to get the keys of the guard-house, for he was come to take the guard of the town that night: but, at the same time, desired his soldiers, quietly, if they inclined to take any small refreshment, by half dozens, they might. He had not been a quarter of an hour at the Cross, when a small body of huzzars came riding down the street in haste, and told him that Cumberland's light horse was in the Fir Park, within rig length of the town; that they had been firing on one another for some time; that they wanted a party of his men to line the horse, and would go into the Park and attack them ... This detachment had waited upon the street about three quarters of an hour, when, in the dusk of the evening, the Major came up with a detachment of Lord Ogilvie's men, about sixteen of the French, (probably from Berwick's) and about twenty or thirty horses of different corps. Upon seeing the party before them, the French officer challenged, Who was there? Captain Stewart answered, it was Colonel Stewart's men. The French officer replied, he was well pleased to see them there, – that was the brave men. The Major called Captain Stewart, told him to allow the French to go in the front, and that they would shew them the way; that Lord Ogilvie's was to follow him in the rear, which accordingly was done. Away they marched, and entered the Fir Park, the horse commanded by Lieutenant (John) Simpson (of Bagot's Hussars), surrounding the same, and searching it out to the other end. Finding none of the enemy, they sat down very quiet, till such time as the horse had patroled the whole bounds, and returned again, finding none of the light horse. Then they began their march again towards Keith; at the same time, Major Glasgoe told Captain Stewart, that the French was to form the advance guard with the horse; that he was to march at a hundred paces distance, which was pointedly observed. Then, upon their way, they got intelligence of their enemy's patrol having passed before them. After five miles marching, they parted from the Keith road, eastward, and passed by Taremore. They searched it; but found none of their enemies there: then passed the water of Illa, at Mill of Keith; made a circle round the town, to the tents of Summer-eve's Fair, as if they had been from Strathbogie. Then Captain Stewart was ordered to close up with his party to the advance guard. As twelve o'clock at night struck, they came near the town. The Campbell's sentry challenged, Who was there? It was answered, Friends – the Campbells. He replied, you are very welcome; we hear the enemy is at hand. On their coming up to him, they seized his arms, griped him by the neck, and threw him to the ground. Then he began to cry: they told him if he made any more noise they would thrust a dirk to his heart. Then Lieutenant Simpson surrounded the town with the horse. The Major, with the foot entered the town, marched down the street, and up to the church-yard; when, finding the guard in the school, and their main body in the kirk, the French began the action with a platoon on the guard; and a general huzza was given, with these words, 'God save Prince Charles!' The action continued very hot on both sides, about half an hour, the fire from the Campbells coming very hard from the windows of the kirk ... At the surrendering of the kirk and guard, the Major sent to Captain Stewart, desiring that he might come with a party of his men, for he was like to be overpowered in the streets, for Kingston's light horse was quartered in the town. Captain Stewart immediately came down the street with a party, where there was a pretty hot action for some time in the street. He vanquished them, and made the whole of them prisoners, carried them over the bridge, and sent back a party to assist in bringing up the rest of the prisoners ...

'In this action, there were nine of Cumberland's men killed, a good number wounded, about eighty taken prisoners, and betwixt twenty and thirty horses, which Major Glasgoe, with his party, delivered at Spey, a little before sun-rising.

'Of the Prince's, there was only one Frenchman killed; but a good many wounded, particularly Lord Ogilvie's men, as they happened to stand in the south side of the kirk-yard, by the firing from the windows of the kirk.'[2]

Bland initially claimed that all 70 of the Argylls were lost. The actual returns record 53 of them killed or missing together with 31 of Kingston's, but it is hard entirely to blame Campbell, 'the mad-headed Highlander who commanded the party.' Such affairs are the ordinary small-change of outpost warfare; he was unlucky and paid for it by being badly 'mangled' and left for dead when he subsequently tried to escape.

Thereafter the countryside between Huntly and Fochabers became something of a no man's land occasionally scoured by patrols from both sides, who generally met each other at Keith and exchanged shots across the river, but made no attempt to cross.

On the 21st of March, two more battalions, Campbell's 21st and Monro's 37th Foot[3], arrived to reinforce Bland and two days later the Earl of Albemarle arrived to supersede him. All was now ready for the final advance.

The operation was an extremely well planned one, reflecting a high degree of staff work. Albemarle's detachment became the 1st Division, comprising Cobham's 10th Dragoons and Kingston's 10th Horse, and the 1st and 3rd Infantry Brigades: 2/Royals, Cholmondley's 34th and Price's 14th; Barrel's 4th, Monro's 37th and Campbell's 21st. Their task was to remain at Huntly until the 10th of April, covering the movement of the three other divisions. Owing to a lack of suitable quarters and a shortage of forage, each had to move northwards independently and there was obviously some danger that a rebel spoiling attack might cause some problems.

Brigadier Mordaunt with the 5th Infantry Brigade – Pulteney's 13th, Battereau's 62nd and Blakeney's 27th – and four cannon, moved off first to their jumping-off point at Old Meldrum on the 23rd, but the operation did not properly begin until the morning of the 8th of April.

Mordaunt's brigade then marched north to Turriff, while Cumberland left Aberdeen with the 3rd Division to take their place at Old Meldrum. It comprised Ker's 11th Dragoons, the 2nd Infantry Brigade – Howard's 3rd, Fleming's 36th and Bligh's 20th – and 6 guns. Lord Sempill's 4th Infantry Brigade – Wolfe's 8th, Ligonier's 59th and Sempill's 25th – also marched on the same day, but their destination was to be Inverurie.

On the 9th, Mordaunt's Brigade moved on to the coastal town of Banff and, as it would have been difficult for Albemarle to support them there, and to cover the other divisions at the same time, Cumberland took the decision to force march the 3rd Division 20 miles to join them there that same night. Sempill however followed at a more ordinary pace and, with no sign of movement from the rebel camp, Cumberland called up Albemarle's men and concentrated the whole army at Cullen on the 11th of April.[4]

Next day the army marched on Fochabers in the confident expectation that the rebels would stand and fight there, in order to defend the Spey crossings. This had indeed been the Jacobites' intention and to that end Lord John Drummond had established a hutted camp on the west bank from Rothes to the river-mouth, known as 'the barracks'. In it were some 2,000 men, made up of the cavalry, the lowland regiments and about half of the French regulars. Unfortunately for the rebels neither the Highland division, nor the artillery train were in position. Some of the Highlanders were in the far north in search of the missing French gold, others were still in Lochaber, returning from the fruitless siege of Fort William, and the rest in Badenoch or the Braes of Atholl under Lord George Murray. The news that Cumberland had left Aberdeen resulted, as we have seen, in the Highland Divisions being ordered to concentrate at Inverness, but they were to be too late to reinforce Drummond.

The Jacobite failure to contest the crossing of the Spey led some of Cumberland's men to speculate that the rebels were deliberately drawing them into a trap, but it was simply down to a lack of proper reconnaissance. Drummond had some inkling of trouble, and patrols had been stepped up since the affair at Keith, but nevertheless, despite repeated orders, in the last few days it all began to fall apart.

On the night of the 11th, a ten-man patrol led by John Daniel of Balmerino's Troop picked up a messenger heading for the Duchess of Gordon's house with a letter ordering supplies to be gathered and advising her that Cumberland intended to force the river that day (the 12th). However, instead of sending this important intelligence back at once, Daniel continued with his patrol and found the army drawn up in order of battle two miles further on. At this point by his account; 'after seeing all we could see, and some bravadoes and huzzas, we retired with all speed, leaving them to wonder what we meant.'[5]

Although he subsequently claimed to have reported all of this on his return to the rebel camp, the upshot of his thoroughly unmilitary behaviour was that Drummond, his elder brother the Duke of Perth, and Colonel John Roy Stuart, were still happily sitting in the minister's house at Speymouth after breakfast, when a countryman burst in with the news that the Enzie (the parish on the east side of the river) was all in a 'Vermine of Red Quites'. At first, despite Daniel's earlier report, they found this hard to believe and somebody flippantly suggested that the dark masses of soldiers seen in the distance were only muck-heaps, whereupon the countryman pithily observed that might very well be so, but he had never seen muck heaps moving before.

As Kingston's 10th Horse, who formed the advance guard, came within half a mile of the river they could see the white colours of the rebel infantry still drawn up on the other side. Accordingly Kingston's troopers halted in a ploughed field and waited for orders, but then as Cumberland's infantry came up, the rebels set fire to the barracks and the Guardhouse, which was correctly interpreted as a sign that they did not intend to fight after all.

'At this Time his Royal Highness gave Orders for the Duke of Kingston's Horse to advance. Accordingly we marched through the Town of Fochabers, which consists mostly of one long Street, where I observed several good Houses, and People of Fashion standing looking at us; but not one Person to wish us good Success . . .'[6]

Surprisingly enough, John Daniel was also still in Fochabers at the time and sound asleep, which rather suggests that he himself had attached no great urgency to the report which he gave to Drummond:

'When fast asleep, a servant came in to tell me that the enemy was in the town, and that it was too late to think of escaping, almost all of our party having already passed the river. However starting up in great confusion, I resolved to risk all rather than fall into their hands, and mounting my horse escaped by a back road.'[7]

Just how he managed to get himself across the river is not explained, which is rather a pity given that the ford was a notoriously difficult one; a point emphasised by the volunteer James Ray, who was riding with Kingston's:

'We entered the River with a Guide, wading on Foot, to shew where the Ford lay; which was bad enough, having loose Stones at the Bottom, which made it very difficult for Man or Horse to step without falling; the Water Belly-deep, and very rapid; the Ford not lying right across, we were obliged to go Midway into the River, then turn to the Right and go down it for about sixty yards, then turn to the Left, inclining upwards to the landing Place. In this Situation had the Rebels stood us here, it might have been of bad Consequence to our Army, they having a great Advantage over us, and might have defended this important Pass a long Time, to our great Loss.'[8]

As the barracks burned, the rebels fell back towards Nairn, and the news of Cumberland's rapid approach led to Colonel Sullivan riding out to assess the situation for himself. Drummond and his brother Perth were actually in the process of pulling their men out of the town just as he arrived, but thinking that they were over-reacting, and aware that the

Highland Division had not yet reached Culloden, he ordered them to halt and take up a covering position.

At this critical point he abruptly fainted – having been bled and purged only a few days earlier he was still feeling rather anaemic – but within half an hour he felt himself sufficiently recovered to take the cavalry out on a reconnaissance across the river. Hardly had they ridden clear of the town however than he saw the British army in full march towards them. This evidently came as a bit of a shock, but he ordered Lord Balmerino to form his little troop of Lifeguards, with the Hussars and Captain Robert Shea's squadron of Fitzjames's Horse, into a single line in order to make as brave a show as possible, then he waited to see what would happen next.

'The Duke (of Perth) & Sullivan waited on a hight neer the bridge until the enemy was very neer them, the Duke and Ld John retired with the foot. Sullivan kept Berwick's piquet with him composed of three officers & twenty-five men; he got the sergeant & some of those men to set two or three little Turf carts on the bridge and set fire to them. This done, the enemy just over against, Sullivan retired, joyned the horse & formed them on the high road, about two musquet shots from the Town and marched. A moment after the enemy's horse appears in the plaine ford & march against us. Sullivan fires his little cavalry likewise, but made a poor figure over against nine squadrons, & sends to the Duke of Perth to pray him, to leave him five hundred of foot.

'Sullivan continued his retraite making volte face from time to time alternatively with the small number of horse he had & those five and twenty men of Berwicks. Four battaillons of the enemy joyns their horse, they continu to pursue Sullivan, firing from time to time but were not near enough to do any hurt. Sullivan sent again to the Duke of Perth to pray him to leave a hundred and fifty men, or even fifty but the Duke and Ld John went to meet the Prince yt was in march towards them with the rest of the Army, & not a soul would wait for Sullivan. He continued his retreat so, for four miles, before he joyned the foot with nine squadrons & four bataillons at his heels, haveing alwaise part of this little Cavalry faceing towards them, & had in all yt time but a trooper & two horses of fitz James wounded.'[9]

Cumberland, as it happened, had only eight squadrons of cavalry, not nine, but otherwise John Daniel, who had been serving with the rearguard since his escape, backs up Sullivan's version and reckoned that the action lasted about three or four hours, although he also suggests that Perth himself may have stuck with the cavalry.

'And here it was his Grace the Duke of Perth and Colonel O'Sullivan gained immortal honour by their bravery and conduct in bringing us off in good order from under the very nose of the enemy; for notwithstanding all their firing upon our rear, and though we were much inferior in numbers, we lost not one man.'[10]

Content for the moment to have driven the rebels out of Nairn, Cumberland encamped his infantry at Balblair, just outside the town, and knowing that a battle was imminent, ordered a day of rest. The rebels meanwhile were faced with two questions; whether or not to fight, and if so where?

As to the first; most of the rebel chroniclers are agreed that it was considered absolutely necessary to fight in order to protect all the ammunition, stores and transport assembled at Inverness. In particular it was necessary to preserve the magazine of oatmeal, since a desperate shortage of ready cash meant that the rebel army was unable to obtain any other food. If Inverness was abandoned to the British army, the rebels would either starve or be forced to disperse in search of food. It is often suggested that the rebel army ought to have retired and conducted a guerrilla campaign in the mountains instead, but this is unlikely to have been a viable operation without the firm prospect of a substantial French landing.

A retreat from Inverness would also quite inevitably have been seen as a major defeat, and although it was subsequently claimed that they might have subsisted on sheep and cattle taken from the hillsides, without gold to pay for them they would very soon have lost any support from the uncommitted civilian population. In any case British army intelligence reports gathered throughout that summer consistently cited a shortage of oatmeal as being the principal obstacle facing those rebel officers trying to reassemble their forces.

Perhaps most crucially of all, the army's ability to operate in the hills has probably been grossly underestimated and, in deciding what course to follow, the Jacobite leaders must have been reflecting uneasily on a raid at the end of February which penetrated deep into upper Strathdon and captured a magazine of Spanish arms and ammunition stored at Corgarff Castle.[11]

Lord Ancrum had marched from Aberdeen on the 28th of February at the head of a mixed detachment of 300 foot and 100 men of Ker's 11th Dragoons, and late the next day arrived at Corgarff, where, according to Captain Alexander Stewart who commanded the contingent of Ker's, 'I dare say never Dragoons were before, nor ever will be again . . .' Suitably impressed the rebels did not stay to meet them and, 'We found it abandoned by the Garrison, but so lately, that the fire was burning, and no living creature in the house but a poor cat sitting by the fire.'[12] Although a false report that Gordon of Glenbucket was in the area led to their dumping most of the ammunition and all but a few hundred firelocks and bayonets in the river, this bold expedition was undoubtedly a success, and if the British army was capable of mounting such a bold incursion in the depths of a Highland winter, there would clearly be little to prevent their repeating it in the summer.

The rebel army therefore assembled on Culloden Moor on the 15th of April to await their fate, and Lord George Murray described the situation thus:

'On Sunday morning, the 13th, it was confirmed that the enemy were coming on, and passed the Spey. Many of our people, as it was seed time, had slipt home; and as they had no pay for a month past, it was not an easy matter to keep them together. On Monday, the 14th, Locheil came up, and that day; his Royal Highness went to Culloden, and all the other men as they came up marched there; and that night, the Duke of Perth came back with all the men he had on Speyside. The Duke of Cumberland . . . encamped this night at Nairn. Many were for retiring to stronger ground till all our army was gathered; but most of the baggage being at Inverness, this was not agreed to. Early on Tuesday morning, we all drew up in a line of battle, in an open muir near Culloden. I did not like the ground: it was certainly not proper for High-landers.'[13]

Murray's criticism of the field appears to have owed more to his insistence on contradicting everything which Sullivan proposed, for on previous experience it fitted the rebel army's requirements in every respect. In order to execute a 'Highland Charge' successfully the rebels needed a clear run at their opponents, as they had on the flat cornfields at Prestonpans, not the broken ground of the defensive position proposed by Murray.

As the morning wore on, however, it began to look as though the question might turn out to be an academic one, for there was no sign of the British army. After a time Lord Elcho was sent forward with a party of horse to find out what was happening, but by about noon it had become obvious that Cumberland had no intention of moving out of Nairn.[14] In the meantime Murray and a number of other Jacobite officers continued to press for an immediate retreat to the high ground across the river Nairn, if only to allow time for the rest of the army to close up. The Camerons had returned from Fort William only the night before, but Keppoch's MacDonalds and reinforcements from Urquhart and Glenmoriston for Glengarry's men were still on their way, as were the Frasers, MacPhersons, and Cromartie's detachment, most of which, unbeknown to them, was at that moment being wiped out by Sutherland's loyalist militia.

Elcho's return with the news that Cumberland and his men were still encamped at Nairn suddenly took some of the heat out of the argument:

'It was then proposed a night attack might be attempted,' said Murray. 'His Royal Highness and most of the others were for venturing it, amongst whom I was; for I thought we had a better chance by doing it than by fighting in so plain a field.'[15]

What Murray disingenuously forbore to admit was that the night attack was in fact his own idea. Elcho quite specifically states that, finding the Prince and his immediate advisers opposed to any notion of retreating into the hills, or even temporarily uncovering Inverness, Murray made a speech:

'... wherin he enlarged upon the advantages Highlanders have by Surprising their Enemy, and rather Attacking in the night time than in day Light, for as regular troops depend intirely upon their discipline, and on the Contrary the Highlanders having none, the Night was the time to putt them most upon an Equality, and he Concluded that his Opinion was that they Should march at dusk of ye Evening, So as that the Duke should not be aprised of it, that he Should march about the town of Nairn and attack them in their rear, with the right wing of the first line, while the Duke of Perth with ye left Should attack them in front, and the Prince Should support the Duke of Perths attack with the Second line.'[16]

Most of those present did indeed agree to the plan. But although, like Murray, they might have thought that anything was better than simply waiting for Cumberland to turn up, it was a quite extraordinary undertaking to contemplate, let alone undertake in their present condition. Perhaps more than any other incident in the campaign, it demonstrates that Murray's military abilities did not always match his conceit. Contrary to his airy assertions, all night operations and more particularly those carried out by large bodies of men actually demand a very high standard of 'discipline' from the troops engaged in them.

The only real point which the plan might have had in its favour was that the British cavalry was encamped out at Auldearn and therefore separated by some two miles from the main camp at Balblair, south-west of Nairn. Nevertheless nobody seems to have considered the likelihood that, if a substantial part of the rebel army was going to march around Nairn in order to attack Cumberland's camp from the east or south-east, they would run the very real risk of having the dragoons coming in on them from the rear while they were engaged with the infantry in the camp to their front. Nor does anybody appear to have voiced serious concern about the even greater probability of Cumberland's outlying picquets being able to detect their approach.

Whatever its chances of success, the venture was also badly timed in that the army had not been fed for two days. There were in fact ample supplies of food in Inverness, including a considerable quantity of salt beef found in Fort George, but no arrangements were made for any of it to be brought forward to the troops. This may simply have been because the battle was expected early on the 15th, but at the bottom of it was bad staff work[17], and as a result Cumberland's unexpected failure to oblige the rebels with a battle on the 15th meant that while their officers wrangled amongst themselves, the soldiers had little to do all day but sit cold and hungry in the wet heather. By evening they were neither physically nor mentally prepared for the ordeal which lay ahead.

Sources:

1. Allardyce Vol.I, p. 299–301.
2. Chambers: *Jacobite Memoirs*, p. 115–120.
3. Now commanded by Louis Dejean, although contemporary narratives continue to refer to the regiment as Monro's throughout the campaign.
4. Allardyce Vol.I, p. 301–3.
5. *Origins*, p. 209.
6. Rae, p. 316.
7. *Origins* op.cit.
8. Rae, op.cit.
9. Sullivan, p. 150.
10. *Origins*, p. 210.
11. This was a cargo landed at Peterhead shortly before the 27th of January.
12. Allardyce, p. 310–11.
13. Murray p. 121. See Sullivan, p. 150–3 for a detailed, and well-argued, criticism of the battlefield proposed by Murray.
14. Elcho, p. 426.
15. Murray, p. 121.
16. Elcho, p. 426–7; Kirkconnell, p. 142–3.
17. It was not, however, Colonel Sullivan's responsibility; his duties as Quartermaster General extended to the 'quartering' of troops and drawing them up on the field of battle, not to providing them with food, boots and other supplies. The man actually responsible was John Hay of Restalrig, who was temporarily standing in for the sick John Murray of Broughton. According to Lord George Murray, Broughton (whom he disliked personally) had been very efficient and it was only when the inept Hay took over that problems arose.

CHAPTER 11
O For Madness
The Night Attack on Nairn

Once the decision to go over on to the offensive again had been taken, hurried preparations had to be made and Colonel Sullivan, in his capacity as Adjutant General, was instructed to prepare fresh orders for the night attack. But at this point, according to his memoirs he received an unexpected rebuff:

> 'Sullivan was commanded to give the orders, and explain what he said in them. Lord George answered that there was no need of orders, yt everybody knew what he had to do.'[1]

Murray may perhaps have been hinting thereby that no prisoners were to be taken[2] or, as is much more likely, simply giving vent to his impatience. Either way it was an unfortunate remark for at this point in time the army stood in very great need of orders, explanations and indeed the professional expertise of trained staff-officers like Sullivan. Moving some 5,000 men across upwards of ten miles of heather moorland at night requires considerably more preparation than a leader boldly striking off into the darkness with the words 'follow me.' The attack on Nairn, put forward more or less on the spur of the moment by Murray, was badly thought out, poorly prepared and incompetently executed, and responsibility for the debacle and its consequences lies squarely with Murray alone.

By way of an elementary security precaution he insisted that the army should delay moving off from Culloden until after dusk. When doubts were expressed in some quarters as to whether the army would then still be able to cover the eight miles or so to Nairn before daybreak, he confidently replied that he would, 'Answere for it', and his stance appeared to be vindicated when the small squadron of naval vessels and transports accompanying the British army hove into view down in the Moray Firth and dropped anchor just offshore at about six o'clock in the afternoon. This delay however fatally compromised the operation and was in any case quite unnecessary, for the army could just as easily have dropped below the skyline towards the south of the moor, and thus been in a position to move forward unseen into a more convenient jumping off point a good deal closer to the objective.

Opinions afterwards varied as to when the march actually began. As Captain Johnstone remembered it, the army was ordered to set off from Culloden at about eight o'clock in the evening[3], which was probably rather later than even Murray would have liked, although this delay did at least give time for MacDonald of Keppoch to come up with his regiment. On the other hand, as soon as the army began assembling it was found that; 'a vast number of men had gone off on all hands to get and make ready provisions; and it was not possible to stop them. Then, indeed, almost everybody gave it up as a thing not to be ventured. His Royal Highness was extremely bent upon it, and said that, whenever we began the march, the men would be all hearty, and those that had gone off would return and follow.'[4]

This confidence was not shared by those officers who actually tried to round up the semi-mutinous stragglers and Lord Elcho reckoned it was not until about nine o'clock in the evening that the Jacobites finally marched off down the spine of the moor, leaving the heather set on fire behind them in the hope of giving the impression to the ships anchored offshore that the army remained encamped around Culloden.[5]

Surviving accounts of the night are pretty unanimous in depicting it as a sorry shambles from its confused beginning to its acrimonious end. The rebel army initially set off in what should have been three columns, following one behind the other. The first was led by Lord George Murray, the second by Lord John Drummond and the third by the Duke of Perth. As the army had earlier been drawn up in its order of battle on the moor, the composition of these columns presumably corresponded with that of the front-line divisions which they were to command in the battle next day. At any rate Lord George Murray's column certainly included his own Athollmen and Locheil's Camerons and closely in the rear of Perth's column came the Prince himself with the cavalry, the remaining infantry regiments, and the French regulars.

Instead of proceeding straight down the main road to Nairn, Murray decided to move across country, thus shunning any houses and people who might be tempted to warn Cumberland of his approach. Ahead of the army therefore went, '. . . about two officers and thirty men of the MacIntoshes in the front as guides, and some of the same were in the centre and rear, and in other parts, for hindering any of the men from straggling.'[6]

Despite this sensible precaution, it soon proved quite impossible to prevent substantial gaps opening up between the columns and between the individual units within the columns. Murray afterwards tried to blame the French regulars and his MacIntosh guides: 'The French piquets

I believe were in the rear, and were not so clever in marching. The moor they went through was more plashy than expected, and they were obliged to make some turns to shun houses, and there were two or three defiles that took up a great deal of time to pass. The guides though they knew the ground very well, yet were not judges what time it would take . . .'[7]

The real problem, familiar to anyone who has ever undertaken a night march, was that obstacles such as walls and ditches invariably took far longer to cross in the dark than in daylight, and once across them, regiments then quite naturally hurried on to make up for lost time, heedless of those still crossing behind them. Murray did his best to keep everything together, and, although Colonel Sullivan also confirms that officers were 'posted all along the road yt the Colomn past by, to make every body follow, yt they may not mistake their way in the moor', their role and that of the guides from Lady MacIntosh's Regiment, seems to have been a passive one and without proper policing of the long column, and supervision of the obstacles, the resultant gaps soon proved virtually impossible to close.

Captain Johnstone had at one time commanded a company in the Duke of Perth's Regiment but, having fallen out with his Colonel at Carlisle, he was now serving as a volunteer and in accordance with the previous day's 'positive Orders that every person attach themselves to some Corps of the Armie', he joined MacDonald of Scotus's company of Glengarry's Regiment. As a result he found himself stumbling along somewhere in the middle of Perth's column and was afterwards able to recall the sorry experience of that night from the viewpoint of an ordinary foot soldier, rather than from the more rarified one of a staff officer. He convincingly describes the endless delays as being due not to the slowness of the French regulars in the rear, but rather to the entirely predictable difficulties experienced by the Highlanders themselves as they floundered around in the darkness:

'This march across the country in a dark night which did not allow us to follow any track, had the inevitable fate of all night marches. It was extremely fatiguing and accompanied with confusion and disorder. The Highlanders, who could not keep together from the difficulty of the roads, were more or less dispersed and we had many stragglers. As there were a great many bad places to cross, it would have been impossible for the best disciplined troops to have preserved anything like order.'[8]

The plain fact of the matter is that, despite Lord George Murray's earlier confident prediction, conducting a night march, and indeed any kind of night operation for that matter, actually demands an extremely high level of training and expertise. Not only was the rebel army simply not up to

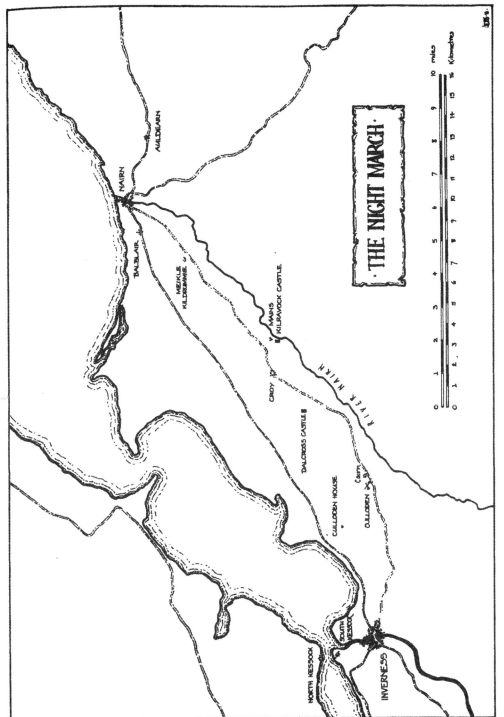

THE NIGHT MARCH

0 1 2 3 4 5 6 7 8 9 10 miles
0 1 2 3 4 5 6 7 8 9 10 11 12 13 14 15 16 Kilometres

NAIRN

BALBLAIR

AULDEARN

MEIKLE KILDRUMMIE

CROY

MAINS KILRAVOCK CASTLE

RIVER NAIRN

DALCROSS CASTLE

CULLODEN HOUSE

Cairn

CULLODEN

NORTH KESSOCK

SOUTH KESSOCK

INVERNESS

The Night Attack 15th/16th April 1746.

135   Map 6

the task, but as the night wore on and the chances of their ever reaching the start line before daybreak slipped further and further away from them, relations between the officers also deteriorated markedly and this in its turn led to yet more delays and confusion.

Murray's own column was supposed to cross the Water of Nairn two miles below Culraick, so that he could attack Cumberland's camp from the south-east, while Perth and his brother, Lord John Drummond, mounted a simultaneous frontal assault. But it became increasingly obvious that this was no longer a practical proposition and at length, with the army held up behind him by the park walls surrounding Culraick Wood, Lord George called a halt to consider the deteriorating situation and sent Locheil back to warn the Prince that it might be necessary to turn back.

'The night being dark, occasioned several halts to be made, for bringing up the rear. When about half way, Lord George Murray ordered Colonel Ker, one of the Prince's aids-de-camp, to go from front to rear, and to give orders to the respective officers to order their men to make the attack sword in hand, which was thought better, as it would not alarm the enemy so soon, and that firearms would be of use to them afterwards. When he returned to the front to inform Lord George Murray of his having executed his orders, he found they were halted a little to the eastward of Kilravock House, deliberating whether or not they should proceed, (having then but four miles to march to Nairn, where the enemy was encamped) or return to Culloden, as they had not at most, or thereabouts, one hour to daylight; and if they could not be there before that time, the surprise would be rendered impracticable, and the more so, as it was not to be doubted that the enemy would be under arms before day-light, as they were to march that morning, to give the Prince battle.'[9]

At this inauspicious moment Colonel Sullivan turned up and 'said he had just come from the Prince, who was very desirous the attack should be made; but as Lord George Murray had the van, and could judge the time, he left it to him whether to do it or not.' Sullivan not surprisingly remembered the conversation slightly differently and in contrast to Murray's rather terse narrative his memoirs recount the resultant exchange in vivid and at times unintentionally hilarious detail. According to the Colonel he warmly pressed Murray to proceed with the attack, and assuring him of the Prince's confidence in him :

'Gad Sr,' says Ld George, swearing, 'I desire no better, speak to those gents.' A Colonel of his Regimt swore & said if they were to be killed yt it wou'd be in plain day, & yt they wou'd see how their neighbours wou'd behave. (This is the Regimt yt must have the right of the first ligne) There was not an officer or soldier of them killed or wounded since the beginning of the Campagne. Another of the Regimt said, 'those yt are so much for fighting, why dont they come with us.' 'I dont know,' says Sullivan, 'to whom this discourse is adres'd, If it be to me, yu know yt it was not the first time yu saw me in the action, yu owned yr self & say'd it openly, yt yu saw no other General but the Prince & me at the battle of Falkirk. If Ld George will permit me, I offer to march in the first rank of his Vanguarde & will give him my head off my shoulders, wch is all I have to loose, if he does not succeed, if he follows, & if he follows, I am sure YU will, Gents;'[10]

What finally settled the matter was the arrival of Perth and his brother, who had gone back to report to the Prince and who now returned with the news that a particularly huge gap had opened up, which, even if the vanguard remained at Kilravock, could not be closed before daybreak. Nevertheless, the abandonment of the operation could still not be undertaken lightly and in the very best 18th-century tradition, Murray first set about obtaining the formal agreement of those officers who were present, presumably (although he later denied it) including Colonel Sullivan.

'It was agreed upon all hands that it must be sunrise before the enemy could reach Nairn and form, so as to make an attempt upon the enemy's camp; for one part was to have passed the water a mile above the town, to have fallen upon them towards the sea-side. The volunteers were all very keen to march. Some of them said that the red-coats would all be drunk, as they surely had solemnised the Duke of Cumberland's birthday . . .

'But the officers were of different sentiments, as severals of them expressed. Locheil and his brother said they had been as much for the night attack as anybody could be, and it was not their fault that it had not been done; but blamed those in the rear that had marched so slow and retarded the rest of the army. Lord George Murray was of the same way of thinking, and said if they could have made the attack it was the best chance they had, especially if they could have surprized the enemy. But to attack a camp that was near double their number in day-light, when they would be prepared to receive them, would be perfect madness.

'By this time Mr John Hay (the Prince's secretary) came up and told the line was joined. He was told the resolution was taken to return. He began to argue the point, but nobody minded him . . . It was about two o'clock in the morning (the halt not being above a quarter of an hour) when they went back in two columns, the rear facing about, and the van taking another way. At a little distance they had a view of the fires of the Duke of Cumberland's camp. Daylight began to appear about an hour after. They got to Culloden pretty early, so that the men had three or four hours rest.'[11]

Andrew Lumisden explains the relatively swift progress in returning to Culloden by their marching back the shortest way 'as we had not the same reason for shunning houses in returning as we had in advancing'[12], but in fact for much of the army the return journey was in some ways just as much of a shambles as the outward one had been and for some a good deal more dangerous.

Having proposed, planned and led the night march in the first place, it undoubtedly took considerable moral courage on Murray's part to abort the operation when it became obvious that it could not succeed. However he now proceeded in his usual careless fashion to make a near fatal blunder. Instead of retracing his steps, he simply turned off to the left to pick up the main road back to Inverness by way of the church of Croy. This was, as Lumisden mentions, a more direct and easier route, but given the known dispersion of the army it was simply asking too much to expect everybody else to follow suit. Colonel Sullivan it is true was sent back with the Duke of Perth to find the Prince, who was marching at the head of Fitzjames's Horse[13], and explain what had happened, but not surprisingly they at first missed him in the dark and fog. Since Murray also neglected the elementary precaution of leaving a picquet drawn from amongst his MacIntosh guides at the point on the road at which he turned off, it was hardly surprising that the second division should have blithely continued on its way, past Kilravock and on as far as Kildrummie, just two miles short of Cumberland's camp at Balblair. In short, while half of the army was making its way back to Culloden, the other half, all unsuspecting, was still marching straight towards the enemy.[14]

As John Daniel of the Lifeguards recalled, it was some time before the rear division actually realised that something was amiss:

'After we had marched till about three o'Clock in the morning, over double the ground that was necessary, we at last came pretty nigh the enemy's camp: and when we were supposing to surround them, and for that purpose in some measure drawing out; my Lord George Murray began to be missing; notwithstanding the Prince's Aides-de-Camp in riding from rank to rank, and asking, for God's sake! what has become of his Lordship, and telling that the Prince was in the utmost perplexity for want of him. In that situation did we remain a considerable time, till, day breaking fast in upon us, we heard that Lord George Murray was gone off with most of the Clans ... But O! for Madness! what can one think, or what can one say here!'[15]

Afterwards there was much talk that, while they waited trying to find out what was going on, they could actually hear the enemy sentries calling out to each other and the Prince was equally unimpressed when

Locheil eventually found him and reported that Lord George Murray and the other officers had resolved to go back. 'The Prince,' said Elcho, who as the commander of his Lifeguard was presumably present during the exchange, 'was not for going back, and said it was much better to march forward and attack, than march back and be attack'd afterwards, when the men would be all fatigued with their night's march. During the time of this Conversation the army, by what means I know not, began to move back;'[16]

Apparently the first positive intimation which the Prince received that the leading division had turned back was when he encountered Perth's Regiment heading back towards Culloden. Hardly surprisingly it was afterwards reported that he called out: 'I am betrayed; what need I give orders, when my orders are disobeyed?' Then Perth himself turned up at last with Colonel Sullivan and confirmed that Lord George Murray had indeed ordered a retreat and was already well out of reach. At this the Prince, although furious, put a brave face on things and replied, 'Tis no matter then; we shall meet them, and behave like brave fellows.'[17]

After this, in Lord Elcho's words, he too turned around, 'and in much Shorter time than they had march'd return'd to the parks of Culloden, where Every body seemed to think of nothing but Sleep. The men were prodigiously tired with hunger and fatigue, and vast numbers of them went to Inverness, and the villages about, both to Sleep and to pick up what little nourishment they Could gett. The principal officers went all to the house of Culloden and were so tired that they never thought of Calling a Council what was to be done, but Every one lay'd himself down where he could, some on beds, others on tables, Chairs, & on the floors, for the fatigue and hunger had been felt amongst the officers as Soldiers.'[18]

Even so, the rebels were not left undisturbed for very long. A party of horse, probably the overworked Hussars, and some of Lady MacIntosh's men 'yt knew the by roads' had been left behind near Culraick Wood to keep an eye on Cumberland's camp, and little more than two hours later they came in with the word that there was a party of cavalry (Kingston's 10th Horse) within two miles and coming on fast, while the main body of the British army was not far behind.

The Prince and his senior commanders thereupon 'all mounted their horses, ordered the drums to beat & the pipes to play, which Alarm Caused great hurry and Confusion amongst people half dead with fatigue'. Murray and Elcho both argued for an immediate retreat across the river Nairn, but the same objections which had driven the Jacobite leaders to the desperate expedient of mounting a night attack still held good, and now moreover if they were to be hustled across the river by even a halfway aggressive pursuit, their already tired and demoralised army might easily have disintegrated as completely as it was to do in the coming battle. What was more, at that point a good part of the army was scattered in houses, barns, thickets and ditches all the way from Culraick to Inverness, and by the time they were all or at least most of them recalled to their colours, the battle was actually beginning:

'The men were scattered among the woods of Culloden, the greatest part fast asleep. As soon as the alarm was given, the officers ran about on all sides to rouse them, if I may use that expression, among the bushes, and some went to Inverness to bring back such of the men as hunger had driven there. Notwithstanding the pains taken by the officers to assemble the men, there were several hundreds absent from the battle, though within a mile of it: some were quite exhausted and not able to crawl, and others asleep in coverts that had not been beat up.'[19] The Prince himself accompanied Locheil's Regiment to the top, doing his best to encourage the men, but according to Sullivan, he; 'in the bottom had no great hopes.' Earlier the Duke of Perth had persuaded the Prince not to go back to Inverness in person to bring forward the desperately needed supplies, but to send Captain Robert Shea, with Fitzjames's Horse instead. On reaching the burgh, Shea apparently decided, sensibly enough, to let his men get some rest before escorting the provisions back to Culloden, but then came the unwelcome news of Cumberland's approach and the inevitable call to boot and saddle.

One of those aroused by this untimely trumpet call was Captain Johnstone, who had earlier decided that he for one had done more than enough soldiering for one night:

'Exhausted with hunger and worn out with the excessive fatigue of the three last nights, as soon as we reached Culloden I turned off as fast as I could to Inverness, where, eager to recruit my strength by a little sleep, I tore off my clothes, half asleep all the while. But when I had already one leg in the bed and was on the point of stretching myself between the sheets, what was my surprise to hear the drum beat to arms and the trumpets of the picket of Fitzjames sounding the call to boot and saddle. I hurried on my clothes, my eyes half shut, and mounting a horse, instantly repaired to our army on the eminence on which we had remained for three days, and from which we now saw the English (sic) army at a distance of about two miles from us.'[20]

In his exhausted condition Johnstone may be forgiven for his assertion that the army was drawn up in the same place as before, but by the time he rejoined, it had fallen back to the west of the battlefield reconnoitred by Colonel Sullivan on the 14th:

'The Prince ordered his men to draw up in two lines, and the few horse he had in the rear towards the wings, and the cannon to be dispersed in the front, which was brought up with great difficulty, for want of horses. As there was no time to march to the ground they were on the day before, they were drawn up a mile farther westward, with a stone enclosure on the right of the first line.'[21]

Murray complained then and afterwards that Sullivan 'did not so much as visit the ground where we were to draw up in line of battle', though given the fact that they did not decide to fall back to it until the morning of the 16th this is hardly surprising, and as soon as the army did fall back Ker of Graden was sent to reconnoitre the enclosures, which at least promised to offer some security for the army's flanks.

While he was engaged in doing this, a fresh dispute seems to have arisen over the question of which regiment should occupy the traditional post of honour on the right of the line. Colonel Sullivan's account of the exchange, although unquestionably partisan in its contrasting of Murray's obstreperous bluster with his own quiet confidence does nevertheless give something of a flavour of that fraught and ill-tempered morning:

'Ld George comes up and tels Sullivan who had the honr to be near the Prince, yt he must change the order of battle, yt his Regiment had the right yesterday. 'But My Ld,' says Sullivan, 'there was no battle yesterday, besides it is no time to change the order of battle in the enemys presence.' 'Laid up the men then, it's your businesse to set them in battle.' 'Yt I will my Ld,' says Sullivan, 'if you'll be so good as to make them follow in their ranks, yt there may be no confusion, for there is nothing more dangerouse, than to change Regimts from one ground to another in presense of the enemy.' The Prince carres'd Ld George, pray'd him to laid the men, & yt he & Sullivan wou'd make them follow in their ranks. 'Gad Sr,' says Ld George swearing, 'it is very hard yt my Regimt must have the right two days running,' when it is he himself wou'd have it so absolutly.'[22]

Oddly enough Sullivan is the only one to suggest that Murray was willing to withdraw the Atholl Brigade from its coveted position on the right. However, although MacDonnell of Lochgarry and a number of others who record it appear to be talking about a dispute which took place that morning, the evidence actually suggests that the arguments had been rehearsed the day before.[23] Although the principle that each regiment should take it in turn to march in the van of the army was established quite early on, in both the previous battles the MacDonald regiments had been given the right wing on the day. Yet when the army drew up on the morning of the 15th, the right was, at Murray's insistence, given to his own Atholl Brigade, a move which was all the more surprising in that hitherto it had always been considered a part of the lowland division and as such posted in the second line.

Having won his point on the 15th, Murray may well have been ready to concede it on the 16th and thus once again preserve his brigade from serious harm. The trouble with that, as Sullivan pointed out, was that there was no time for a major redeployment with the British army approaching, particularly as withdrawing the brigade to its accustomed place in the second line would leave an already thin front line far too badly stretched.

Undisturbed by nocturnal alarums and excursions, Cumberland's men had toasted his birthday with brandy and an extra ration of cheese before settling down to a good night's sleep. Reveille was sounded in Nairn at four o'clock in the morning of the 16th of April, and by a quarter past five the British army was on the march towards Inverness.

With both armies now committed to battle, Cumberland saw no point in taking chances. His men halted frequently to dress their ranks and catch their breath, and marched with 'arms secured and Bayonets fixed' which Alexander Taylor, a private soldier in 2/Royals, considered a very 'uneasy' way of marching.[24] By way of an advance guard, Lieutenant-Colonel John Campbell, younger of Mamore, commanding the Argyll Militia and three companies of Loudon's 64th Highlanders, was sent ahead with his own men and a Troop of Kingston's 10th Horse 'to Examine the Roads and woods in the way.' Not far beyond Kilravock they caught sight of the rebels, halted and sent back word to Cumberland.

The thin mists of the previous night had given way to a cold, raw gusting wind out of the north-east, bringing occasional 'smart' showers of rain and sleet. When Cumberland heard from Mamore that the rebels were assembling up on top of the moor, rather than in front of Culloden House, he swung his army to the south in order to keep the wind in his back as he approached.

As the moor rose above them like a hill, Cumberland and his staff could see the rebels posted amongst some old walls and houses, and with no further need for them, the units of the advance guard were recalled. Mamore was then ordered to divide his Highlanders between the right and left flanks until the battle actually began, at which point he was to retire to guard the baggage. This was a sensible precaution since only the regulars of the 64th Highlanders wore red jackets and the others might easily be mistaken for rebels in the confusion of battle. As it was, some of them were to see a good deal more fighting than they had bargained for.

When the army finally deployed at the foot of the moor, Mamore, on the right, dutifully led his men back to the wagon lines, but on the left Major General Humphrey Bland ordered one of the 64th officers, Captain

Colin Campbell of Ballimore, to stand fast with his half battalion. Ahead of them lay the high dry-stone walls of the Culwhiniac enclosures and if Bland was to get through them he was going to need infantry support.

Sources:

1. Sullivan, p. 154.
2. Speck, p. 155.
3. Johnstone, p. 116.
4. Murray, p. 122.
5. Elcho, p. 427. On the other hand John Daniel (*Origins* p. 211) puts their departure at about seven o'clock which sounds rather on the early side.
6. Murray – letter of 16th May 1746 *IN* Charles *Transactions* p. 319 Lumisden *IN Origins*, p. 415, Lady MacIntosh's Regiment had of course been raised locally, but Murray notes that 'though they knew the ground very well, yet were not judges what time it would take.'
7. Murray, op.cit.
8. Johnstone, p. 116.
9. Ker of Graden, p. 138–9.
10. Sullivan, p. 156–8.
11. Murray – letter of 16th May – p. 313–4.
12. Lumisden, p. 416.
13. Sir John McDonnell *IN* Sullivan, p. 157.
14. George Innes (*Lyon in Mourning*), p. 288–9.
15. Daniel, p. 211; Johnstone, p. 117–8. It is hardly surprising that there should be such a strong tradition afterwards that Murray was a traitor, although Johnstone stated that, 'knowing him perhaps better than any other person, I can only attribute his disobedience to the Prince's orders to the violence and impetuosity of his character.' In a rather incoherent memorandum written in March 1759 the Prince went so far as to say that 'he (Murray) turned a crose Rode to retret back, so that Clenronald's Regiment not knowing ye trick advanced ye write rode and came to spake to ye senteris whom he found quite surprised ... Ld G's vilany proved out of all dispute.' Elcho, p. 453.
16. Elcho, p. 428.
17. Innes, p. 290.
18. Elcho, p. 428–9.
19. Kirkconnell, p. 148.
20. Johnstone, p. 118–9.
21. Ker of Graden, p. 140–1; Murray, (p. 123) also confirms that, 'we drew up in the muir, a little back from where we had been the day before.'
22. Sullivan, p. 160–1. It is entirely possible that knowing Murray's volatile nature, Sullivan was adopting an air of unconcern precisely in order to needle him.
23. Lochgarry's letter *IN* Blaikie *Itinerary* p. 120–1. 'The McDonnells had the left that day, the Prince having agreed to give the right to Ld George and his Atholemen. Upon which Clanranald, Keppoch and I spoke to his RHs upon that subject, and begg'd he wou'd allow us our former right, but he intreated us for his sake we wou'd not dispute it, as he had already agreed to give it to Lord George and his Atholemen; and I heard HRHs say that he resented

it much, and should never doe the like if he had occasion for it.' However Murray (16th May) disingeniously says; 'I cannot justly tell what order they were drawn up in; there had been some disputes a day or two before about the rank, but nobody, who had any regard for the common cause insisted upon such things on that occasion.'

24. Taylor's letter is in Leask & McCance *Historical Records of the Royal Scots*. A slightly shorter version is also to be found in the *Scots Magazine*. In describing it as an 'uneasy' way of marching he was talking quite literally, for in the 'Secure Arms' posture the firelock was carried muzzle downwards with the lock tucked under the armpit – the object being to prevent rain-water from getting at the lock or running down the barrel. Ordinarily a firelock could be carried in this manner without difficulty, but with an additional 17 inches of bayonet fixed on the end, there was every chance of inadvertently digging it into the ground, particularly on rough moorland.

CHAPTER 12

High Noon

The Battle of Culloden Part 1

'There is a rising ground, (between) Culloden and the river Nairn, which reaches a great way towards the town of Nairn; the ascent is steep on both sides, particularly from the shore; towards the town of Nairn the hill dies away insensibly; the top is a level moor, about half a mile broad.'[1]

On one side of the moor lay two stone-walled enclosures, the Culwhiniac Parks, running downhill to the river Nairn, and on the other side were the walls of the Culloden Parks, attached to the Lord President's house. At the northern end of the Culwhiniac Parks another, turf-walled, enclosure belonging to a steading called Leanach, jutted out into the moor by about 50 or 60 yards. Two other steadings on the moor were to play some part in the battle; one was Culchunaig, which stood just beside the south-west corner of the Culwhiniac wall, and the other was Balvraid, lying nearly 1,000 yards to the west. The ground itself was all rather boggy, with a fair amount of standing water, particularly to the north of the road which slashed diagonally across the moor.

The rebel army took its stand facing north-east, with its right wing anchored on the south-west corner of the Culwhiniac Parks and its left similarly anchored on the north-east corner of the Culloden Parks 1,100 yards away on the other side of the moor. On the right of the army stood Lord George Murray's Athollmen, three battalions which should in theory have totalled some 500 men.[2] Next came 600 Camerons under Donald Cameron of Locheil, 150 men from Appin led by Charles Stewart of Ardshiel, 500 Frasers under an Aberdeenshire laird, Lieutenant-Colonel Charles Fraser of Inverallochy, another 500 men in Lady MacIntosh's Regiment, commanded by Colonel Alexander McGillivray of Dunmaglass, 150 Deeside men under Lieutenant-Colonel Francis Farquharson of Monaltrie; 182 men in a combined battalion of MacLeans and MacLachlans; 100 Chisholms, 200 MacDonalds under Keppoch,. another 200 in Clanranald's Regiment and finally 500 men in Glengarry's Regiment, commanded by Donald MacDonnell of Lochgarry.[3] All in all there ought to have been something in the region of 3,800 rank and file in the front line.

The second line was very much smaller, comprising a scatter of units formed in columns to act as a tactical reserve for the front-line regiments. Behind the right wing stood the two remaining battalions of Lord Lewis Gordon's Regiment: 200 men of the Aberdeen battalion led by Lieutenant Colonel James Moir of Stonywood, and 300 men of the Strathbogie battalion led by Lieutenant Colonel John Gordon of Avochie.[4] Standing more or less in the centre were half a dozen battalions under Colonel John Roy Stuart: Two battalions of Lord Ogilvy's Regiment mustering some 500 men between them; his own 200 men; Lord Kilmarnock's Footguards; John Gordon of Glenbucket's Regiment and the Duke of Perth's Regiment. The latter numbered about 300 men while the others all had about 200 apiece. Stuart's 'reserve' was flanked on the right by the two French regular units; the *Royal Ecossois* on the right and the Irish Picquets on the left. The Marquis D'Eguilles later put the strength of these units at 350 and 302 rank and file respectively.[5]

Standing a short distance behind these regiments was a scattering of mounted units; Lord Elcho's Lifeguards and most of the mounted element of Fitzjames's Horse were brigaded on the right, while Strathallan's Horse and the Hussars appear to have been brigaded on the left. Each 'brigade' according to Sandby was about 70 strong and in the centre was the Prince's escort comprising 16 troopers of Fitzjames's Horse under Captain Robert Shea and probably a similar number of men belonging to Lord Balmerino's troop of Lifeguards.

As for the rebel artillery, most plans show twelve guns, sometimes grouped in two or three batteries, although Thomas Sandby (a surveyor on Cumberland's staff and perhaps best placed to know) shows an irregular scatter of cannon spread most of the way across the front of the army. Three are shown on the right, five more or less in the centre and three others towards the left. These were presumably the eleven 3-pound cannon afterwards reported as having been captured, and the twelfth gun, shown by Sandby on its own at the extreme left of the line, just by the Culloden Parks wall, must have been a 'Swedish' 4-pounder which was brought up after the battle had started by a French engineer named Du Saussay.[6]

Having taken up their position, the rebels did not stay in it for very long. Murray was concerned about the way the turf-walled Leanach enclosure threatened to impede the Atholl Brigade's intended line of advance. Moving forward to demolish it before the British army arrived appeared impractical and so he compromised by leading the brigade about halfway down the Culwhiniac wall and forming them into columns – six men deep rather than the customary three – in order to make it easier for them to manoeuvre around the obstacle when the time came. Unfortunately, since the MacDonald regiments on the left flank refused

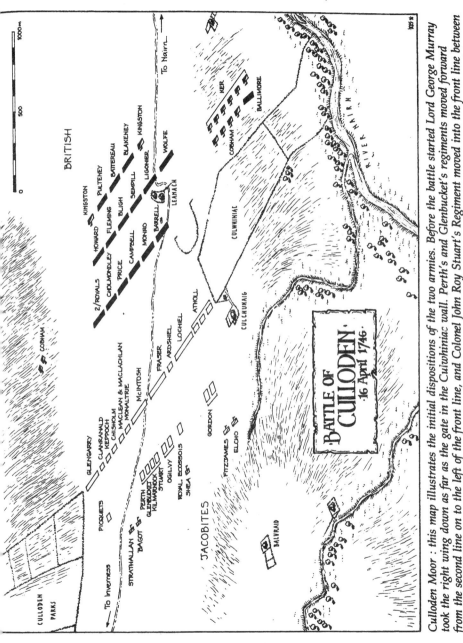

Culloden Moor : this map illustrates the initial dispositions of the two armies. Before the battle started Lord George Murray took the right wing down as far as the gate in the Culwhiniac wall. Perth's and Glenbucket's regiments moved forward from the second line on to the left of the front line, and Colonel John Roy Stuart's Regiment moved into the front line between Ardshiel's Regiment and the Frasers. On the other side of the battlefield, Pulteney's and Battereau's regiments moved in to the right of the first and second lines, and Kingston's Horse also prolonged the right.

to conform to this move as it would mean their leaving the protection of the Culloden Parks walls, the whole line was thrown badly askew and stretched to a degree that Colonel Sullivan was astonished to hear cries of 'Close, close!' and on investigation discovered 'intervals, yt he had not seen before.'

As the MacDonalds remained unco-operative there was no alternative but to fill those gaps by bringing up some regiments from the second line 'for there was no time to be lost, to fill up the vacansy yt was left (by Ld George's changement) . . .' Consequently John Roy Stuart's Regiment was brought forward to fill a gap between the Appin men and the Frasers, while two more battalions, Perth's and Glenbucket's, were posted on the left, and thus, as Sullivan recalled: 'The McDonels by this had no more the left, they were almost in the Center' [7]

Over on the other side of the moor, the British army's deployment was proceeding rather more smoothly. It marched from Nairn in four columns, three of them comprising five battalions ranked one behind the other, and the fourth being made up of the three cavalry regiments. All that was required in order to deploy for battle was for the even-numbered battalions to move out to their left and then forward into the gaps between the odd numbered battalions. By this means the army was ready, if unexpectedly attacked, quickly to form two lines each of six battalions, with a third, reserve line of three battalions. This pre-planned deployment was practised as soon as they were ready to leave Nairn and again, briefly, on their first sighting the rebel army. With no sign of the Jacobites coming forward to meet him, Cumberland then continued up the moor to near the Leanach steading, and there deployed into line for the third time.

The left-hand battalion of his front line, Barrell's 4th Foot stood astride the moor road about 300 yards forward of the steading, and then Monro's 37th, Campbell's 21st, Price's 14th, Cholmondley's 34th and, on the right of the line by virtue of seniority, the Second Battalion of the 1st or Royal Regiment of Foot. Two 3-pound field-guns were placed in the gaps between each battalion. The second line, standing about 300 yards further back and positioned so that each battalion covered the gaps between those in front, comprised from left to right; Wolfe's 8th Foot, Ligonier's 59th, Sempill's 25th, Bligh's 20th, Fleming's 36th and Howard's 3rd(Buffs). The third line, flanked by the two squadrons of Kingston's 10th Horse, was made up of Blakeney's 27th, Battereau's 62nd and Pulteney's 13th Foot. Finally, positioned between the first and second lines, and rather to the right of the army, were six Coehorn Mortars.[8]

This neatly balanced arrangement did not last very long however, for at about this point Lord George Murray began his 'changement', which was interpreted by Cumberland and his staff as a general shifting to the rebel left, which needed to be countered by bringing forward two of the reserve battalions, Pulteney's 13th and Battereau's 62nd to prolong the right of the British first and second lines respectively. At the same time both squadrons of Kingston's 10th Horse were also brought forward to cover the over-exposed right flank, and were joined there by two troops of Cobham's 10th Dragoons who had been scouting towards the north.

Meanwhile the remainder of Cumberland's cavalry, the other four troops of Cobham's 10th and all six troops of Kerr's 11th Dragoons,[9] together with four Highland companies[10], were standing to the south-east of Leanach, facing the six foot high walls of the Culwhiniac Parks, and it was they who began the battle.

'From this place,' wrote Captain Duncan Campbell, in command of a company of militiamen from Glenorchy, 'we sent to acquaint General Bland that the Horse could go further. He came up to the ground and ordered us to pull down the wall, which was done so that the squadron could march abreast.'[11]

General Hawley's Aide de Camp, Major James Wolfe, wrote the next day that the two cavalry regiments had originally been posted on the left simply because that was where the ground was firmest. But peering interestedly over the wall Humphrey Bland could now see that the Culwhiniac enclosure appeared to be undefended and he thereupon sent to his immediate superior, General Hawley, advising him that it appeared to be possible to outflank the rebels by moving through it. By the time Hawley and Wolfe came down to have a look for themselves the wall had been successfully breached and the General promptly took charge of the operation, ordering Ballimore's Highlanders to demolish the far wall as well. At this stage Hawley's prospects must have seemed quite promising. If the rebel right flank could indeed be turned, not only would their defeat be doubly assured, but there was also every prospect that it would then be possible for him to cut off any line of retreat across the Nairn to the hills beyond, thereby forcing them back on Inverness. The imminent possibility that the British army might well attempt to try something of this sort had not been overlooked by the Jacobite leaders either, as John Cameron, later an officer in Lord Ogilvy's French regiment recalled.

'This made Locheil send to Lord George Murray, then on the left with the Duke of Perth, to tell him of the danger. Lord George Murray [whom I heard formerly say the park would be of great service to prevent our being flanked] on this took a narrower view of it and sent three gentlemen, viz., Colonel Sullivan, John Roy Stewart, and Ker of Grydan to view it down to the Water of Nairn. At their return they said it was impossible for any horse to come by that way.'[12] Nevertheless, Lord George Murray remained worried about it and forcefully taxed Sullivan on the subject as the rebels took up their positions on the moor. The Colonel's account of the discussion is, as usual, surprisingly instructive:

'The enemy appeared plainly in battle array, upon two lignes, and in very good order, as they were near the river side Ld George thought they were coming to take him in flank 'Never fear yt My Ld' says Sullivan 'They cant come between yu & the river, unlesse they break down the walls of those two parks yt are between yu & them, but yu can prevent them, but as I am sure they will not, & yt certainly their left will be against this park where yr right is. My advise wou'd be, as all their horse is at their left, yt we shou'd make a breach in this wall, & set in this park Stonywood & the other Regimt yt is in Colloum behind yu, who will take their horse in flank, without fearing in the least yt they can come upon him. If the horse is taken in flanck, with such a wall as this between them, & those yt fires on 'em Il answer they'd break. If they are once broak, the foot will not stand, besides my Ld, if yu march to the enemy, as yu have no other party to take, for I suppose yu don't pretend to measure yr fire wth the English troops; in case yu are repulsed those same troops yt you'l set in the park will protect yr retrait.'[13]

The north wall was indeed quickly breached by Ballimore's Highlanders thus allowing the dragoons to penetrate into the upper enclosure, but their advance was therefore made along the bottom of the upper one, visible to the Jacobite right wing and in particular in sight of those units which Sullivan had posted to deal with the threat – James Moir of Stonywood's and John Gordon of Avochie's battalions of Lord Lewis Gordon's Regiment.

Unfortunately neither battalion was actually posted inside the enclosure, as he had recommended. George Innes, a local Presbyterian minister, subsequently wrote that; 'Some of Stoniewood's Regiment assert that Colonel Bagot had advised to post them along the outside of that parkdyke, which probably would have prevented a good deal of mischief these Campbells and dragoons afterwards did; but that Lord George Murray would not hear of it.'[14] Sullivan posted them instead in what he calls a 'hollow way', advising Stonywood, 'a very brave man', to keep a sentry posted on the top to warn of any approaching trouble.[15]

Murray may well have feared that if the battalions were actually posted inside the enclosure they might be cut off, or would be unable to support the main battle on the moor. But whatever his reasoning, the entirely predictable result was that Ballimore's Highlanders and the two regiments of dragoons following them were able to traverse the enclosure unmolested and break through the south wall as well. Harry Ker of

150

Graden rather sourly commented on the fact that they did so, 'without receiving one shot from the two battalions that were placed to observe their motions', but as the Aberdeenshire men were standing too far up the hill and on the wrong side of the wall to intervene, this criticism seems rather harsh.

Instead, after breaking through the wall and swinging westwards to come up on to the moor in the rear of the Jacobite army, they were brought to a halt in front of what was variously described as a 'hollow way' or a 'ditch'. Most modern accounts of the battle firmly place the ensuing action across a sunken road bending around the Culchunaig steading and more specifically in the gap between the steading and the Culwhiniac enclosure walls. However this gap is only a hundred yards wide, allowing barely sufficient room for the deployment of the two troops making up a single squadron of dragoons. Given the obvious impossibility of squeezing no fewer than ten troops of dragoons into such a confined space, let alone the four infantry battalions and the two troops of cavalry which eventually opposed them, it is clear that the fighting actually took place not around Culchunaig itself, but instead across the prominent re-entrant running roughly from east to west, more or less on a line stretching between Culchunaig and the much larger steading at Balvraid, about 500 yards to the south-west. This re-entrant is formed by a stream which later turns south to run more or less parallel with the Culwhiniac enclosure wall, at a distance varying from about four to five hundred yards.

At any rate Captain Duncan Campbell of the Argyll Militia stated that; 'The Dragoons went out and formed at a distance, facing the rebels,' while Thomas Sandby depicts the dragoons taking up their battle positions wide of the steading and on the far side of the stream.

Had General Hawley simply come storming up the hillside within the enclosure, Stonywood's and Avochie's battalions, securely lining the outside of the wall, ought to have been quite sufficient to stop him, but once the dragoons instead broke through the south wall and passed out on to the open slopes beyond, the threat to the Jacobite right wing and rear assumed a much greater significance. The two battalions were swung around to face downhill and Lord George Murray responded to the threat by ordering Lord Ogilvy's two battalions to march across from the reserve in the centre of the first line; 'and to Lord Ogilvie said, he hoped and doubted not but he would acquit himself as usual.'

Meanwhile, Hawley, as yet unable to see the full strength of the defensive line being thrown together against him, was making a serious blunder. Instead of keeping Ballimore's Highlanders with him, he now ordered them to remain within the Culwhiniac Parks. Why he did this is not entirely clear. He may simply have wished to secure his own flank, or more probably he may have considered it safer to leave them mewed up in the enclosure where, lacking uniforms, they were less likely to be mistaken for rebels than on the open moor. Whatever his reasoning it was a mistake which Hawley was soon to have cause to regret.

There is also a little doubt as to where Ballimore's Highlanders eventually came into action, since a scatter of graves lying just inside the former Leanach enclosure wall are, it is true, traditionally identified as being those of some of the Campbells who broke the park walls. However only six men of Ballimore's battalion were killed and he himself is recorded as having been buried in Inverness. Moreover, for any of the Highland companies to have ended up in the Leanach enclosure they must have either retraced their steps back through the breaches, or else passed through the gate in the upper part of the enclosure, and crossed the lane separating the two. This is certainly not impossible, but Captain Duncan Campbell makes no mention of it, and both Sandby's and Finlayson's maps how them to have remained within the Culwhiniac enclosure.

Campbell of Airds' account clearly relates that, 'Ballimore & his command were ordered to break down them Dykes & make way for the Horse which they Executed, & taking advantage of the Second Dyke as a Breast Work fire Closs on a strong party of the Rebels that then formed the Right, Composed of Lord John Drummond's men being part of the Enemy's second line.' Although Airds watched the battle from the comparative safety of the baggage train, he evidently got the details of this particular struggle from those of his comrades who were there, and just as importantly, the fact that they engaged Drummond's *Royal Ecossois* rather than the Highlanders in the rebel front line also points to their having stayed within the Culwhiniac enclosure.

This, however, is to anticipate matters a little. Having thus rather short-sightedly dispensed with their infantry support, Generals Hawley and Bland crossed the stream where it ran parallel to the wall, swung northwards and then deploying into two lines found their path blocked by the Jacobite regiments standing along the line of the re-entrant between Culchunaig and Balvraid. Included amongst them now were two small cavalry units, and James Maxwell of Kirkconnell, Major of Elcho's Lifeguards, recorded that:

'he (Murray) made Avuchie's battalion advance towards the Campbells, but they had already broke into an enclosure towards the river, and made a passage for the dragoons, who came round the right of the Prince's army and formed in the rear of it. Upon which Lord George ordered the Guards and Fitzjames's horse quite to the right flank, and made them form opposite to the dragoons, upon the brink of a hollow way; the ascent was somewhat steep on both sides, so that neither could pass safely in presence of the other. The Campbells advanced no farther, and Avuchie's battalion was ordered to watch their motions.'[16]

Both Kirkconnell's and Lord Elcho's accounts suggest that only the Life-guards and seventy troopers of Fitzjames's Horse, supported by John Gordon of Avochie's Regiment, stood between the dragoons and the moor. But had this been so it is unlikely that Hawley would have been held up for very long, and in fact three other Jacobite infantry units can be firmly identified as having taken part in the action. Since Avochie's battalion is specifically mentioned it must presumably have been standing next to the cavalry, while Stonywood stood on Avochie's left. Lord Ogilvy's two battalions appear from contemporary maps to have ended up on the right of the cavalry.

This was very much more formidable than either Hawley or Bland had bargained for. In order to force their way across such an obstacle they would almost certainly require some kind of infantry support. Ballimore's men might have been able to provide it, but they had been left behind in the enclosure and were probably by now beyond recall. As Wolfe was serving on General Hawley's staff at Culloden he must have taken part in this particular action, and writing the next day to a friend, Major Henry Delabene, he noted that once in position, Hawley halted the brigade and made no attempt to get across the re-entrant until the sound of firing begin to slacken over on the moor.[17]

Afterwards there was considerable disagreement amongst the participants as to what time that firing actually began, but on balance it looks to have begun around about one o'clock, and there is complete agreement that it was the rebels who fired the first shot. It is common to dismiss the effect of the rebel bombardment as being wholly insignificant and some secondary sources blithely refer to only a couple or so men being killed by it. There is no doubt that the exchange was somewhat uneven, but the rebel guns were not wholly ineffective. It is in fact fairly easy to obtain a reasonably accurate picture of the damage which was done by the Jacobite artillery; Battereau's 62nd Foot had an officer, Captain Carter, and two men wounded, Howard's 3rd (Buffs) had one man killed and two others wounded, one of whom must subsequently have died as only Private Charles Appleton, disabled in the right hand, survived to claim a pension, while Fleming's 36th had six men wounded. All three regiments stood in the second line and were not subsequently engaged by rebel infantry units, so all of these casualties can confidently be attributed to artillery fire.

It is very much more difficult to assess the scale of the casualties inflicted on the rebels by the British guns. Captain Godwin began firing a few moments after Finlayson – the Reverend George Innes's account says that the Jacobite guns fired in a ripple across their front twice before Captain-Lieutenant John Godwin replied with his ten 3-pounders[18] – but just as few people were afterwards able to agree when the firing began, there is similar disagreement over the duration of that firing.

James Wolfe, who as a staff officer was supposed to take especial note of such things, reckoned afterwards that: 'The cannon in particular made them very uneasy, and after firing a quarter of an hour obliged them to change their situation and move forward . . .'[19] Some, however, thought that even less time elapsed before the commencement of the rebel assault. Whitefoord states that when the rebel guns opened fire: 'Ours were not then ready' and goes on to say that the rebels, 'broke into Columns from the moment our cannon began to play'. Another staff officer, Joseph Yorke, who was one of Cumberland's aides, wrote that: 'When our cannon had fired about two rounds, I could plainly perceive that the rebels fluctuated extremely, and could not remain long in the position they were then in without running away or coming down upon us; and according as I thought, in two or three minutes they broke from the centre in three large bodies . . .'[20]

There is in fact a general consensus on the part of British officers that the attack was made within a very short time of Godwin's opening fire, but perhaps the most precise estimate came from Campbell of Airds, safely back with the baggage and therefore able to view the exchange with a certain degree of detachment. He opined that, 'The Cannonading Continued about nine minutes.' To have noted the time so precisely Airds must have been consulting his watch. Wolfe, one might suppose was doing the same, but he was listening to rather than watching the battle on the moor when he claimed that the guns were firing for upwards of fifteen minutes.

Nevertheless, if a period of some fifteen minutes of uninterrupted bombardment by the British guns is accepted – allow for those rounds actually fired into the rebels as they advanced – it is possible to arrive at a rough estimate of the likely number of casualties suffered by the rebels.

Although Captain Godwin's men were better trained than their rebel counterparts, their target was still over 500 yards away and perhaps as much as 700 yards away on the right. It was therefore edging into the outer limit of the effective range of the little 3-pound cannon. Theoretically each gun could be loaded and fired twice a minute and, if each round struck home on the rebel front line, it might kill or maim three or even six men in its passage through the ranks. It can safely be assumed, however, that while the rebels remained standing at the top of the moor, Godwin will have opted for a slower but steadier rhythm of fire, maintaining a rate of only one round per minute from each of his ten guns. If the cannonade was indeed maintained for fifteen minutes, then some

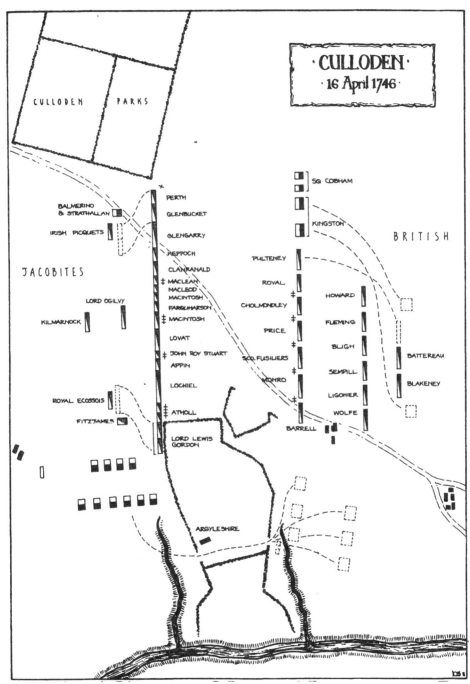

Composite of Thomas Sandby's contemporary sketches of Culloden, showing the locations of the guns on both sides and Hawley's thrust into the Jacobite rear.

Map 8

150 rounds of ball ammunition will have been fired in that time.

Statistical analysis of the hits recorded by similar artillery pieces at this range in contemporary tests, suggests that in ideal conditions some 40% of these rounds should strike their target. Unfortunately for the British gunners, the conditions at Culloden were far from ideal and there is ample testimony on the Jacobite side that many of the rounds were going over the heads of the clansmen. George Innes, for one, wrote unequivocally that: 'many of the balls went quite over the Highland lines.'[21] Some of them landed about the Prince and he himself afterwards claimed to have had a horse shot from under him (it survived), while a groom named Thomas Ca was killed while leading a sumpter horse just a few yards away.

Captain Godwin therefore will have been doing well to average just one casualty for each round fired. In other words, over the fifteen minute period during which the bombardment probably lasted, his men are unlikely to have inflicted more than about 150 casualties of all kinds on the rebels, and if the bombardment was actually shorter, as seems quite possible, then proportionately far less. Although this was obviously of little comfort to those men actually maimed or killed by the incoming rounds, it hardly represents the bloody massacre so often pictured by later writers and there is certainly no question, as at least one has suggested, of as many as a third of the men in some regiments being killed or incapacitated at this time. In any case, as we shall see, the location and the distribution of the known mass graves clearly point to most of the rebel casualties having been suffered after the charge began rather than while they were still standing at the top of the moor.

Nevertheless, if the physical effects of the British bombardment have largely been overestimated by earlier historians, there is no doubting its psychological effects on the Jacobites and soon they were clamouring to be led forward.

Sources:

1. Kirkconnell, p. 141.
2. Unless otherwise noted Jacobite strengths are taken from Thomas Sandby's excellent map of the battlefield, which to all appearances took its figures from captured Jacobite documents. The proviso must be added however that there is general agreement that the notional strength of all units was considerably reduced by straggling following the abortive night march.
3. The figure of 500 men – higher than Sandby's estimate – is given by Lochgarry.
4. There does not appear to be any evidence that Lord Lewis Gordon himself actually took part in the battle.
5. *Origins*, p. 178. The Picquets were not as strong as they might appear, for D'Eguilles' figures include 42 men from the Regiment Berwick who landed

in February and 148 press-ganged prisoners and deserters – largely men from Guise's 6th Foot captured at Fort George and Fort Augustus. On the other hand a dismounted element of Fitzjames's Horse should also be added. Similarly the *Royal Ecossois* had been making good their own losses through recruiting for a second battalion.

6. As all the guns originally emplaced on the moor were 3-pounders there would clearly have been no confusion over the ammunition supply as some modern accounts cheerfully suggest.

7. This is confirmed by Sandby's and Finlayson's plans as well as by a sketch drawn by Lieutenant-Colonel Whitefoord.

8. *A Return of the officers and men in each battalion on the day of the battle of Culloden.*

Regiments		Field Offs.	Capts.	Subs.	Serjs.	Drums	R&F
Royals	(1st)	2	5	19	29	25	401
Howard	(3rd)	2	4	10	21	14	413
Barrel	(4th)	2	5	13	18	10	325
Wolfe	(8th)	1	7	14	17	11	324
Pulteney	(13th)	2	6	14	23	19	410
Price	(14th)	2	7	14	21	11	304
Bligh	(20th)	2	5	13	22	13	412
Campbell	(21st)	1	5	13	21	14	358
Sempill	(25th)	3	5	15	20	14	420
Blakeney	(27th)	2	4	14	24	12	300
Cholmondley	(34th)	2	7	15	21	15	399
Fleming	(36th)	2	6	18	25	14	350
Monro	(37th)	2	6	15	23	19	426
Ligonier	(59th)	3	5	16	21	16	325
Battereau	(62nd)	1	7	19	24	18	354
Total		29	84	222	330	225	5,521

To this should be added as many as 32 Sergeants, 30 Corporals, 9 drummers and 430 of the Highland companies, besides 10 officers and 106 NCOs, gunners and matrosses of the Royal Artillery.

9. Cobham's 10th Dragoons had 276 officers and men present at Culloden, though 60 of them were detached on the right wing. Kerr's 11th Dragoons according to a return dated 28th March 1746, had 267 soldiers present and fit for duty besides 18 sick and a further 26 sick left behind. Kingston's 10th Horse mustered 211 officers and men.

10. They comprised three companies of the Argyll Militia led by Captain John Campbell of Achnaba, Captain John Campbell of Achrossan and a Captain Duncan Campbell, together with a company of Loudon's 64th Highlanders under Captain Colin Campbell of Ballimore. As a regular officer Ballimore had seniority and therefore took command of the provisional battalion.

11. This and other accounts by Argyll Militia officers can be found in National Library of Scotland, *NLS*, 3733–5.

12. Forbes *Lyon in Mourning*, p. 86–7.

13. Sullivan, p. 163.

14. Forbes, p. 291.

15. Sullivan op.cit.

16. Kirkconnell, p. 151.

17. Willson, *Life and Letters of James Wolfe*, p. 63.

18. Although Major William Belford was serving as Cumberland's CRA (Commander Royal Artillery) at Culloden, the artillery company was actually led by Captain-Lieutenant John Godwin.
19. Willson, p. 65.
20. Whitefoord, p. 78, Yorke is quoted in Black, p. 170.
21. Forbes, p. 291.

CHAPTER 13

The Bloodiest Battle in the Memory of Man

The Battle of Culloden Part 2

Time spent under fire is always subjective and it is hardly surprising that the Jacobites afterwards thought that they had been shot at for longer than the 10–15 minutes recorded by more dispassionate eyewitnesses on the other side. What is surprising, however, is that Lord George Murray should have delayed so long under that fire before giving the order to advance. He himself merely states with his usual blandness that: 'The Highlanders were much galled by the enemy's cannon, and growing so impatient, that they called out for the attack; upon which it was judged proper to attack and orders were given accordingly.'

Charles appears to have been sending him orders to do just that for some time. First by Colonel Sullivan, then by Colonel Stapleton. A third messenger, Captain Lachlan McLachlan of Inishconel is said to have been decapitated while carrying the order forward. Eventually, 'Lord George Murray . . . sent Colonel Ker to know if he should begin the attack, which the Prince accordingly ordered. As the right was further advanced than the left, Colonel Ker went to the left, and ordered the Duke of Perth, who commanded there, to begin the attack, and rode along the line till he came to the right, where Lord George Murray was, who attacked, at the head of the Atholl men.'[1]

The Highland charge had begun, but within a few short minutes a number of factors saw it begin to degenerate into a bloody shambles.

On past experience the rebel line might have been expected to have advanced fairly steadily at first to within musket shot of the British front line, fired, and then rushed in under their own smoke. Instead, when the order was given, they immediately surged forward at a run. Many of the front rank men simply broke ranks, threw down their firelocks without discharging them, and drew their swords at once. To Joseph Yorke and some of the other eyewitnesses who saw them come on, the rebels certainly appeared to be coming down upon them in a very disorderly manner; 'they broke from the centre in three large bodies, like wedges, and moved forward. At first they made a feint, as if they would come down upon our right, but seeing that wing so well covered, and imagining that they might surround the left because they saw no cavalry to cover it, two of these wedges bore down immediately upon Barrell's and Monro's regiments, which formed the left of the first line; and after firing very irregularly at a considerable distance, they rushed furiously in upon them, thinking to carry all before them, as they had done on former occasions.'[2]

Once the rebels came down within yards of the British front line, Captain Godwin's men stopped firing ball and loaded with canister instead. The effect was devastating. Allowing for the likelihood of the four guns positioned in the gaps between 2/Royals, Cholmondley's and Price's regiments being aimed rather towards the rebel left, the six guns firing on the centre and right divisions were now, very suddenly, killing or wounding something in the region of sixty to eighty men every twenty seconds. Moreover, given that the Atholl Brigade under Lord George Murray, was at first partially sheltered by the turf wall of the Leanach enclosure it is probable that all six guns were in fact firing on Locheil's Camerons and part of the centre division, commanded by Lord John Drummond.

This storm of canister fire had two immediate effects. The rebel officers were accustomed to leading from the front and therefore suffered disproportionately high casualties. Locheil himself went down with both legs broken by canister-shot. Secondly, Lady MacIntosh's men in the centre then appear to have shied away from the guns, inclining towards their right instead of coming straight on. In so doing however, they not only lost contact with the other units on their immediate left, who, for reasons of their own which will shortly be examined, were already hanging back, but they then came into violent collision with Murray's right-hand division, which was simultaneously moving out to its left in order to clear the protruding Leanach enclosure wall.

The result was that by the time the Highlanders eventually reached the British line they may well have received something in the region of five or even six discharges of canister and consequently suffered anything up to about 300 casualties without inflicting a single one in turn.

Moreover, once they came within about 50 yards of the British front line, this particular body of rebels was also fired into by at least three infantry battalions, Barrell's 4th, Monro's 37th, and Campbell's 21st. Between them these regiments mustered some 1100 bayonets and an unnamed Corporal in Monro's related that they had time to fire one round apiece as the rebels came in, and then give them another in their teeth:

'they began to play their Cannon very briskly upon us; but as soon as we saw them pointed, we stoop'd down, and the Balls flew over our Heads. Two Pieces of our Cannon play'd from our Left to their Right, which kill'd many of them, and made their whole body determine to come down upon our Left, compos'd of Barrel's, Monro's, and the Scots Fusiliers. When we saw them coming towards us in great Haste and Fury, we fired at about 50 Yards Distance, which made hundreds Fall; notwithstanding which, they were so numerous, that they still advanced, and were almost upon us before we had loaden again. We immediately gave them another full fire . . .'[3]

He may not have been exaggerating, for even allowing for as little as one round in every ten being fired at point blank range actually finding its mark (as contemporary tests suggest), the initial ripple of platoon volleys alone will have dropped about a hundred of the oncoming rebels. Notwithstanding these losses the Highlanders on the right and in the centre at least pressed forwards, running across the front of Campbell's and Monro's to fall upon the 325 rank and file of Barrell's Regiment, standing on the extreme left of the British front line.

Cumberland's own official account of the battle pays tribute to the way in which Barrell's and Monro's 'fairly beat them with their bayonets: There was scarce a soldier or officer of Barrel's and that part of Monro's which engaged, who did not kill one or two men each with their bayonets and spontoons.'[4] Another letter related: 'That general Barrell's regiment gained the greatest reputation imaginable in the late engagement; the best of the clans having made their strongest efforts to break them, but without effect, for the old Tangierines bravely repulsed those boasters, with a dreadful slaughter, and convinced them that the broad sword and target is unequal to the musket and bayonet, when in the hands of veterans, who are determined to use them – After the battle there was not a bayonet in this regiment but was either bloody or bent.'[5]

Afterwards Barrell's returned sixteen men killed, besides Captain Lord Robert Ker, together with a further five officers and 103 men wounded. Amongst those injured was their commanding officer, Lieutenant-Colonel Robert Rich, who went down with a hand sliced off and half a dozen cuts on his skull as he tried to save one of his regiment's colours. Defending the same colour, Ensign Browne was trampled underfoot and badly knocked about, but nevertheless he still managed to cling on to it.

Against all the Highlanders' expectations, Barrell's refused to run, but then, almost at once, the rebels lapped around their flanks, overrunning Sergeant Edward Bristo's two guns and fatally wounding the Sergeant and five of his men:

'Making a dreadful huzza, and even crying 'Run, ye dogs!', they broke in between the grenadiers of Barrel and Monro; but these had given their fire according to the general direction, and then parried them with their screwed bayonets. The two cannon on that division were so well served, that when within two yards of them they received a full discharge of cartridge shot, which made a dreadful havoc; and those who crowded into the opening received a full fire from the centre of Bligh's regiment, which still increased the number of the slain. However, such as survived possessed themselves of the cannon, and attacked the regiments sword in hand;'[6]

As Barrell's fell back, the weight of the rebel attack now fell upon Monro's Regiment to their immediate right, but as the Corporal records, this battalion managed to hold its ground; 'the Front Rank charged their Bayonets Breast high, and the Center and Rear Ranks kept a continual Firing ... the Rebels designing to break or flank us; but our fire was so hot, most of us having discharged nine Shot each, that they were disappointed.'[7]

It was one of the officers of Monro's who left what is perhaps the most spirited and vivid account of the battle in a letter written to a brother officer stationed in Newcastle-upon-Tyne:

'The Hurry I am in going to collect the number of killed and wounded, scarce allows me time to tell you, that Yesterday we had the bloodiest Battle with the Rebels that ever was fought in the Memory of Man. The same Morning we march'd from Nairn, and met the Gentry about Noon near Culloden, the Lord President's House, three Miles from hence, where we cannonaded each other for some Time; at last the Rebels advanc'd against the Left of our Line where was Barrel's Regiment, and the late Sir Robert Monro's, now Col. De Jean's. Barrel's behaved very well, but was obliged to give Way to their Torrent that bore down upon them; Their whole Force then fell upon the Left of ours where I had the Honour to command the Grenadier platoon; our Lads fought more like Devils than Men. In short we laid [to the best of my Judgement] about 1600 dead on the Spot, and finished the Affair without the Help of any other Regiment. You may judge of the Work, for I had 18 men killed and wounded in my Platoon. I thank God I escaped free, but my Coat had six balls thro' it. I must now tell you, that in the Midst of the Action the Officer that led on the Camerons call'd to me to take Quarters; which I refus'd, and bid the Rebel Scoundrel advance, he did, and fir'd at me; but providentially miss'd his Mark: I then shot him dead, and took his Pistol and Dirk, which are extreamly neat. The French have all surrendered Prisoners of War: We have taken their Cannon and Baggage; Lords Kilmarnock and Cromarty are among the Prisoners of Distinction. Our Regiment had ample Revenge for the Loss of our late Colonel, Sir Robert, and the rest of our Officers, whom the Scoundrels murdered in cold blood, but (as I told Lord Kilmarnock) we had ample Revenge in hors. For I can with great Truth asure you, not one that attack'd us escaped alive, for we gave no Quarters nor would accept of any. Our Regiment took three Stand of colours. Our Wounded are Capt. Kinnier and Lieuts. Lort and King, and Ensign Dally kill'd. I now give you Joy of the Day; and be assur'd never was a more compleat Victory gained – Our Gaols are full of them and they are brought in by Hundreds.'[8]

It was perhaps a pardonable exaggeration in the circumstances, but in those first few moments of the Highland attack Monro's men were falling quickly. Besides the officers, fourteen men were returned as killed (just two less than in Barrell's) and 68 wounded. Left to their own devices for very much longer, they too might have been swept aside like Barrell's, but the gallant stand by both regiments gave 'Daddy' Huske time to prepare a counter-attack. Even as Barrell's began to give way under the pressure, he swung Wolfe's 8th and Ligonier's 59th Foot around to the left and brought up Sempill's 25th and Bligh's 20th Foot as well to seal off the penetration.

Modern accounts of the battle, following the version in Home's *History of the Rebellion in the Year 1745*, state that Wolfe's Regiment was positioned forward of the rest of the front line and at a right angle to it, some time before the rebel assault began. But in point of fact every writer in the British ranks who refers to the crucial part played by Wolfe's tells how they only marched up into a flanking position *after* Barrell's were hit.

One of them, James Wolfe, was on the other side of the Culwhiniac enclosures by this time, but he held a Captain's commission in Barrell's and naturally took a great interest in what happened both to that regiment and to his father's one, commanded that day by Lieutenant Colonel Edmund Martin:

'The Regiment (Barrell's) behaved with uncommon resolution ... they were however surrounded by superiority, and would have all been destroyed had not Col.Martin with his Regiment (the left of the 2nd line of Foot) mov'd forward to their assistance, prevented mischief, and by a well-timed fire destroyed a great number of them ... '[9]

Indeed one of Sandby's preliminary sketch maps even shows Wolfe's wheeling in on the extreme left while Ligonier's men are at the same time dividing themselves into two wings in order to be able to clear the Leanach steading to their immediate front.[10] In any case the matter is quite conclusively settled by a letter from Captain-Lieutenant James Ashe Lee of Wolfe's Regiment:

'Poor Barrell's regiment were sorely pressed by those desperadoes and outflanked. One stand of their colours was taken; Collonel Riches hand cutt off in their defence . . . We marched up to the enemy, and our left, outflanking them, wheeled in upon them; the whole then gave them 5 or 6 fires with vast execution, while their front had nothing left to oppose us, but their pistolls and broadswords; and fire from their center and rear, (as, by this time, they were 20 or 30 deep) was vastly more fatal to themselves, than us.'[11]

Indeed it was. Ensign Robert Bruce was the only casualty subsequently returned by Wolfe's Regiment and Ligonier's had none at all, probably because the rebels by this time were halted on either side of the Well of the Dead. Sempill's Edinburgh Regiment on the other hand lost one man dead and thirteen more wounded, but at least some of these may have been the result of artillery-fire, since it is otherwise difficult to account for the bruise which rendered Private John MacDonald unfit for any further service.[12]

Bligh's, coming up on the right of Sempill's to plug the gap between them and Monro's, suffered more heavily than any other regiment in the second line with four men killed and sixteen wounded besides Lieutenant Trapaud. Once again some of these casualties might be attributed to artillery fire but others were certainly suffered at this time. Joseph Simmers for example was wounded in the head, and Archibald Smith had the misfortune to be 'shot in the mouth and wounded in the side.'[13]

The losses being suffered by the British regiments on the left were as nothing however, by comparison with the terrible casualties which they were inflicting upon the clansmen opposite. If Barrell's, with 17 men killed and 108 wounded out of 325, are discounted as being temporarily out of action, the rebel column was now partially surrounded by no fewer than 1,900 men of Wolfe's, Ligonier's, Sempill's, Bligh's and Monro's regiments. Even though the front rank stood fast with charged bayonets – as described both by the Corporal of Monro's and an officer in Wolfe's, who declared that they, 'plied them with continual fire from our rear and fixt bayonets in front' – that still meant something like 1,200 men were firing into the rebels at point blank range.

The Corporal of Monro's reckoned that he and his comrades fired off about nine rounds apiece in the course of the battle, including the two volleys with which they saluted the rebels as they approached. In the second line, Captain Lee of Wolfe's reckoned that five, or perhaps six volleys were fired by his regiment before the rebels broke. Once again, if only one round in ten took effect, in just two terrible minutes as many as 700 rebels may have been killed or wounded. Later they were buried where they fell and it is no coincidence that the macabre outline of this

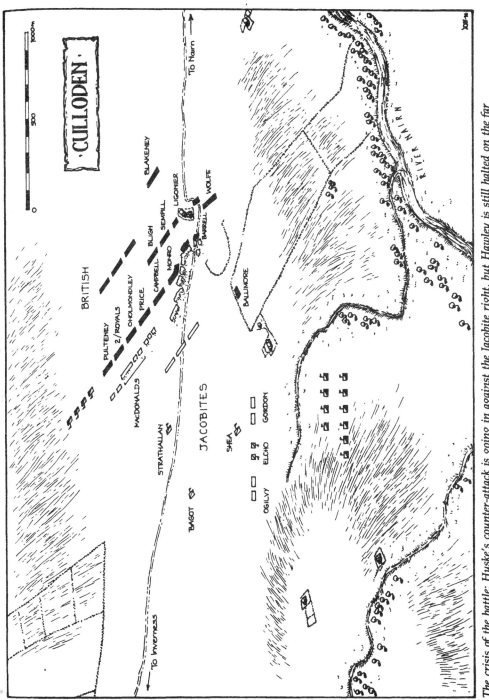

The crisis of the battle: Huske's counter-attack is going in against the Jacobite right, but Hawley is still halted on the far side of the re-entrant near Culchunaig.

165   Map 9

great column can still be traced today in the long slew of mass graves running westwards from the Well of the Dead.

Meanwhile their swing to the right ought to have resulted in Lady MacIntosh's Regiment and the Frasers attacking Campbell's Scots Fusiliers, but once again they shied away from the regular platoon volleys. Instead the clansmen followed the Camerons and the Stewarts into the great hole torn in the British front line. At least one of them, Major Gillies McBean of Lady MacIntosh's Regiment, was later seen lying dead some distance beyond Sergeant Bristo's guns, but as they fought their way past Campbell's and Monro's they continued to suffer terrible casualties and both regiments lost their commanding officers; Lieutenant-Colonels Alexander McGillivray of Dunmaglas and Charles Fraser of Inverallochy. The Frasers also lost their colours, for 'A blew silk colours with the Lovat arms, *Sine Sanguine Victor*' must have been one of the three trophies afterwards claimed by Monro's. Another was presumably the 'white silk colours with the Stewart's Arms, *God Save King*', lost by John Roy Stuart's men,[14] but the third remains unidentified since those carried by both Lady MacIntosh's and the Appin Regiment are known to have been saved.

Further towards the Jacobite left it was a different story. Despite Ker of Graden's sensible precaution of passing on the order to advance to the left wing first, their subsequent advance was slow and hesitant. This was largely due to the nature of the ground which they had to cross. Captain Johnstone, who was with Glengarry's men went so far as to say that the ground was not only marshy, but 'covered with water which reached halfway up the leg.' Indeed, unlike many writers both then and afterwards, he thought the bog 'well chosen to protect us from the cavalry of the enemy.'[15] But despite this so-called advantage, the MacDonalds and some of the units on their immediate right advanced much more slowly and eventually halted altogether once they came under fire from the British front line.

'Sullivan was at the left, with the Duke of Perth & Ld John where they had only foot over against, & of consequence most of the fire. Our left flinches, the Duke of Perth runs to Clenronald's Regimt takes their Collors & tells them from that day forth he'l call himself MccDonel if they gain the day. Lord John & Sullivan brings up the left again.'[16]

But still they would not close. 'They came running on in their wild manner,' wrote Cumberland. '& upon the Right where I had placed Myself, imagining the greatest Push would be there, they came down three several Times within a Hundred Yards of our Men, firing their pistols and brandishing their Swords, but the Royals and Pulteneys hardly took their Firelocks from their shoulders . . .'

One of those standing in the ranks of the Royals was an Ayrshire man named Alexander Taylor, and he afterwards wrote to his wife, telling her of the battle and how the Highlanders; 'came running upon our front line like troops of hungry wolves, and fought with intrepidity. But the thunder of our fire, and the continuation of it, began to slacken their fury . . .'

It was the wet ground which doomed their assault, for the MacDonalds advanced no less bravely than their comrades on their right and encountered the same remorseless platoon fire rippling up and down the ranks of Cholmondley's and Price's regiments. But while Lord George Murray's men were still carried forward through it by the sheer impetus of their charge, the Jacobite left wing was literally bogged down and shot to pieces without ever making contact.

This is starkly evident from the casualty lists of the four regiments facing them; Pulteney's suffered no casualties at all, Cholmondley's had one man killed and two wounded, Price's had Captain Andrew Simpson and eight men wounded, while the Royals returned a mere four men wounded. Two of them, Alexander Buchannan and John Reynolds were both wounded in the left leg, but how John Ross came to be disabled by a rupture at Culloden must remain a minor mystery.[17]

It is evident both from Cumberland's remark that the Royals and Pulteney's, 'hardly took their Firelocks from their shoulders.' and a similar statement by Whitefoord that Perth's and Glenbucket's regiments must have been hanging back. Few officers from either battalion are known to have been hit, although Major Robert Stewart of the former had his horse shot from under him and was left pinned to the ground underneath it. By contrast Colonel Lachlan MacLachlan was badly injured by a cannonball, and all the officers in the little independent company formed by the Chisholms of Strathglas were killed or wounded. Their white linen colours with the motto '*Terrores Furio*' were later pulled from underneath a pile of bodies. The Farquharsons were even more badly hit with at least thirteen officers killed, and they too lost their white linen colours.

The MacDonalds may not have been quite so badly hit, but even so Keppoch was shot down and Clanranald received a nasty head wound. Although the third commanding officer, Lochgarry, escaped unscathed many of the other MacDonald officers were killed or wounded including Captain Donald MacDonnell of Scotus. Johnstone was standing beside him when he fell, just twenty paces short of their objective and still believing that they could yet win the battle, when to his dismay he realised that the right wing was giving way.

Lord George Murray meanwhile was trying desperately to retrieve the situation over there:

'Our men broke in upon some regiments on the enemy's left; but others came quickly up to their relief. Upon a fire from these last, and some

167

cannon charged with cartouch shot, that they had, I think, at their second line, (for we had passed two that were on their front) my horse plunged and reared so much, that I thought he was wounded; so quitted my stirrups, and was thrown.'

Kirkconnell testifies to the fact that the second line had been following closely behind the first, but most of its regiments had already been called away to defend the threatened right flank, or else brought forward to reinforce the first line. Just three regiments now remained, of which the Irish Picquets were too far away to be of help, leaving only Lord Kilmarnock's Footguards and the *Royal Ecossois*. 'I brought up two regiments from our second line, after this,' said Murray, 'who gave their fire; but nothing could be done – all was lost.'[18]

The Jacobite collapse came very suddenly. The right wing, caught in that terrible crossfire, was the first to run – 'which by the way,' crowed Campbell of Airds, 'was the pleasantest sight I ever beheld.'[19] On the left, Perth's men were still holding together, but recognising that his moment had come, Cumberland himself galloped across to the two troops of Cobham's 10th Dragoons and in the admiring words of an eyewitness, 'clapping some of them on the shoulders, call'd out 'One Brush, my Lads, for the Honour of Old Cobham'; upon which, rather like Devils than Men they broke through the Enemy's Flank, and a total Rout followed.'[20]

Both Glenbucket's and Perth's regiments were already retreating so Sullivan ran to Captain Shea, who commanded the Prince's escort squadron and rather breathlessly announced: 'yu see all is going to pot. Yu can be of no great succor, so before a general deroute wch will soon be, Sieze upon the Prince & take him off.' The Prince was at that time trying to rally the broken right wing, but 'sees this Regimt of horse very near our left wch was the MccDonels, yt were quite uncovered, sees it is time & retirs.'[21] He got clean away, escorted for at least part of the way by Glenbucket's and Perth's regiments, but behind him the battle was still raging.

The Picquets too were retiring towards their original position, somewhere in the vicinity of the Kings Stables cottage. But when Cobham's and Kingston's came down on the MacDonalds' flank, they halted and turned at bay. 'Stapleton makes an evolution or two, fires at the Dragoons & obliges them to retire . . .' At much the same time the French engineer officer Du Saussay turned up to assist them with a field-gun, but their stand was a short one and Sullivan, who may have been the only eyewitness simply says that after firing their volley, they 'throws themselfs into ye Park yt was on our left, continues there fire where Stapleton was wounded, & are at last obliged to give themselfs up as prisoners of war.'[22] It was clearly a one-sided fight for the French paymaster, Captain James

Hay of the *Royal Ecossois* afterwards opined that about 100 were killed or wounded – nearly half their strength at Culloden. The cavalrymen on the other hand came out of it virtually unscathed. Kingston's 10th Horse returned only one man wounded and lost three horses, while Cobham's 10th Dragoons had one man killed and nine horses killed or wounded, including one ridden by Trooper Enoch Bradshaw:

> '. . . we lost but one man,' he wrote to his brother, 'tho I fear I shall lose my horse, he having at the moment of writing a ball in his left buttock 'Twas pritty near Enoch that time, but, thank God, a miss is as good as a mile, as we say in Gloucestershire.'[23]

Across on the other side of the moor it was pretty much a similar story. Having fired a token volley at long range, Kilmarnock's Footguards and the blue-bonneted mercenaries of the *Royal Ecossois* started falling back. '. . . when the second Line, where I was, broke, I was next to Lord John Drummond's Regiment, and went with them and the other Low Country Foot along the Wall to the South of the Field of Battle which covered us from the Cannon shot of the Duke's Army.'[24] They were not, however, covered from Ballimore's loyalist Highlanders standing behind the park walls. Earlier they had been firing on the Jacobite regiments still drawn up by Culchunaig, but now Ballimore fired a volley into the flank of the *Royal Ecossois* and promptly led his men out through the gate.

It proved to be a fatal decision, for the *Royal Ecossois* still had a lot of fight in them and as Campbell of Airds reported: 'It was in passing a slap (opening) in the second Dyke that Ballimore was Shot Dead, and that Achnaba received his wound of which he Dyed next day.'[25] Six others in Ballimore's company were also returned as dead and two more wounded as they ducked back behind the wall. One of the surviving Campbell officers afterwards reported that his men had only fired four rounds apiece, but it was sufficient to drive the *Royal Ecossois* away from the wall and straight into the path of Hawley's dragoons.

Thus far the General had been reluctant to cross the re-entrant, not because he was intimidated by the opposition, but simply because he was unable to see what lay on the other side of the crest. The initial advance through the Culwhiniac Parks had been led by the four troops of Cobham's 10th Dragoons, but now the six troops of Kerr's 11th passed through their intervals to take the lead as they went up the slope. '. . . as soon as the Rebels began to give way and the Fire of the Foot slacken'd, he (Hawley) ordered Genl Bland to charge the rest of them with three squadrons, and Cobham to support him with two. It was done with wonderful spirit and completed the victory with great slaughter.'[26]

It was not entirely one-sided. Kerr's 11th Dragoons had three men killed and three others wounded, and no fewer than 19 horses were lost, which strongly suggests that they got in the way of a volley from Lord Lewis Gordon's men. This seems to have blunted their enthusiasm somewhat, for Gordon's and Ogilvy's men were then allowed to retire unmolested. The *Royal Ecossois* were not so lucky. Still trying to catch up with the Aberdeenshire men, they were intercepted and surrounded by Cobham's 10th Dragoons. In the fight that followed about 50 were killed or wounded, including their commanding officer, Lord Lewis Drummond. A substantial number of them then surrendered, although others, led by Major Hale, succeeded in escaping across the river Nairn with the wreck of the right wing.

Some of Cobham's 10th were already chasing the fleeing rebels down the Inverness road; now Bland was ordered to support them with the rest of the cavalry and 'gave Quarter to None but about Fifty French Officers and Soldiers He picked up in his Pursuit.' James Wolfe, who was probably riding down the road himself, remarked to his friend Major Delabene: 'The Rebels, besides their natural inclinations, had orders not to give quarter to our men. We had an opportunity of avenging ourselves for that and many other things, and indeed we did not neglect it, as few Highlanders were made prisoners as possible.'[27]

Just how many rebels were killed or wounded must to some extent remain a matter of conjecture. George Innes, the Jacobite-leaning Presbyterian minister, asserted that one of Cumberland's surgeons had very carefully counted some 750 bodies lying on the moor, besides those dead or dying on the roads. All in all most estimates agree on a figure of around 1,500 in addition to 154 rebel and 222 'French' prisoners.[28] A great many of these prisoners were also described as 'terribly wounded', disproving later claims that the Jacobite wounded were systematically butchered on the field. Some men undoubtedly were finished off in the days which followed, but upon closer examination these appear to have been relatively isolated incidents on the fringes of the battlefield, and usually involving stray burial parties not under the direct command of officers.[29] Indeed a letter written by a Sergeant in Howard's 3rd (Buffs) two days after the battle speaks of wounded rebels still being brought in.[30]

By contrast the British army lost just 50 dead and 259 wounded.[31] But, although the battle had been won, the rebellion was not yet over.

Sources:

1. Sullivan, p. 163–4; Murray (16th May), p. 316; Graden, p. 142; Kirkconnell, p. 151. The whole question of the order to attack is rather mysterious. Sullivan and Kirkconnell are both positive in stating that Murray was ordered to attack at the outset of the battle, while Ker implies that orders were not

forthcoming until he went to get them. Murray too says nothing about having received orders, but as usual his account is suspiciously bland. Kirkconnell suggests that he delayed attacking either because he considered the enemy to be too far away and was also worried about the Culwhiniac parks. More plausibly still perhaps he may have been hoping that a second battalion of the Frasers, led by the Master of Lovat, would arrive in time. Whatever his reasoning, however, it is odd that having decided to go forward, he then sent Ker to ask for permission, instead of taking his earlier orders as *carte blanche* to proceed.

2. Quoted *IN* Black, p. 170.
3. *Newcastle Journal.*
4. Charles, p. 295–302.
5. *Newcastle Journal.*
6. Michael Hughes *IN* Tomasson & Buist, p. 181.
7. *Newcastle Journal.*
8. Ibid.
9. Willson, p. 62–5.
10. JSAHR Vol.35, p. 22.
11. O'Callaghan, p. 450. NB: Lee is referred to therein as *Thomas* Ashe Lee, but the Commission Register in WO.25 gives his Christian name as James.
12. WO.120 (Chelsea Registers).
13. Ibid.
14. There is however a tradition that Stuart's colours were green and were saved from the debacle by a man named James MacIntyre.
15. Johnstone, p. 122.
16. Sullivan, p. 163–4.
17. WO.120.
18. Murray (16th May), p. 317; Kirkconnell, p. 154.
19. NLS 3733–35.
20. *Newcastle Journal.*
21. Sullivan op.cit. There is no evidence to support suggestions that the Prince was already back at Balvraid.
22. Ibid.
23. Forbes *Lyon in Mourning*, pp. 380–3. It is not clear whether Bradshaw was serving with the two troops on the right, or with the four under Hawley on the left. However the troops on the right do seem to have been more heavily engaged.
24. Lord Kilmarnock *IN* Allardyce, Vol.I, p. 322–3.
25. NLS 3733–5.
26. Willson, p. 63. See also Elcho's plan of the battle which depicts Kerr's in the front.
27. Ibid. There is an apocryphal tale of Wolfe refusing Cumberland's order to execute Fraser of Inverallochy, but it seems clear from these sentiments that he would actually have obeyed such an order without compunction.
28. The figure of 326 rebel prisoners is given in Cumberland's official dispatch, but the actual roll of prisoners compiled on 19th April (Allardyce p. 611–4) contains only 154 names, to which may be added the 172 prisoners taken at Dunrobin to arrive at the official total of 326. See Appendix 4.
29. Although there were certainly some stories of atrocities circulating at the time most of the evidence concerning the alleged killings was later collected by a Jacobite clergyman named Robert Forbes. While his *Lyon in Mourning* is an

important source of eyewitness accounts of other episodes in the rebellion, his 'evidence' gathering is decidedly suspect in regard to Culloden.

30. *Newcastle Journal*. One of those brought in that day was a Captain Ranald MacDonald of Bellfinlay who later provided a graphic, if not entirely consistent, story of the atrocities which he claimed to have witnessed while lying on the moor. A number of British wounded were also taken in to Inverness on the 18th.

31. For full details of British army casualties see Appendix 2.

CHAPTER 14

Putting an End to a Bad Affair
The Counter-insurgency Campaign
and Afterwards

The first priority, clearly, was the capture of Inverness. Not surprisingly the Highland capital was in a state of bedlam. As the Prince left the field he ordered Captain Felix O'Neill of the Regiment Lally to ride there and warn his supporters to make their escape. It is likely however that he was preceded by the first of the fugitives and amongst them the enigmatic figure of Simon Fraser, the Master of Lovat. According to Lord George Murray, he and his men arrived on the field in time to take part in the charge[1], but local tradition holds that the Master was still on the march when he met the fleeing remnants of the Jacobite left wing. Thereupon he is said to have faced his men about and marched, with his colours still flying and pipes still playing, straight back to Inverness.[2]

The first of the dragoons cannot have been very far behind, but they met no resistance and Captain James Campbell of the 25th took formal possession of the burgh at about 4 o'clock that afternoon. Despite Captain O'Neill's warning, the streets were still filled with Jacobite non-combatants: 'There were vast numbers of them, some crying, some mourning, some stood astonished and did not know whither to turn themselves.' There were others, however, who viewed the sight of red coats in the burgh very differently. Confined in the church were a fair number of British prisoners, taken for the most part when Fort Augustus surrendered.

The treatment of these men had been far from gentle and a number of them were driven to enlist with the Irish Picquets 'for mere subsistence.'[3] At one point they were even stripped of their coats by a Jacobite officer anxious to clothe his own new recruits.[4] Indeed, an unnamed officer declared: 'Our Men have really been pretty severe, and gave little Quarter, being exasperated at the Treatment our Prisoners met with, they being found in dark Dungeons at Inverness, almost naked and eat up with Vermin.'[5] Not surprisingly the army now took some considerable satisfaction in thrusting the hundreds of rebel prisoners into those self-same dungeons.

Meanwhile, having fled the field, most of the clansmen appear either to have dispersed, or else made for Fort Augustus where they met with Barisdale's men and the MacGregors, but the lowland regiments from the right wing held together and spent the night of the battle at Corrybrough, some four miles south-east of Loch Moy.[6] From there they made their way to a rendezvous at Ruthven Barracks. Upwards of 1,500 men assembled there; about half of them from the four battalions which formed the rearguard at Balvraid, but elements of the *Royal Ecossois* under Major Hale, the Duke of Perth's Regiment, and most of the surviving Jacobite cavalry are also known to have been present, along with Cluny's Regiment, which had not taken part in the battle.

The Prince, however was not present. During the retreat he had paused by the ford at Faillie for a brief conference with some of his surviving officers. Not surprisingly it soon turned into an acrimonious affair and became even more so when the Prince declined to accompany the remnants of his army southwards to Ruthven. He had already determined to escape to France. Lord Elcho, the hot-headed commander of his own Lifeguard was so disgusted that he took his leave with the memorable retort: 'There goes a damned Italian coward!'[7]

Nevertheless there was at first some brave talk at Ruthven of continuing the fight, but then orders arrived from the Prince, directing them to 'shift for themselves'. Destitute of food, ammunition, money and now the will to fight, they dispersed on the 18th.

'At first we had great hopes of rallying again,' said John Daniel, 'but they soon vanished, orders coming for every one to make the best of his way he could. So some went one way, some another: and those who had French Commissions surrendered; and their example was followed by my Colonel, Lord Balmerino, tho' he had none. Many went for the mountains, all being uncertain what to do or whither to go.' One of them was Daniel himself, who stuffed his troop's standard into his coat pocket and set off to an eventual rendezvous with two French ships.[8]

Those officers and men belonging to the *Royal Ecossois* and Fitzjames's Horse who were confident of being treated as prisoners of war, retraced their steps and gave themselves up at Inverness on the 19th, while the others, presumably deserters or other recruits picked up since their regiments came to Scotland, attempted to escape singly. Not all of them made it. Major Hale for example was killed in the sea-fight at Loch nan Uamh. The paymaster, Captain James Hay gave himself up in Edinburgh on the 29th, and a stray trooper of Fitzjames's named Lawrence Clerk turned up in Aberdeen on the 5th of May.[9]

In a final flourish, Lord Ogilvy's Regiment marched off home in a body, by way of Braemar, where Mr Garden, the Minister of Birse, saw them pass through 'some with Arms, many without, some wounded and all in the greatest Confusion' and eventually they disbanded at Clova on the 21st. The two Aberdeenshire battalions on the other hand appear to have been disbanded at the barracks, for Ensign John Martin of Stony-wood's subsequently confessed that: 'he was at Ruthven after the Battle, where there were several hundreds of the Rebels, and that Stonnywood his Commander came and told his People that orders were given that they should all disperse and shift for themselves, and that he saw Stonny-wood tear the Collours from the staff.'[10]

Had the rebellion ended at Ruthven Barracks on the 18th of April, the story of the next few months might have been a very different one. Having decisively beaten the rebels, Cumberland's regiments were urgently needed in Flanders where the French were about to open their summer campaign. Naturally wishing to avoid seeing his men sucked into an open-ended counter-insurgency campaign in the hills, Cumberland halted in Inverness for a month, waiting to see if a general surrender would follow.

In February he had issued a proclamation; 'requiring all common and ordinary People who have borne Arms, and been concern'd in the rebellion, to bring in their Arms to the Magistrate or Minister where the Notice shall reach them, and give in their Name and Place of Abode, and submit themselves to the King's Mercy.'[11] For the most part, those who did so were treated very leniently, although due to a misunderstanding 81 men from Glemoriston and Glen Urquhart who surrendered at Inverness on the 5th of May ended up being transported to Barbados. Generally speaking, however, they were normally left alone, or if brought to trial were acquitted if they could prove that they had surrendered in accordance with the proclamation. These terms were not extended to the rebel officers, but now, in an effort to bring the rebellion to a speedy conclusion, Cumberland may secretly have taken the bold step of putting out secret feelers, offering an amnesty to the leaders as well if they would submit promptly. Surprising though this offer might seem in view of what followed, it is mentioned both by Drummond of Balhaldy (admittedly perhaps not the most reliable of sources) and in a memorial apparently drawn up by Locheil in April 1747, which stated:

'It was at this point that the Duke of Cumberland offered Mr Cameron of Locheil very favourable terms to try to win him over, and it was made known to the other chiefs that the Duke, greatly impressed by their bravery, would use his good offices in their favour if they would only resolve in good faith to lay down their arms. Locheil rejected these overtures with disdain, and none of the chiefs would hear of surrender. On the contrary they were convinced that France would not leave them in the lurch . . .'[12]

175

The promise of French aid had been a recurrent theme throughout the rising, and, apart from Drummond's Regiment and the Picquets, it had invariably proved illusory. Now, however, when it was far too late, two French frigates, the *Mars* and the *Bellona*, nosed into Loch nan Uamh on the 30th of April. On the 2nd of May they were gallantly but unsuccessfully attacked by three Royal Navy sloops, the *Greyhound*, *Baltimore* and *Terror*. After a six-hour battle in the narrow confines of the loch, the three sloops drew off to lick their wounds and the Frenchmen hastily sailed before they could return with reinforcements.[13] On board they carried a number of prominent Jacobite leaders, including the Duke of Perth (who died on the way back to France) his brother Lord John Drummond and Lord Elcho, but behind them on the beach, packed in six casks, they left £35,000 in gold.[14]

Before the arrival of the frigates, Locheil (who was still crippled by his Culloden wounds) and the other chiefs might well have been disposed to respond positively to the offer of an amnesty. But now, with their pockets full of French gold[15], they took the fatal decision to fight on. At a meeting of the remaining Jacobite leaders at Muirlaggan, near the head of Loch Arkaig on the 8th of May; Locheil, Lochgarry, Clanranald and Barisdale all agreed to raise their men once more, bring them to a rendezvous ten days later at Invermallie, and then to join with Keppoch's and Cluny's men in order to resume the campaign.[16] Significantly, in the meantime, Locheil sent a desperate appeal to Cluny, begging for a supply of meal with which to feed his men.

In the end, after having been postponed for a week, it turned into a complete fiasco. Locheil was reported to have brought in about 300 men, but none of Clanranald's people turned up, while Lochgarry and Barisdale raised only about 150 men apiece. Many of Lochgarry's, particularly those from Glen Urquhart and Glenmoriston had already surrendered, and now as soon as he got their arrears of pay, he moved off again in search of food with a vague promise to return in a few days. Barisdale too judged it prudent to make his excuses and left Locheil at Achnacarry. What he may or may not have known was that Fort Augustus had been re-occupied on the 17th of May by three regular battalions – Howard's 3rd (Buffs), Price's 14th, Cholmondley's 34th and eight Highland companies – and that Cluny's MacPhersons surrendered to Loudon on the same day.

Next morning, a body of Highlanders appeared on a nearby hill. Locheil at first supposed them to be Barisdale's men returning as he had promised; 'but he was soon undeceived by some out-scouts he had placed at proper distances who told him these men were certainly Loudon's, for they saw the red crosses in their bonnets.'[17] At this unwelcome news, Locheil at last recognised that the game was up and dispersed his remaining followers without offering resistance. Unfortunately the damage was done and Cumberland himself followed with the greater part of his army a week later, intent on stamping out the last desperate embers of rebellion.

In the weeks which followed, the clans of Lochaber and the Great Glen were subjected to one punitive expedition after another, largely carried out by the Highland Independent Companies, who now that the Jacobite field army was destroyed at last came into their own. In Badenoch and elsewhere in Scotland, however, the process of 'pacification' was much more lenient in character and it is clear, therefore, that much of the responsibility for the sufferings of their clansmen must be borne by Locheil and the other chiefs, for wantonly attempting to prolong the rebellion.

By July the Highlands were as secure as they were ever going to be and Cumberland departed for the south, turning over command of the army in Scotland to Lord Albemarle. Almost all the regular troops had now been withdrawn from the hills: Houghton's 24th (who had sat out the rebellion in Bristol) were in garrison at Fort William, with a rather lonely detachment of ten men under Captain Powell at Bernera, while two Culloden regiments; Blakeney's 27th and Battereau's 62nd, held Inverness. Five more; Handasyde's 16th; Mordaunt's 18th (both newly arrived); Dejean's (formerly Monro's) 37th; Fleming's 36th and Sackville's (formerly Bligh's) 20th; were spread out along the coast between Nairn and Dundee. Two battalions, 2/Royals and Skelton's 12th (also newly arrived) were in garrison at Perth and two more, Price's 14th and Conway's (formerly Ligonier's) 59th, at Stirling. As for the rest, five companies of Barrell's were quartered in Linlithgow and the other five at nearby Bo'ness, the Scots Fusiliers lay at Glasgow, and Lee's 55th remained in Edinburgh.

With the Argyll Militia disbanded this left the Highlands to be policed by Lord Loudon's Regiment and seventeen Highland Independent Companies. These were based at Fort Augustus, but had numerous small detachments scattered throughout Badenoch and as far south as Blair, while the three Additional Companies of the 43rd Highlanders were deployed at Ruthven, Taybridge and Inveraray respectively.[18]

By this time too the prisoners had all gone south to face trial. The limited amount of secure accommodation available in Inverness was soon exhausted and, after the first few days, many of the wounded who were adjudged too badly injured to escape seem to have been farmed out to private houses. Even this expedient – and a high degree of mortality – failed to alleviate the growing problem of overcrowding and the prisoners were first transferred to the transports which had accompanied the army along the coast, and then shipped southwards in the custody of the Vestry Men from Handasyd's 16th and Mordaunt's 18th Foot.[19]

The disposal of these and all the other prisoners taken at one time or another during the rebellion was naturally a very protracted affair, and some individuals were still in custody two years later! As to their eventual fate, some 120 officers and men were executed (including a number of deserters retaken at Culloden), 88 others are known to have died in custody, 936 were transported to the West Indies or to the American colonies, and at least 58 managed to escape by one means or another, including James Miller, a trooper in Bagot's Hussars who calmly walked out of the Edinburgh Tolbooth two days before Culloden dressed in women's clothing.[20]

No fewer than 1,585 of the prisoners were released, conditionally or otherwise, at the end of the day, but the fate of some 700 others is uncertain. A good many of them, particularly the wounded from Culloden, may well have died in prison, and the chances are that over 130 others, detained for the most part on suspicion, were equally casually released. However the majority of those unaccounted for, ironically enough, probably ended up in the ranks of the British army.

On the 31st of July 1746 it was ordered that 250 rebel prisoners were to be sent to Antigua to bring Dalzell's long-suffering 38th Foot back up to strength, 100 more were similarly to go to Trelawney's 63rd in Jamaica, and 200 each to Shirley's 65th and Pepperell's 66th at Cape Breton. Then, in June 1747, at least two of the twelve Independent Companies being raised for Boscawen's expedition against Pondicherry in far-off India, were also ordered to be recruited from Jacobite prisoners. The extent to which these various quotas were actually filled at the end of the day is uncertain although the numbers of men thus enlisted clearly exceeded the 65 identified by Seton and Arnot.[21]

Many of those who got away also, perforce, had to go as a soldier but in the French Service. Colonel John Sullivan, his reputation undiminished in that quarter at least, was again employed as a staff officer and is known to have been with the French Army at Lauffeldt in 1747, when Marechal Saxe fought Cumberland to a bloody draw. James Johnstone too, having made his escape, served on General Montcalm's staff at Quebec in 1759 and thus had the rather unusual, if decidedly dubious, experience of fighting on the losing side in two of the British army's most famous 18th-century victories.

If the second battalion of Drummond's *Royal Ecossois* was ever formed in the first place, it was disbanded after the rebellion. Instead, two new Scottish regiments were raised; one commanded by Lord Ogilvy and the other, the Regiment *d'Albany*, raised for Prince Charles himself and given to Locheil in partial recompense for his financial losses. The Regiment *d'Albany* never saw action and, with the Prince banished from France, it was disbanded in 1748. The *Royal Ecossois* and the Regiment *d'Ogilvy* however still soldiered on until 1763, providing useful employment for a considerable number of Jacobite refugees. John Daniel, despite being court-martialled on the beach for his enterprising but unsuccessful attempt to steal some of the gold landed at Loch nan Uamh, served as a Captain in Ogilvy's Regiment, and another of its officers was John Cameron, the sometime Presbyterian minister who furnished Robert Forbes with material on Culloden and afterwards for *The Lyon in Mourning*.

Perhaps one of the better known members of the Regiment *d'Ogilvy* was Alan Breck Stuart, generally held to have been the murderer of Colin Campbell of Glenure.[22] The man actually hanged for the deed was one James Stewart 'of the Glens', and in one of history's odd little ironies the prosecuting counsel in the case was none other than Simon Fraser, sometime Master of Lovat and once a Colonel in the Jacobite Army!

Simon Fraser had inherited all his father's slippery character and his speedy rehabilitation in the eyes of the authorities was nothing short of astonishing. Ostensibly it was managed through the interest of the Duke of Argyll, but one cannot help feel that some of his actions on the 16th of April were equivocal to say the least. At any rate, having thus decisively declared for the Government, Simon went on to raise a Highland regiment which he led at Quebec in 1759. Significantly, a considerable number of the officers and men serving in Fraser's Highlanders, were, like their 'hard and rapacious' Colonel, former rebel soldiers from the Jacobite heartland in the Great Glen. Now they had made their peace with the government and, where once upon a time bold young men would have sought service abroad in the mercenary regiments of Holland, France and Sweden, now, increasingly they turned to the British army instead and made it their own.

In 1747 the Chiefs' heritable powers of 'Pit and Gallows' were taken away from them. No longer were they able to rule their people in a despotic manner and pull them out, willingly or otherwise, on to the heather. This measure, it is said, by destroying the paternalistic attachment of the Chief to his clansmen, eventually paved the way for the Clearances, but it was the people themselves who first took the initiative and the years which followed the '45 were characterised above all by a growing independence on the part of many Highlanders. Freed of the dead hand of their Chieftains they sought their own destiny. To the impotent fury and despair of those who had once held the power of life and death over them, they turned their backs on their old masters and emigrated in their thousands, seeking a better life in the Americas, or taking service with the mighty East India Company. Indeed, by the early 1800s, the Company was widely regarded as a Scottish mafia and one of its most influential directors, Charles Grant, was the son of a clansman from Glen Urquhart who stood in the ranks of Glengarry's Regiment at Culloden. The bitter pain of the 19th-century Clearances might capture the imagination and rightly excite indignation, but by then far more people had already left the Highlands of their own free will than were ever evicted by force.

While the Highlands certainly changed after Culloden, it was a gradual process which had begun long before the Prince stepped ashore, and it is questionable whether the terrible defeat of some of the Highland clans there did much to hasten that change. It is perhaps all too easy to draw a direct link between Culloden and the infamous Highland Clearances, and the sad fact is that economic pressures upon the chiefs-turned-landlords would have still brought about the Clearances had the battle never been fought.

There have been far too many 'ifs' and romantic conjectures as to what might have happened if events had turned out differently, and perhaps the last word on the matter should be left to John Murray of Broughton: 'The Actions of Gladsmuir (Prestonpans) Cliftonmoor, Falkirk, and Culloden, are fought over at every Tea Table, with so much address and Gallantry and with such substantial and solid remarks upon the bad Conduct of our Leaders; that some of both Sexes seldom or never fail to convince the Rest of the Company of their Military genius, and occasions a full and ample Declaration of their Sincere regret that her Ladyship had not the Command, concluding with what pity it was that, this and t'other, had not been done, for sure never was anything more obvious and easy.

'The Castle of Edinburgh is starved before the punch Bowl is empty. The Batteries against Stirling erected anew, and the Garrison made Prisoners of War by the time it is replenish'd.

'The Prince and Council are perswaded to wait Cumberland's Approach at Bannockburn, and taught how to rout his Army whilest the fine Lady sips her Hyson; and the passage of the Spey pronounced impracticable with a look of Scorn and flirt of the Fan.

'A parcel of Antiquated Attorneys, with the help of a black Gentleman in a gown and Cassock, will march us to Derby, from thence make our way straight and easy to the Capitall, render the March of the Enemy impossible, rouse the Sleeping English, seize the Treasury, make the two Armys under Cumberland and Wade disband, their Officers sue for Pardon, and the Fleet send their Submission, erect Triumphall Arches, and make the Mayor and Aldermen meet us with the Regalia of the City, which with their Charter returnd, and protection promised, compleat the Cavalcade to St. James's.'[23]

Sources:

1. Murray (16th May), p. 315–6.
2. Chambers *History of the Rebellion* pp. 300, 311. The Master's conduct on the 16th of April was decidedly ambiguous. On the whole it seems unlikely that he actually fought at Culloden, but there is a tradition that he and his men were seen on the bridge over the river Ness, proclaiming their intention to defend it. Again there seems no reason to doubt it but it may reasonably be questioned whether it was their intention to hold it against the British army, or against their fellow Jacobites. As it happens there is also a strange story that some of the Argyllshire men infiltrated the town to seize the bridge and close it against the fugitives. Moreover, Captain Johnstone [p139] recalled hearing 'a brisk firing in the town which lasted a few minutes.' Putting two and two together it looks very much as if the Master changed sides, or at least tried to on the afternoon of the 16th of April. At any rate it is hard otherwise to account for his freedom from prosecution and an amazing rehabilitation which saw him die as a Member of Parliament and a Major General in the British army.
3. Chambers *Jacobite Memoirs*, p. 298.
4. Murray, p. 129. 'An officer of our army had got a corps new raised, and they were very ill- clothed. What possessed him, I cannot tell; but a complaint was brought to me, that he and his men were stripping the prisoners in the church of their coats, to clothe his own men. I immediately went to the Prince, and an order was sent to stop it. Before the order came, they had got off most of the coats; but they were all immediately returned. This was a week before the battle of Culloden.' Although Murray does not identify the officer concerned, it seems clear from the reference to his regiment being 'new raised', that he must have been Lord Kilmarnock.
5. *Newcastle Journal*. This was the same officer who described how Cumberland galloped over to Cobham's and ordered them to charge the rebel left flank. Presumably therefore he was an officer in that regiment.
6. *Orderly Book of Lord Ogilvy's Regiment.*
7. There are various versions of this exchange, and denials that it ever took place, but see Alice Wemyss' comments IN Scott-Moncrieff, p. 98.
8. *Origins*, p. 216. The standard, 'a curious fine' one taken from Gardiner's Dragoons at Falkirk was subsequently lost when the coat was stolen by two stragglers from the Picquets. Oddly enough it may be possible to identify them, for a Joseph Boes of the *Royal Ecossois* and a William Boes of the Regiment Rooth, two brothers from Westmeath, who had deserted before Culloden, were picked up in Moidart in June 1746. ·
9. Hay was initially sentenced to death as a rebel, but eventually repatriated as a French prisoner of war. Clerk's fate is unknown, although he does not appear in a list of prisoners held in Aberdeen on the 16th of May. (Allardyce p. 253–9)
10. Allardyce, p. 247.
11. *London Gazette*: the proclamation was actually issued at Montrose on the 24th of February 1746.
12. Gibson, *Locheil*, p. 174. Authorship of the memorandum has also been attributed in the past to Lord John Drummond.
13. A useful account of the action can be found in Gibson's *Ships of the '45*, p. 36–41.

14. One of the casks containing the gold was promptly stolen by John Daniel and an unnamed Irishman. A drumhead court-martial followed, but both were released after Daniel revealed to a priest where they had hidden the loot. Daniel himself glosses over the incident (*Origins* p.221–2) but a more factual account is to be found in Chambers *History of the Rebellion*, p. 522–3.

15. Some of the gold was divided out amongst the commanding officers by way of pay for those men wounded at Culloden and for the widows of the dead. Lists were apparently drawn up, of which only that prepared by Ardshiel survives (Rosebery & McLeod p. 383–5) showing that his battalion lost 90 killed and 65 wounded.

16. Broughton, *Memorials*, pp. 275–277. *Lyon in Mourning*, p. 88.

17. *Lyon in Mourning* op.cit. Those Highland Independent Companies lacking uniforms had a red saltire badge pinned to their bonnets.

18. Terry, C.S. (Ed.) *Albemarle Papers*, p. 202–3.

19. Ibid. p. 206.

20. Sir Bruce Gordon Seton and Jean Gordon Seton's *Prisoners of the '45* is quite invaluable, but does need to be treated with some considerable care. In the first place it appears to be far from complete as it includes only a small minority of the 'French' prisoners, and omits the names of a considerable number of those known from other sources to have been taken prisoner at Culloden. On the other hand at least 50 out of the 3,471 names appear twice (albeit with varying spelling) and 310 men, women and children are clearly civil prisoners, or were picked up on suspicion. Some indeed had no discernible connection with the rebellion, but merely happened to be locked up at the time.

21. Atkinson, pp. 296, 297.

22. Stewart seems to have been a rather unprepossessing character and Stevenson's fictional character is actually based on Colonel John Roy Stuart, once captain of grenadiers in the *Royal Ecossois*.

23. Broughton, p. 257.

APPENDIX 1

The British Army

At the outbreak of the rebellion in the summer of 1745, the British army comprised 66 regiments of the line and 22 regiments of cavalry besides the Footguards and other Household troops, although a very considerable proportion of them were serving overseas.

Its ranks were for the most part filled by voluntary enlistment. In the middle of the 18th century, the coming Industrial Revolution and the coincidental unemployment created by contemporary agrarian reform had not yet swelled the ranks of the urban poor to any great degree and most recruits were still countrymen or discontented tradesmen picked up at markets or hiring fairs. The Duke of Argyll, it is true, claimed in 1740 that they were for the most part men who were 'too stupid or too infamous to learn or carry on a Trade', but their recorded behaviour rarely bears out the frequently expressed contention that the army was the last refuge of the desperate and the criminal classes.

Even so, the written instructions issued to recruiting parties invariably warned them against enlisting Roman Catholics (technically quite illegal though often winked at), foreigners, boys, old men, idiots, the ruptured and the lame. Besides these rather obvious categories of undesirables, there was also a certain and quite understandable reluctance on the part of most recruiting officers to entertain 'strollers, vagabonds, and tinkers'. This was a great pity since these individuals were of course exactly the sort of *mauvais sujets* whom the local magistrates were all too keen to dump on the army. Indeed the instructions issued to recruiters for the 93rd Foot in early 1760,[1] ruled that they should only take such men 'as were born in the Neighbourhood of the place they are Inlisted in, & of whom you can get and give a good Account.'

Agricultural labourers might predominate, but those enlisting in the army also included, to give just some examples; substantial numbers of tailors and other clothworkers, carpenters, gardeners, shoemakers, together with the occasional mason, tobacconist, brickmaker or butcher. There might well be some regional and seasonal variations on this particular sample, taken from a 1775 company roll,[2] and the high preponderance of agricultural labourers might perhaps also be explained by the inevitable laying off of casual workers after the harvest.

However, not all of the recruits gathered into the ranks of the infantry during the last Jacobite Rising were willing volunteers. Two Acts were to be hastily rushed through Parliament in 1745, encouraging magistrates to impress all 'able-bodied men who do not follow or exercise any lawful calling or employment' and 'all such able-bodied, idle and disorderly persons who cannot upon examination prove themselves to exercise and industriously follow some lawful trade or employment, or to have some substance sufficient for their support and maintenance.'

For each reluctant recruit thus delivered up to the army, the parish officers received the not inconsiderable reward of £1 sterling and a further £3 was also paid at the same time into the vestry account. In theory this sum was intended to provide for the upkeep of any dependants left behind as a burden on the parish, but by way of an incentive to voluntary enlistment the whole of the £4 was payable directly to the man concerned if he managed to offer his services to a recruiting party before the sexton and his mates got their hands on him.

This measure was a typically inept politician's response to a crisis, and these 'Vestry Men' were probably more of a liability than an asset to the army, since both Acts also very considerately provided that unless regularly enlisted, they were entitled to be discharged again within six months, or at the end of the rebellion. Not surprisingly the regimental returns for the battalions still quartered in Scotland in September and October 1746 show that those Vestry Men who had not already been discharged by their units were employed in the undemanding and unpopular job of prisoner handling[3] – and a brutal job they seem to have made of it.

A rather more positive move was to be the temporary brigading of 'Additional' or depot companies into provisional battalions, and the authorisation of the raising of Provincial regiments, again for the duration of the emergency. Officially these would comprise the 67th to 79th Regiments of Foot, and the 9th and 10th Regiments of Horse, all raised in England. Of limited value, both the provisional battalions and Provincial units were normally employed in garrison duties, releasing the better trained regulars for service in the field. Similar units, which saw rather more action, were raised in Edinburgh, Glasgow and Argyllshire although they were not allocated numbers, and both north and south of the border a considerable number of loyalist volunteer units of generally dubious military value also appeared.

While the role played in the suppression of the rebellion by the Argyll Militia, at least, and particularly at Culloden, is well known, one other category of British soldier needs to be described if only because he is all too often forgotten: the Invalid. As their designation implies Invalids were old soldiers, worn out or crippled by wounds or disease. Generally unfit for active service they were employed instead as the permanent garrisons of forts and castles. Although occasionally denounced as 'useless', or 'old and decrepit' some of them were to prove a lot tougher and more resolute than they looked.

Ideally, training ought to have occupied a good deal of a regiment's time, particularly since most units saw a very brisk turnover in personnel. Unfortunately, it was very rare for a regiment to be fully recruited up to its authorised strength at the best of times. Units returning from overseas were virtually at skeleton strength and frequently had to be built up almost from scratch. Even then there was no certainty that they could hang on to their new recruits since other battalions suddenly ordered overseas before they were ready might be authorised to bring themselves up to strength by taking drafts of men from those units remaining at home.

There was, therefore, a constant need to recruit men and to conduct intensive training at every level within a regiment, but in practice it was often surprisingly difficult to find that time, or even for that matter the space in which to conduct it. Most regiments tended to be widely dispersed in peacetime. Each year for example a whole battalion was scattered across the length and breadth of the Highlands manning the various forts and police posts. Otherwise the lack of proper barracks meant that units had to be accommodated in civilian billets which again necessitated considerable dispersion and a consequent falling off in military efficiency.

The problem was obviously even more acute for cavalry regiments. Not only did they require larger quarters since not only the trooper but his horse had to be accommodated and so they were consequently even more scattered than their pedestrian counterparts, but the nature of their peacetime duties also generally saw a wider dispersion of regiments in tiny detachments, serving as a rural constabulary or as a back up for the overstretched customs service. As if this were not enough, in the summer months it was also the practice wherever possible to put the horses out to grass and train the otherwise idle troopers in the infantry platoon exercise.[4]

Assuming that an infantry battalion was sufficiently concentrated to permit such exercises – and this was seldom the case in peacetime with companies dispersed in billets over a wide area – some three to four hundred odd rank and file (the average strength of the battalions at Culloden) required a field 200 yards broad simply in order to be able to draw up in a straight line, let alone to find enough room in which to carry out their required repertoire of manoeuvres. Consequently, although small arms drill – the 'manual exercise' as it was referred to – was generally practised to a high standard, the overall level of training in many units was often quite abysmal. In one of his more vitriolic

outbursts, James Wolfe, a brigade major at Culloden and later the cele-
brated, albeit posthumous, conqueror of Quebec, wrote;

> 'I have but a very mean opinion of the infantry in general. I know their
> discipline to be bad, & their valour precarious. They are easily put into
> disorder, & hard to recover out of it; they frequently kill their Officers
> thro' fear, & murder one another in their confusion . . .' [5]

Although Wolfe was a notably efficient battalion commander in his time,
he was also prone to these ascerbic outbursts and as ever the standard
of training actually depended very much on the quality and professional-
ism of the officers serving in a particular regiment.

The British army's officers came from a wide variety of backgrounds
in the 18th century, but by and large it was only the aristocrats and
landed gentry who made it to the very top. They had both the money
to purchase promotion and, much more importantly, the 'interest', that
is they could rely upon patronage and the influence of friends and
relations to facilitate their upward progress.

By far the greater number of ordinary regimental officers, however,
were simply 'private gentlemen' (always a rather elastic term in the 18th
century) generally of good family, but seldom possessed of very much
in the way of either money or prospects. They belonged in short to what
are now regarded as the middle classes, rather than the aristocracy. Not
unnaturally, a substantial number of them were themselves the sons
of army officers, but clergymen, doctors and other professionals and
substantial tradesmen also contributed their sons as well. A quite dispro-
portionate number of officers, perhaps at times as many as a third, were
Scots, and Anglo-Irishmen were nearly as common.

Finally, a far from negligible group of officers were promoted rankers,
given free commissions in recognition of their ability, or exceptional
service. An Ensign Wilson, who testified at the inquiry into Cope's
debacle at Prestonpans, had actually taken part in the battle as Sergeant
Major of Lee's 55th Foot, and Lieutenant Terence Molloy of the same
regiment was made up from Sergeant after his successful defence of
Ruthven Barracks shortly before. Frequently such officers were employed
as Adjutants, since they obviously knew the workings of the army inside
out, but some, like Molloy, did occasionally serve as line officers and in
time they often obtained commissions for their own sons.

Such promotions almost invariably occurred in wartime, especially
when a regiment was being raised from scratch, and consequently in
desperate need of experienced officers. In peacetime, the majority of
officers' commissions were purchased, though it is hard to say what the
true cost actually was to the individual. Although there was an officially
regulated scale, prices of commissions sometimes varied from regiment

to regiment, but the actual sums which changed hands often tended in practice to be less than a superficial perusal of the official scales might suggest.

An officer named Samuel Bagshawe explained it thus in a memorandum written sometime in 1742:

'... When a Capt. has leave to quitt the Service & dispose of his Commission 'tis generally done in this manner, the Lieutenant recommended either gives him his [own] Commission and the difference between the Commissions of a Capt. & Lt. or a certain sum of money in which last case the Lt. has the disposing of his own Commission which if sold to an Ensign, that Ensign acts in the same way that is, gives the Lieutenant his Ensign's Commission and the difference or else a certain Sume & sells the Colours himself, So that the price of a Captain's Commission is either a certain Sume, or is compos'd of the difference between a Capt. and a Lieutenant's Commission, the difference between a Lieutenancy and a pair of Colours & the Colours. Now suppose a Company is dispos'd of in this last way & sold for eleven hundred pounds the Case stands thus

The Difference between the Captains & theLt's Commission £600
The Diff. between ye Lieutenancy & ye Colours £100
The Colours £400
£1100[6]

Once the initial investment had been made in an Ensign's commission (and of course in the cost of his not inconsiderable kit) it was relatively easy subsequently to obtain promotion to Lieutenant, although a Captaincy and the command of a company which came with it was rather more difficult, unless ready money was at hand to purchase the 'step' or a non-purchase vacancy appeared.

Not all commissions however were purchased. If an officer died in harness, or was dismissed from the service by the sentence of a court-martial, his successor, normally the most senior officer in the rank below, stepped into his boots gratis. Although further promotion was certainly not barred to the holders of free commissions (whatever their source), it was much more difficult for them subsequently to proceed up the ladder as they generally could not offset the value of their commission against the cost of the next step. Nevertheless, meritorious officers could and did rise quite high in their profession, presumably because their commanding officers ensured that they stepped into any non-purchase vacancies which might arise.

The purchase system has traditionally been attacked as a wholly bad practice which denied promotion to those deserving officers who lacked the necessary cash, but in fact it is remarkable how well it actually worked. To the politicians the great virtue of the purchase system was that it was self-financing, and just as importantly it kept the army firmly in the hands of 'men of family and fortune' who might be relied upon to preserve liberty and property, rather than in the grubby hands of unreliable 'mercenaries' who might be rather more prone to destroying or making off with it.

Not surprisingly, most officers advanced fairly slowly in peacetime and on average it seems to have taken about ten years to achieve promotion to Captain and thus to take command of a company or troop. Indeed during the long peace which followed Queen Anne's War and the Jacobite Rising of 1715, there was considerable stagnation, and most of those officers 'in post' in 1740, just before the war, had taken nearly twice as long to climb each rung of the ladder.[7] The outbreak of war with France shortly afterwards did speed up the rate of promotion, especially in newly raised regiments, but there were still some very old officers around in 1745, like John Crosbie who had been a Captain in Campbell's 21st (Scots Fuziliers) for twenty-one years, and whose first commission was dated 1st of March 1704.

At the end of his service an officer would normally provide for his retirement by selling his commission and acquiring an annuity with the proceeds. In order to do this he normally needed to have purchased his commission in the first place, but holders of non-purchase commissions could be permitted to sell after twenty years' service.

The alternative was to exchange on to the Half-Pay list. This pension had originally been granted as a concession to the officers of disbanded regiments since it would clearly be impossible for them to recover their original investment by finding buyers for their now empty commissions. However, if an officer from a disbanded regiment still wished to stay on the active list there was nothing whatever to prevent his exchanging with an officer in a standing regiment who wished to retire, but for one reason or another could not find a suitable buyer for his commission. As for the holder of a non-purchase commission, since he could not normally sell it, he had no guarantee of a pension but it was generally found expedient to transfer a retiring officer on to the Half-Pay list of a long defunct regiment thus leaving behind a non-purchase vacancy in his original corps which could be filled by another deserving but impecunious young man.

Artillery officers on the other hand were in some measure a law unto themselves since they came under the control of the Board of Ordnance rather than the Horse Guards. This distinction was very pointedly emphasised by their wearing of dark blue uniforms rather than the red ones traditionally worn by the rest of the army. Moreover, since their branch of the service naturally demanded a certain level of technical competence somewhat above that commonly required of infantry and cavalry officers, commissions could not be purchased. Instead, an aspiring gunner had first to join the Royal Regiment of Artillery as a cadet and learn the , intricacies of his craft before being let loose on the world. Once he did reach commissioned rank, promotion came strictly by seniority and was in consequence ponderously slow.

INFANTRY

Ordinarily a regular infantry regiment comprised ten companies with an average strength of around 30 to 40 soldiers apiece, besides the officers, sergeants and drummers, making up something over 300 or 400 men in total. One of the companies was the grenadier company and the others were officially termed battalion companies. However this being a rather clumsy term the soldiers belonging to these companies were colloquially referred to as 'hatmen' to distinguish them from the mitre-capped grenadiers. Except in newly raised units, the grenadiers were not as is often said selected from the tallest and strongest men in a battalion but rather were formed of the older and steadier men who could be relied upon in a crisis.

Three of the ordinary, or so-called battalion companies were notionally commanded by what were called field officers. The senior of these was the Colonel himself, who gave his name to the regiment and was often a General officer and not infrequently aged and infirm. He was in consequence rarely to be seen with his regiment and for example only four out of fifteen regular battalions at Culloden were to be led by their Colonel in person. In practice most units tended to be commanded on a day to day basis by his deputy, the Lieutenant Colonel, or even by the Major. The latter, assisted by the Adjutant, was also particularly responsible for the regiment's training and discipline.

The seven remaining companies (including the grenadiers) were commanded by Captains, each of them, like the field officers, assisted by a Lieutenant and an Ensign, except for the grenadiers who had a second Lieutenant instead of the Ensign, since a greater degree of self reliance was expected of that company. Because the Colonel, whether he was actually present or not, generally had rather more important things to worry about, his own company was actually commanded by the regiment's senior Lieutenant. For his not inconsiderable pains this officer received the curious title of 'Captain-Lieutenant', but was addressed and treated as if he were a Captain in almost every particular except his pay.

Companies were merely administrative sub-units and the tactical organisation of infantry units, that is the manner in which they were actually arranged for fighting, was quite different. Just how they were organised depended both on the strength of the individual battalion, and to some extent on the particular system of drill favoured by the Colonel.

Most regiments conducted themselves more or less in accordance with the King's regulations of 1728, which were in turn largely cribbed from Humphrey Bland's 'Treatise of Military Discipline', first published in the previous year and going through nine editions until 1762. These regulations were however complicated and consequently very much open to individual interpretation. Many units simplified them or developed what became known as 'traditional manoeuvres', and indeed as late as 1782 the satirical 'Advice to the Officers of the British army' cheerfully recommended to Colonels: 'When promoted to the command of a regiment from some other corps, show them that they were all in the dark before, and overturning their whole routine of discipline, introduce another as different as possible.'[8]

Nevertheless the basic principles were essentially retained. When preparing for action (usually at least the night before, rather than on the day itself) the whole battalion was lined up in three ranks and the men evenly told off into platoons by the Major and his faithful assistant, the Adjutant – around thirty men apiece being reckoned by Bland to be about the minimum required for each platoon. These platoons were at the same time numbered off and allocated to 'Firings', of which there were normally three, besides a reserve.

The grenadier company, however, formed no part of the 'Firings', but was instead itself divided into two small platoons, one of which was posted out on each flank of the battalion to act independently as circumstances required.

The reason for this rather complicated arrangement was to permit the employment of what was called 'Platoon Firing', a system which in theory allowed an infantry battalion to maintain a steady and effective fire in battle, but which in practice all too often broke down with frightening rapidity.

All infantrymen were armed with the Land Pattern firelock, a fairly sturdy muzzle-loading weapon with a 46" long barrel, to which a 17" long bayonet was invariably fitted in action. It fired a .75 calibre (12 bore) soft lead ball weighing one and one third ounces, which produced a terrible wound. A well-trained individual could comfortably fire his weapon twice in a minute, and in extremis might manage to do even better over short periods. It was reasonably accurate in the hands of a good shot up to fifty yards or so, but could still be effective beyond that distance against the massed targets provided by infantry battalions or cavalry regiments. It is easy to compare it unfavourably with more modern weapons, but the fact remains that almost all battles of the period were decided one way or another by the application of infantry firepower, rather than by the somewhat overrated qualities of cold steel.

Should every man in a battalion discharge his firelock at the enemy upon a single word of command, the effect might be suitably devastating. On the other hand, if the immediate results were less than impressive – and the great Marechal Saxe acidly commented that he had seen battalion volleys which killed no more than four men – then that battalion was clearly going to be in deep trouble if the enemy continued to advance while they frantically reloaded their firelocks. Platoon firing was intended to obviate such a danger.

When the decision was taken to open fire, normally well within a hundred yards of the enemy (General Hawley reckoned in 1746 that sixty yards was a 'large Musket shot'), the three ranks were tightly locked up, that is the front rank went down on one knee, the second rank closed up and moved half a pace to the right, in order to aim his firelock through the gap between the front rank men and his neighbour, while the soldier in third rank closed up and moved a full pace to his right, aiming his firelock over the head of the front rank man in the neighbouring file.

On the word of command actually being given to open fire, only the various platoons scattered up and down the line belonging to the first 'firing' initially did so, either all together or in a sequenced ripple. As soon as they had fired, the platoons of the second firing then blasted off their own volleys and so on until by the time the platoons of the third 'firings' had discharged their weapons in the general direction of the enemy, the platoons of the first 'firing' had reloaded and were ready to begin the cycle again.

Such at least was the theory. In practice it was usually difficult to control and rarely so neatly done. More often than not after the first couple of volleys had been fired in their proper sequence, each platoon and ultimately, if the firefight lasted long enough, each individual soldier usually ended up loading and firing as fast as possible without much regard to precedence. Consequently fire control could normally only be effectively maintained by platoon commanders simply directing their men to fire a given number of rounds at the enemy. Even Humphrey Bland, whose 'Treatise of Military Discipline' formed the basis for these drills, recognised that controlled Platoon Fire was something that British soldiers were only 'With difficulty brought to, from a natural Desire and Eagerness to enter soon into Action,' and as one account of the battle of Dettingen in 1743 recalled;

> 'They were under no command by way of Hyde Park firing, but the whole three ranks made a running fire of their own accord, and at the same time with great judgement and skill stooping as low as they could, making almost every ball take place.' [9]

Perhaps paradoxically the lack of proper training facilities may actually have helped to develop the effectiveness of British infantry firepower.

Unable to practise large scale drills and evolutions to any great extent the training was perforce concentrated on individual weapon-handling skills. As a result their ability to manoeuvre may not have been very good, but in a firefight this emphasis gave them a real edge throughout the 18th century.

Firepower normally decided the outcome of conventional battles but if cold steel was called for it was almost always the bayonet, rather than the soldier's largely decorative sword or hanger, which was used. Even so its effects were still generally more psychological than real. It comprised a 17″ long triangular blade affixed to an iron tube which slotted over the muzzle of the firelock. The blade was offset to the right and slightly angled outwards so that the weapon could still be loaded and fired after the bayonet was locked on. It was not, therefore, a particularly handy weapon and its usefulness was also significantly undermined by its usual loose fit on the end of the barrel.

Contemporary bayonet fighting drills were very largely defensive in nature and reflected and stressed the need for soldiers to act in concert rather than individually. Essentially, they were no more than an adaptation of the old pike fighting drills employed in the Great Civil War of a hundred years before.

On the command being given to 'Charge your Bayonets breast high', the soldier took a half turn to his right and levelled his firelock breast high, with the point of balance resting in his left hand, up under the chin and his right hand grasping the butt. On the further command 'Push your Bayonets', he did just that; stamping forward in unison with his comrades on either side and thrusting the firelock forward by means of a vigorous push with the right hand. A barking shout was naturally a recommended accompaniment to this rather impressive movement.

Clearly this style of bayonet fighting was best suited to a static position although it is possible to undertake a slow and steady advance. Not until the late 1750s would the bayonet be levelled waist high, permitting the more rapid advance into a bayonet charge which to some extent was be the trademark of the British regular during the American War.

CAVALRY

In 1745 the British army had two types of cavalry besides the Household troops; Horse and Dragoons. The first category was originally formed in the 17th century as heavy battle cavalry. They were big men on big horses trained as shock troops in much the same manner as Napoleon's later *cuirassiers*. Dragoons had originally been no more than mounted infantry riding cheap nags, but faced with the choice of being both second-rate cavalrymen and second-rate infantrymen, they not surprisingly elected to become cavalrymen first and foremost. Nevertheless in 1745 they were still equipped for their original role and trained both for mounted action and in the 1728 infantry platoon exercise.

All cavalrymen were very heavily armed, perhaps too heavily armed. Each soldier carried a basket-hilted broadsword which was not so very different from the weapon carried by many Highlanders, and a very solid pair of pistols. Both broadsword and pistols could be used on horseback according to circumstances, although contemporary tactical doctrines, in the British army at least, preached reliance on the sword alone. In addition the Dragoon also carried a firelock strapped to his saddle, and a bayonet at his belt, in case he should be called upon to fight on foot. Except for a .65 bore and having a 42" barrel it was virtually identical to the firelock carried by infantrymen. troopers of Horse on the other hand had a fairly large carbine, but no bayonet.

The battlefield organisation and tactical handling of the cavalry was rather more straightforward than that of the infantry. Normally a cavalry regiment comprised six troops, each being the equivalent of an infantry company. Depending upon the number of men actually available, two or occasionally three troops were normally banded together to make up a squadron, which would be commanded either by one of the field officers or by the senior captain.

There was however a fair bit of flexibility in this regard with the British cavalry at Prestonpans and Falkirk being drawn up in squadrons, but for the most part fighting in individual Troops at Culloden. Again, while an infantry regiment would invariably be drawn up in one three-deep line, a cavalry regiment normally tried to have two squadrons up and one in reserve with sufficient intervals left between the Troops or Squadrons in order to to allow fresh reinforcements to come up into the front line, or permit blown ones to retire and rally behind the second line.

ARTILLERY

A fairly wide variety of guns were employed by the Royal Artillery during the 1745 campaign, ranging from 18lb siege pieces to obsolete little one and a half pounder battalion guns intended to give close support to infantry units. Some considerable use was also made of mortars. In general the artillery trains were decidedly light by continental standards but this was pretty largely a reflection of the state of Scotland's roads rather than a commentary on the condition of the Royal Artillery.

The mortars, of which there were two varieties, the Royal and the rather lighter Coehorn, were stubby bronze pots set in solid wooden blocks and lobbed spherical explosive shells or 'bombs'. Looking remarkably like those wielded by cartoon anarchists, these bombshells can have had only a limited effect in the field since the mortar was designed to provide indirect fire, dropping the shells over walls to explode in confined, built-up spaces.

Far more effective were the light battalion guns firing either one and a half pound, or three pound, solid iron roundshot. They were capable of firing two or three rounds every minute, but unlike modern artillery rounds these did not explode on impact but instead skipped and bounced rather like a flat stone skimming across a pond, smashing anything and everything in their path. On soft ground, however, they tended to bury themselves and did not bounce so far. At close range, (say about 300 yards) the gunners switched from ball to case or cartridge shot. This was a linen or even a paper bag, tightly packed with musket balls which burst on firing, turning each cannon into a huge shotgun with murderous effect.

Until the climactic battle of Culloden the artillery, as we shall see, had little chance to make its presence felt except in siege work. At Prestonpans, Sir John Cope had no proper gun crews, being forced to rely instead upon an unreliable collection of volunteers, seamen and Invalids, while at Falkirk the artillery never came into action at all. At Culloden however it was to be a different matter entirely. Important though the artillery's role in that battle may have been, in the end it still came down to the regiments of infantry and cavalry to win it.

Sources:

1. Bagshawe, p. 210–212.
2. Actually for Captain Hamilton Maxwell's company, raised in Banffshire for the 71st Highlanders. SEE J.M.Bulloch's *Territorial Soldiering in North-East Scotland*, p. 34–5.
3. SP Scot, 34/19 & 34.
4. SEE Houlding *Fit For Service* for a very thorough discussion of this.
5. Houlding, p. vii.
6. Bagshawe, p. 97.
7. Houlding, p. 108–110.
8. *Advice*, p. 27.
9. Houlding, p. 351.

British Casualties at Culloden

Regiment	Killed	Wounded
2/Royals	0	4
Howard's	1	2
Barrell's	17	108
Wolfe's	0	1
Pulteney's	0	0
Price's	1	9
Bligh's	4	17
Campbell's	0	7
Sempill's	1	13
Blakeney's	0	0
Cholmondley's	1	2
Fleming's	0	6
Monro's	14	68
Ligonier's	1	5
Battereau's	0	3
Loudon's	6	3
Argyll Militia	0	1
Royal Artillery	0	6
Kingston's Horse	0	1
Cobham's Dragoons	1	0
Kerr's Dragoons	3	3
Horses:		
Kingston's	2	1
Cobham's	4	5
Kerr's	4	15

The above figures are inclusive of officers, and a fair number of those returned as wounded are known to have subsequently died. The names of casualties given below are taken from the London Gazette, the Chelsea Hospital Registers (WO.120) and the pay-rolls for Captain-Lieutenant John Godwin's Artillery Company (WO.10/28–34).

Royals
Alexander Buchannan disabled in left leg
John Reynolds wounded in left knee
John Ross disabled by a rupture at Culloden

Howard's (3rd)
Charles Appleton disabled in right hand

Barrell's (4th)
Lieutenant Colonel Robert Rich wounded
Captain Lord Robert Kerr killed
Captain John Romer wounded
Lieutenant James Edmonds wounded
Ensign John Browne wounded
Ensign James Campbell wounded
Corporal John Adams lost the use of his right hand
Corporal John Griffith lost the use of his left leg
William Alexander wounded at Culloden
Thomas Appleton lost the use of his left arm
David Bairnsfather wounded in the right leg
Peter Burford disabled in his left hand
James Buttler lost his left arm
Matthew Chappington lost the use of his right arm
Simon Crocker lost the use of his right hand
John Dills unfit for service by wounds received at Culloden
David Drenan disabled in the right thigh
John Fawcett wounded at Culloden
Thomas Harris wounded in the left leg
John Hobbs wounded at Culloden
Samuel Hunt wounded in the head and right hand
Ralph Jackson disabled in his left hand
John Jenkins lost the use of his left arm
Thomas Kelly lost the use of his left leg
Thomas Knight disabled in the right leg
John Lee lost his right arm
David Lotty shot through the right arm
John Low shot through the left leg and thigh
John Messenger wounded at Culloden
Isaac Midgely disabled in the left hand at Culloden besides 14 more wounds
Thomas Pritchard wounded at Culloden
Jonathan Scoon wounded in the head
John Telford wounded at Culloden

John Tinlims disabled in his right hand and shoulder
George Webb shot through the left arm

Wolfe's (8th)
Ensign Robert Bruce wounded

Price's (14th)
Captain Alexander Grossett murdered, probably in mistake for his brother Walter Grossett
Captain Andrew Simpson wounded
Richard Dennison lost his left leg
John Ross wounded in the right ankle
Mark Berry lost his right leg

Bligh's (20th)
Lieutenant Trapaud wounded
Corporal John Fowkes disabled in right leg
John Byrom disabled by a wound in his right foot
Joseph Simmers wounded in his head
Archibald Smith shot in the mouth and wounded in the side
Robert Spence lost his right arm

Campbell's (21st)
Mark Whitehead wounded in the thigh

Sempill's (25th)
Thomas Haskin wounded in his right thigh
John Lemmon wounded in the right thigh
John McDonald unfit by reason of a bruise at Culloden

Munro's (37th)
Captain William Kinier wounded
Lieutenant King wounded
Lieutenant Lort wounded
Ensign Dally killed*
Ensign Mundock wounded
* originally returned as wounded, but named in the grenadier officer's letter as killed
William Ashmore disabled in left hand and shoulder
Arthur Buchan disabled in the right thigh
Luke Cunningham shot through the body
John Davidson disabled in left hand and shoulder
John Dollaway disabled in left thigh

197

Robert Farrington disabled in left leg
William Gill shot through the right elbow
Thomas Grant disabled in both thighs
Isaac Gregg disabled by fall at Culloden
Thomas Griffith shot in the left knee
John Guest disabled in the right arm
John Hawson shot in the left knee
William Irwin lost use of left leg
Thomas Lowns disabled in left leg
Charles McLeland shot through the right ankle
Edward McMullen disabled in several parts of his body at Culloden
Richard Moulton disabled by a shot in his right leg
John Perry disabled in right leg
John Tovey jaw shot away at Culloden – the register also records that
he was 59 years old and had been 'born in the army'.

Ligonier's (59th)
Captain Spark wounded
William Knight was disabled in the right foot

Battereau's (62nd)
Captain Carter wounded
Will Matthews wounded in his right side
Daniel McIntosh lost his left leg

Loudon's (64th)
Captain Colin Campbell of Ballimore killed
Dougal McPhail was disabled in the left shoulder and thigh

Argyll Militia
Captain John Campbell of Achnaba mortally wounded

Royal Artillery
Sergeant Edward Bristo died of wounds
Bombardier William Sanderson do.
Bombardier Joseph Turner do.
Gunner John Illingworth do.
Gunner William Shepherd do.
Gunner Thomas Todd do.

APPENDIX 3

The Jacobite Army

'All was confused,' wrote Colonel Sullivan, describing the levies who assembled at Glenfinnan. 'They must go by tribes; such a chiefe of a tribe had sixty men, another thirty, another twenty, more or lesse; they would not mix nor seperat, & wou'd have double officers, yt is two Captns & two Lts, to each Compagny, strong or weak. That was uselesse, & became a great charge afterwards to H.R.Hs. They wou'd follow their own way, but by littel & littel, were brought into a certain regulation.'[1]

The last Jacobite army drew its personnel from four principal sources. First there were those men, mainly Highlanders, who joined in the rebellion, or in the language of the time 'came out', because they were told to by landlords, employers, feudal superiors, or clan chiefs. The bulk of the men standing in the clan regiments clearly fell into this category, but it is difficult to assess the actual enthusiasm of their participation.

Many of those who were taken prisoner during or after the rebellion testified that they had been forced out by the Jacobites, either by means of threats that their homes would be burnt and their cattle taken, or even because they were simply beaten up if they held back. Typical and vivid evidence of this came from the Reverend James Robertson, who testified that Keppoch and some of his men arrived in Lochbroom on the 17th March 1746, and;

> 'unexpectedly surprized the poor people, snatching some of them out of their beds. Others, who thought their old age would excuse them, were dragged from their ploughs ... while some were taken off the highways. One I did myself see overtaken by speed of foot, and when he declared he would rather die than be carried to the rebellion, was knock'd to the ground by the butt of a musket and carried away all bleed.'[2]

Unsurprisingly the courts almost invariably declined to admit evidence of coercion unless it could also be shown that the individual concerned had subsequently made every effort to escape. In other words the material fact considered at the end of the day was not the manner of their recruitment, but the question of whether or not they were taken in arms; in

199

other words whether or not they were actually serving as rebel soldiers when they were captured. Nevertheless, the frequency with which this particular defence was advanced suggests that a very high proportion of rebel soldiers were pressed men rather than volunteers. A second, and rather similar, category of recruits were those men who after Prestonpans were raised in the lowlands of Scotland as fencibles or militiamen. Using the existing tax records, the Jacobite authorities demanded that land-owners should supply an able-bodied man, suitably clothed and accoutred, for every £100 [Scots] of valued rent. Alternatively they could simply pay £5 sterling in lieu of a man, and allegations were rife at the time that the rebels were actually much more interested in getting the money than in gaining recruits. Notwithstanding these quite understand-able suspicions, a considerable number of men appear to have been raised by this means and old John Gordon of Glenbucket for one refused offers of money instead of men.[3]

In a confidential letter to one of his officers, Lord Lewis Gordon, the local Jacobite commander in the North-east of Scotland, wrote in December 1745:

'Although I have got some voluntiers, I assure you that att least two thirds of the men I have raised is by the stipulation att first agreed on, and all those that have not as yet sent their quotas, have been wrote to in very strong terms.'

Equally strong deeds were also required from time to time and just as in the Highlands, there was a certain amount of 'forcing' to fill the required quotas. After a brief experiment with quartering Highlanders on the refractory, Lord Lewis Gordon took to naked threats of burning, and as a contemporary remarked;

'This soon had the desired effect, for the burning of a single house or farm stack in a Parish terrified the whole, so that they would quickly send in their proportion, and by this means, with the few that joined as volunteers, he raised near 300 men called the Strathboggy Battalion in the country thereabouts.'[4]

Naturally enough many landlords were decidedly unwilling to send their tenants off into the rebellion, but rather than defy the Jacobites and incur the threatened penalties, they often turned to the third category of recruit; men hired on the open market. Most lists of rebels compiled for the Government after the rebellion fail to distinguish between the various categories, but the one for the Banff area is quite revealing. It shows that officers aside, no fewer than a third of the known rebels in that locality were mercenaries 'hired out by the county'.[5] Interestingly, to judge from their subsequent fate, the Government appears to have shown little interest in pursuing these men. This was in marked contrast to how they viewed the fourth, and most dangerous category, the volunteers.

The volunteers formed a far from negligible group who not only provided the Jacobite army with its officers, the cavalry, and many of the men in the lowland units, but who also did most of the fighting. After the skirmish at Inverurie just before Christmas 1745, even the Jacobites themselves admitted that the greater part of their men had hidden amongst bushes and in ditches until it became clear to them that they were on the winning side.

The reasons why men volunteered were of course many and varied. Some, like Lord Pitsligo, genuinely believed in the justice of the Pretender's cause and were prepared to risk everything in his service. Many others, however, it is clear joined the rebellion hoping to repair shattered fortunes. One was John Hamilton, Factor to the Duke of Gordon, of whom it was said that although he was long suspected of being a Jacobite, 'the reason of his commencing adventurer was generally imagined to be owing to the disorder of his affairs'. A very similar case was James Moir of Stonywood: 'This gentleman very early imbibed the Jacobite principles and was entirely educated in that way; his fortune also was greatly embarrassed so that his going off was no great surprise.' [6]

Also found amongst the volunteers were a number of deserters from the British army, though it is easy to overestimate their importance. A considerable number appear to have been enlisted from amongst the prisoners taken at Prestonpans, if the testimony of a mariner named Robert Bowey is reliable:

> 'On Friday last 27th Sept. he was at Edinburgh and there saw about 200 soldiers with the livery of H.M. King George go down under guard to the Abby, and shortly after saw about 40 carried away under guard . . . and the remainder were set at liberty, and this deponent saw many going about at large with white cockades along with the rebells, by reason whereof it was said that they had all initiated with the Pretender and were in his service.' [7]

They actually appear to have been enlisted into the Duke of Perth's and Colonel John Roy Stuart's Regiments for there are two references in a surviving orderly book to the 'Red Coats of Perth's' (and Stuart's as well) while they were still quartered in Edinburgh. [8] By Culloden, however, most of them had evidently escaped, for only a very few of Cope's men can be identified amongst the prisoners taken there.

Substantial numbers of men also deserted from the 64th (Loudon's) Highlanders, early in the rising, including some officers such as MacDonnell of Lochgarry and Cluny MacPherson. Both appear to have taken their companies with them, although since they obviously also took their company books with them it was quite impossible afterwards to identify the individuals concerned. A number of other later deserters from Loudon's 64th Highlanders were however identified in the ranks of Lord Cromartie's Regiment, when it was captured at Dunrobin, but the largest single group out of the ninety-eight deserters actually recorded as retaken at Culloden belonged to Guise's 6th Foot. These men were captured for the most part at Fort George and Fort Augustus, and afterwards they were coerced into enlisting in the two French battalions then serving with the Rebels; the Irish Picquets and *Royal Ecossois*.[9]

All of the Jacobite army's recruits, whether they were serving willingly or otherwise, were enlisted into regiments which were at least notionally organised on conventional lines, even to the extent in at least three recorded cases – Locheil's, Lord Ogilvie's and Macdonnell of Glengarry's Regiments – mustering grenadier companies.[10]

Nevertheless, as Colonel Sullivan complained, one of the Jacobite army's besetting problems was an overabundance of officers and a proliferation of small and militarily quite useless regiments. To a considerable extent this was a result of granting commissions to anyone and everyone with pretensions to being a gentleman, as much perhaps in order to gratify their vanity as for any better reason; but at the same time it was perhaps inevitable that with a pressing need to recruit men the net had to be cast very widely indeed. While some officers might be successful in bringing in sufficient volunteers to justify their commissions. Others, perhaps with the best will in the world, were markedly less successful. Some Highland units in particular appear to have been over-officered to a quite ridiculous degree. Not until April 1746 are there clear indications that the Jacobite leaders were getting on top of the problem by amalgamating some of the smaller units, or even simply absorbing them into larger formations.

A good example of this sensible process can be seen in Lord Kilmarnock's Foot Guards. Originally this had been a cavalry regiment, but in February 1746 the remaining troopers gave up their horses in order to mount the newly arrived Fitzjames's Horse.

Kilmarnock then proceeded to recruit an infantry regiment around a nucleus of his old troopers and some other soi-disant cavalrymen from Lord Pitsligo's Horse. Judging by those identified as serving in the unit, by far the greater number of the new Footguards were enlisted in the Buchan district of Aberdeenshire, where Kilmarnock had family connections – not the least of whom was the formidable Lady Erroll. A small and badly disciplined company raised some time earlier in Aberdeenshire by James Crichton of Auchengoul also seems to have been joined with the Footguards; at any rate a Jacobite soldier named William McKenzie, from Bruntbrae in Aberdeenshire, confessed after Culloden that 'he did bear Arms in a Company of Kilmarnock's Rebel Regiment, commanded by James CRICHTON of Auchingowl, Captain.'

Judging by the considerable diversity of units represented at the battle of Culloden, the process does not however appear to have done anything much to reduce the numbers of officers, or to have entirely removed the anomaly of Colonels commanding what were little more than independent companies.

The officers themselves naturally varied considerably as to the experience and expertise which they brought to the job. Very few of them had actually seen much service in either the British or the French army, and fewer still had advanced beyond subaltern rank – even Lord George Murray for example had merely been an Ensign (the lowest commissioned rank) in the Royals between 1712 and 1715, thirty years previously. As for the rest, only two other regimental commanders; John Roy Stuart and MacDonnell of Keppoch, had any military experience and once again it was at a junior level. Stuart, for example, was a captain of grenadiers at Fontenoy.

In Highland units in particular, military rank was all too often simply a reflection of social standing and it is doubtful if many of the officers were really up to the job. They were no doubt brave enough and possessed of at least some management skills; after all they ran families, farms and sometimes small businesses, but this did not always fit them for military command. The surviving Jacobite orderly books are full of complaints of routine orders being disregarded or neglected and punctuality appears to have been an alien concept to many.

Sir John McDonnell commented that Gordon of Glenbucket was; 'the only Scot I ever knew who was able to start at the hour fixed,'[11] but Lord George Murray's comments are perhaps more telling:

'I not only wrote the orders myself when I commanded a separate corps of the army, or directed them, but to any officer that was to go upon a party, or upon an outpost, I endeavoured to explain every thing that might happen, and answered any objections that could be started, besides giving the orders in writing, by which means there was no mistake or confusion, and the officers did their duty with cheerfulness, and made their reports with exactness. Mr.O'Sullivan's manner was – when he had parties to send, or a post to occupy, it was mentioned in the general order of the day, only mentioning the regiment that was to furnish so many officers and men. This might have done well in a very regular army, but in ours more exactness and attention was necessary. Much confusion and mistakes happened by it; and it was often night before a party went that should have gone in the morning.'[12]

All in all the picture which so clearly emerges is of officers who were brave and willing enough to lead their men into battle, but who were unable or at best disinclined to apply themselves to the more mundane aspects of soldiering. Given that hardly any of them had any previous military service this is perhaps not surprising, but while a newly commissioned subaltern in a regular regiment could look to his fellow officers (and probably more importantly to his sergeant) for advice and assistance, no such support was available to most Jacobite officers.

Nevertheless some attempt was made to 'discipline' or train the men, and there is no question of the Jacobite army having simply been little more than the howling mob of clansmen so beloved of film-makers and romantic novelists. Lord Ogilvy's Regiment, a lowland unit largely raised in Forfarshire had a French regular officer, Lieutenant Nicholas Glasgoe of Dillon's Regiment, attached to it to 'discipline' the men and act as what would now be called an Operations Officer. This particular regiment also benefited from the expertise of a Chelsea out-pensioner named James Webster who acted as a drill instructor and taught the men the firelock exercise.[13]

Such efforts were not however confined to the lowland regiments and all of them at one time or another tried to drill properly, as one witness, Allan Stewart, a sometime sergeant in Ardshiel's regiment, testified;

> 'Some days before the battle of Culloden I remember to have seen said Colonel Francis Farquharson with a big blue coat on, at the head of his own regiment which was then drawn out with Ardshiel's regiment and some of the McLeods upon a plain about a mile from Inverness, and that they went through their exercise and were reviewed by the pretender's son.'[14]

INFANTRY

The Jacobite infantry were loosely organised in two divisions, a Highland one and a lowland one, of which the former was certainly stronger and regarded itself as the elite of the army. Despite a policy of attempting to clothe the whole army in Highland dress, contemporary observers on both sides were usually able to readily distinguish between the two. Whether, at the end of the day, there was very much to choose between them is perhaps a moot point.

The Jacobite leaders were certainly in no doubt as to how their men were to be clothed and equipped. On the 6th of December 1745 Lord Lewis Gordon issued the following instructions:

'All men are to be well cloathed, with short cloathes, plaid, new shoes and three pair of hose and accoutred with shoulder ball gun, pistolls and sword.'[15]

While this might have been regarded as the ideal, and is certainly how Jacobite soldiers are commonly envisaged as being dressed and equipped, the available evidence suggests that most lowlanders wore breeches, and that on the whole all Jacobite infantrymen, both Highland and lowland were in actual fact fairly conventionally equipped. In 1927 Sir Bruce Seton drew attention to the fact that the traditional picture was not supported by the relative quantities of arms actually surrendered by parties of clansmen after Culloden.

For example on the 15th of May 1746, 77 of Glengarry's men handed in 65 firelocks, 26 swords and 4 dirks, while 98 of Keppoch's men turned in a firelock apiece, but only 22 swords and a dirk. Two days later, on the 17th, 44 men surrendered 27 firelocks, 3 swords and 6 pistols, and a fourth group gave up 10 firelocks, 4 swords and 2 pistols. Twenty of the Appin men surrendered with 16 firelocks and 2 swords, and twenty Camerons also gave up 16 firelocks but only one sword. Only in one instance, a party of twenty-three Mackintoshes, who also surrendered on the 17th of May was there anything like parity between the numbers of firelocks and swords handed in; 16 firelocks and 13 swords.[16]

With the exception of this last group, rather less than a third of all the men concerned had broadswords. It is possible that while they were ready enough to surrender firelocks, swords which might have a sentimental or even mystical value were hidden, but this is not borne out by the return of weapons actually recovered by Cumberland's men from Culloden Moor itself.

In his official report compiled on the day after the battle, Cumberland reckoned that the Jacobites had lost some 2,000 men, including nearly 600 taken prisoner. Not surprisingly therefore 2,320 firelocks were reported picked up from the moor, but in contrast to this only 190 broadswords and blades were found. Even if a certain allowance is made for casualties amongst lowland units and for French regulars who are known not to have been armed with broadswords, this suggests that out of something like 1,000 odd Highlanders killed or wounded on the moor, or on the road to Inverness, only about one in five had a broadsword – a figure entirely consistent with the later surrenders. It is also consistent with General Hawley's well-known remarks, made shortly before his debacle at Falkirk, in which he claimed:

'They Commonly form their Front rank of what they call their best men, or True Highlanders, the number of which being allways but few, when they form in Battallions they commonly form four deep, &

these Highlanders form the front of the four, the rest being lowlanders & arrant scum.'

Making due allowance for hyperbole, Hawley's description matches both the evidence quoted as to the relative numbers of weapons recovered, and other accounts of clan warfare. The front rank of a Highland regiment comprised 'gentlemen', armed with the full panoply of weapons: firelock, pistols, broadsword and targe. But those standing behind, the ordinary clansmen, the tenants, servants and dependants of the gentlemen, were armed only with firelocks and bayonets. In the lowland regiments broadswords were probably confined to the officers.

The firelocks carried by Jacobite soldiers appear for the most part to have been French or Spanish ones. The hostile author of the Woodhouslee Ms. described how the Highlanders who took Edinburgh were armed with a startling collection of antique weapons: 'they were guns of diferent syses, and some of innormows length, some with butts turned up lick a heren, some tyed with puck threed to the stock, some withowt locks and some matchlocks.'[17] The rebels subsequently captured numbers of British land pattern firelocks, and Murray of Broughton states that both Gordon of Glenbucket's Regiment and the first battalion of Lord Ogilvie's Regiment, were both equipped with arms captured from Cope's army at Prestonpans.[18] But other evidence suggests that by the time Culloden was fought the rebels had largely discarded these in favour of the foreign arms. At any rate, three days after the battle Cumberland issued an order to the effect that:

'French or Spanish firelocks or bayonets and cartridge boxes to be delivered by the Train to Ensign Stewart of Lascelles' Regt.; he is to distribute them to the Prisoners of our Army released here.'[19]

Had British Land Pattern firelocks been recovered in any number there would obviously have been no need to re-arm the released prisoners with French or Spanish military ones.

Large numbers of French firelocks and bayonets were in fact supplied to the rebels in the course of the campaign, and 1,500 to 1,600 stand of arms (firelocks and bayonets complete) were landed at Montrose in October alone. These were probably the Model 1717, (rather than the more modern Model 1728) which superficially resembled the Land Pattern in appearance save that there was a single iron barrel-band halfway to the muzzle, and that the sling was fastened to the side rather than the underside of the weapon. The important difference lay in the fact that it was of .69 calibre (16 Bore) and the decision to standardise on this weapon and the very similar Spanish firelocks – also of .69 calibre – landed at Peterhead,[20] must have been made in order to avoid any problems arising from two quite different calibres of small-arms ammunition being used.

As for the more mundane articles of military equipment, 6,000 canteens were requisitioned while the army was in Edinburgh, and the ever observant John Bisset noted in his diary that when the Jacobites marched out of Aberdeen to fight McLeod at Inverurie, a few days before Christmas 1745, they all had on their 'wallets and pocks in a posture of marching.'

The tactical doctrines adopted by the rebel forces were very different from those practised by the British army. In the lowland units at least, the available evidence suggests that French teaching prevailed. This generally called for manoeuvring in column, (Sullivan referred at one point to 'Stonywood & the other Regimt yt is in Colloum behind you'), stressed the use of a four-deep fighting line (as described by Hawley) and preached reliance upon shock action with the bayonet, rather than relying upon firepower. This fitted in very well indeed with Highland notions of how to fight a battle.

The old Highland way of fighting was to advance quickly towards the enemy without paying much regard to preserving a line, fire a hasty volley at fairly close range and then run in under the smoke led by the swordsmen. Popularly, they are also said by way of a refinement to have thrown themselves flat, or gone down on one knee, when the enemy fired, before springing up and attacking as they desperately struggled to reload. However, since the regular army's drills stressed the importance of maintaining a steady rolling fire, rather than blasting off everything at once, the likelihood of such a cunning plan actually working out in reality may be guessed at.

The Highland charge worked, when it did work, by intimidating the opposition in exactly the same way that the French revolutionary armies were to do in the 1790s, that is, by storming forward in deep columns (indeed accounts from the receiving end of Highland charges invariably describe how the clansmen came forward in columns or wedges), and for that the bayonets carried by the majority of Jacobite soldiers worked just as well as the broadswords waved so frighteningly by the gentlemen in the front rank. At Prestonpans, General Cope's raw Scots recruits had indeed been intimidated and stampeded into a rout, and much of Hawley's army at Falkirk would be similarly panicked. Significantly, however, those regular units which did not run away were left well alone.

Considering the resultant confusion at Falkirk, Lord George Murray afterwards declared that, effective though Highlanders might be in launching the first onset, the Jacobite army required more regular troops if their successes were to be properly exploited:

'. . . the best of the Highland officers, whilst they remained at Falkirk after the battle, were absolutely convinced, that, except they could attack the enemy at very considerable advantage, either by surprise or by some strong situation of ground, or a narrow pass, they could not expect any great success, especially if their numbers were no ways equal, and that a body of regular troops was absolutely necessary to support them, when they should at any time go in, sword in hand; for they were sensible, that without more leisure and time to discipline their own men, it would not be possible to make them keep their ranks, or rally soon enough upon any sudden emergency, so that any small number of the enemy, either keeping in a body when they were in confusion, or rallying, would deprive them of a victory, even after they had done their best.'[21]

A couple of interesting points stand out in this analysis. Firstly, and despite the evident successes which they had gained at Prestonpans and now partially at Falkirk, the commanders of the Highland regiments were evidently well aware of the shortcomings of their men, and apparently considered that if there was the time for it they should be properly trained or 'disciplined'. Secondly, aware that this was not in the circumstances a practical proposition (although as we have seen a number of regiments were observed drilling just before Culloden), more regular troops were required – presumably, though it is not explicitly spelled out – French ones.

CAVALRY

The Jacobite cavalry has never had a particularly good press and there is no doubt that even at their peak they were incapable of fighting regular cavalry on anything like equal terms. Indeed two regiments, Lord Pitsligo's Horse and Lord Kilmarnock's Horse Grenadiers, were dismounted a couple of months before the battle of Culloden and their remaining mounts turned over to Fitzjames's Irish regulars. Although it is easy therefore to dismiss their contribution as insignificant, this is completely to misunderstand their real role, which was in fact confined to providing reconnaisance and security patrols.

Lord Strathallan's Perthshire Squadron was the senior of the rebel cavalry units and probably typical of all of them. It was first raised shortly before the battle of Prestonpans and a surviving muster roll dated 7th of February 1746 lists eighty-two officers and men serving in two troops. For some reason the designations or occupations of the officers and troopers are recorded in this roll:

Apparently some twenty-five of them could be considered as being gentlemen since they either bore the prefix Mr, or were described as being 'of' a particular place. Six others were professional men, mainly writers (solicitors), while another twenty were servants, presumably attending upon the gentlemen in the troop. The remainder were small tradesmen, such as tailors, wrights (carpenters), slaters, shoemakers, and there was even a solitary labourer.[22]

The Prince's Lifeguards, perhaps predictably, appear to have taken the view that their principal role lay in lending some tone to the proceedings. The names of some 112 Lifeguards are known – a high proportion of the total – and where Strathallan's men were gentlemen of small estate, with a heavy admixture of tradesmen, the Lifeguards were very largely young men chiefly drawn from Edinburgh and Dundee 'society'. A considerable number were identified as being gentlemen's sons, while the greater part of them were 'merchants' and writers, and of course their servants.

In complete contrast, Bagot's Hussars seem to have gone very much out of their way to cultivate a distinctly raffish air. This troop was originally raised in the Edinburgh area by John Murray of Broughton, but he remained no more than a titular commander and, after a somewhat less than distinguished record during the march into England, the Hussars were taken over by Major John Bagot, an officer in the Irish regiment Rooth, and given a thorough re-organisation. The original aristocratic troop leaders either conveniently got themselves captured or found staff appointments and were replaced by other Irish officers. Under their professional leadership the Hussars' performance improved quite dramatically.

Major Bagot had no illusions whatever about their fitness to stand in the line of battle and instead he trained them very effectively as light cavalry or hussars in the continental manner. Their primary role was intelligence gathering, often in small patrols and according to the admiring Lancashire Jacobite, John Daniel:

'A set of braver fellows it would be very hard to find; many of them having mounted themselves on horses which they had taken from the enemy. Their Commander also was a wise, courageous virtuous man, and behaved himself in his station to the admiration of all, regulating his corps with such order as to make our enemies and the country, even fifty miles distant from us, have more fear of them than almost the whole army. In fine, he was of infinite service to the Prince, as also were his horse; for their conduct was daring, and their courage was steeled, and few of them there were, who would have scrupled to go, if possible to hell's gates to fetch away the keys.'[23]

ARTILLERY

If the Jacobite cavalry was poor, its artillery often seems to have been regarded by historians as a sick joke. Throughout its short existence, the rebel army always contrived to have some guns with it although the effort expended on them was rarely if ever justified by results. In the first place, except for some heavy pieces landed by the French and abandoned after Falkirk, the Jacobite guns were for the most part too light for siege work – though they did have their occasional minor success. In the second place the tactical doctrines espoused by the the rebels left very little room for artillery on the battlefield and indeed the only occasion when guns were deployed by the Jacobites in the field was at Culloden.

After Culloden Cumberland happily reported the capture of no fewer than 22 artillery pieces of assorted calibres, and eight swivel guns. They were in fact a heterogeneous collection of French and captured British guns and the multiplicity of calibres has spawned the quite unfounded idea, amongst some historians, that this severely hampered the performance of the rebel artillery at Culloden. In actual fact it is clear from contemporary sketches that only eleven cannon were deployed by the rebels at the outset of the action and that all of them were 3-pounders.

Sources:

1. Sullivan, p. 60–1.
2. Seton & Arnot, *Prisoners of the '45*, Vol.I, p. 270.
3. Ibid., p. 273.
4. 'Memoirs of the Rebellion in Aberdeen and Banff' (anonymous but probably the Rev. John Bisset] *IN Origins*, p. 129.
5. *List of Persons Concerned in the Rebellion*.
6. *Origins*, p. 116, 119.
7. Seton & Arnot, Vol. I, p. 274–5.
8. *Orderly Book of Lord Ogilvy's Regiment*: JSAHR Vol. II, Appendix p. 5.
9. Seton & Arnot var. *Newcastle Courant* – list of English deserters at Culloden.
10. *Albemarle Papers*, p. 327, Seton & Arnot var.
11. Sullivan, p. 60.
12. Murray, p. 125–6.
13. Seton & Arnot Vol. III, p. 396–7.
14. Allardyce, *Historical Papers*, Vol. II, p. 479.
15. Tayler, A&H *Jacobites of Aberdeenshire and Banffshire*, p. 28.
16. Seton & Arnot, Vol. I, p. 288–290.
17. Woodhouslee Ms. p. 25.
18. *Origins*, p. 220.
19. Seton & Arnot, Vol. I, p. 290.
20. 600 of the French firelocks were ordered to be delivered to Moir of Stonywood on the 21st of October 1745, which would have been sufficient for both

his own Gordon of Avochie's battalions of Lord Lewis Gordon's Regiment. *Spalding Club Miscellany,* Vol. I, p. 401.

21. Quoted IN J. Black; *Culloden and the '45,* p. 139–40.
22. Livingston, Aikman & Hart *Muster Roll,* p. 53–55.
23. *Origins,* p. 202.

APPENDIX 4

Men and materials captured at Culloden

Cumberland's official report on the battle concluded with a suitably impressive list of captured personnel and equipment. Heading the list was an impressive bag of French prisoners of war. Many of them had laid down their arms on the battlefield, but as Major General Bland approached Inverness he was met by a drummer, sent out by Sir John McDonnell, bearing the formal surrender of all the French officers and soldiers there.[1] Next day they signed their parole:

Stapleton, Brigadier of the Armies of the Most Christian King, and Lieutenant Colonelof Berwick's Regiment[2]

Jean McDonell, Colonel of Fitzjames's Regiment of Horse

Le Marquis de Guilles, Captain in the Marine Regiment[3]

Francois Nugent, Captain of Fitzjames's Regiment of Horse, appointed to exercise the Function of Quarter-master in the French Troops in Scotland.

Patrice Nugent, Captain of Fitzjames's Horse

N(icholas) Comerford, Captain of Bulkley's Regiment

(Francis) Cusack, Captain of Dillon's Regiment

Richard Bourke, Captain of ditto.

Jean McDonagh, Lieutenant of ditto.

Michael Burke, Lieutenant of ditto.

Edouard de Nugent, Captain of ditto.

Carbery Fox, Lieutenant of ditto.

Thomas McDermott, Captain of Rothe's Regiment

Dudley McDermott, Lieutenant of ditto.

Peter Taafe, Lieutenant of Rothe's Regiment

(Nicholas) de la Hoyde, Captain of Berwick's Regiment

Patrick Clargue, Captain of ditto.

Thomas Goold, Lieutenant of ditto.

Pierre O'Reily, Lieutenant of ditto.

Robert Stack, Captain of Lally's Regiment, being wounded, Murphy signed for him

Richard Murphy, Captain of ditto.

Miles Swiny, Lieutenant of ditto.

Patrick Sarsfield, Lieutenant of ditto.

Jacques Grant, Lieutenant of ditto.
Jean O'Bryen, Captain of the Regiment of Paris Militia
(Francis) O'Donoghue, Captain of the Regiment of Royal Scots[4]
Douglas, Captain of ditto.
Alexander Gordon, Chaplain of the French Troops
Pierre Colienno, Second Captain of a Spanish Ship
(Basil) Barnaval, Lieutenant of Fitzjames's Regiment
Robert Shee, Captain of ditto, Horse
Thomas Bagot, Captain of ditto.
Mark Bagot, Adjutant of ditto.
Alexandre Geoghegan, Captain of Lally's Regiment D'Andrion, Officer
of Artillery
Jean Nugent, Lieutenant of Fitzjames's Horse De Cooke, Cornet in ditto.
John Dillon, Captain of Dillon's Regiment
Thomas Scott, Volunteer in Bulkley's Regiment Du Saussay, French
Engineer d'Hortore, Captain of the Royal Scots Dicconson, Lieutenant of
ditto
(John) Nairne, Lieutenant of ditto.
Damary, Lieutenant of ditto.
O'Daniel, Lieutenant of Bulkley's Regiment
Charles Guillaume Douglass, Captain in Languedoc
Jean St.Leger, Captain of the Royal Scots
Eugene O'Keaffe, Lieutenant of Berwick's Regiment
Charles Bodin, Officer of Artillery
Philippe Molloy, Quarter-master in Fitzjames's
Lord Lewis Drummond, Captain of the Royal Scots[5]

This list does not of course include the 222 rank and file belonging to
the 'French' regiments, or those officers seconded to rebel units, such as
Major John Bagot of the Hussars (who was badly wounded at Culloden)
and Nicholas Glasgoe of Lord Ogilvy's Regiment. Oddly enough, neither
man appears amongst the list of rebel prisoners either.

*A Return of the Rebel Officers and Soldiers now Prisoners in Inverness, 19th
April 1746.*

Men's Names	Station	Regiment	County
Lord Kilmarnock	Colonel		Stirlingshire
Francis Farquharson	Colonel		Aberdeenshire
James Stewart	Major	Duke of Perth's	do.
MacLachlan	Colonel[6]		Inverness-shire

Men's Names	Station	Regiment	County
John Farquharson	Captain	Colonel Farquharson's	Aberdeenshire
Duncan MacGregor	Ensign	do.	do.
Sir John Wedderburn	Life Guards	Elcho's	Angus
Andrew Wood	Captain	John Roy Stewart	Glasgow
Alexander Cuming	Captain	Duke of Perth's	Perthshire
George Lauder	Surgeon		Edinburgh
John Rattray	Surgeon		do.
John Findlason	Engineer	Artillery	do.
Andrew Spruel	Captain Pitsligoe's	Glasgow	
James Lindsey	Ensign	Lord Strathallan's	Perthshire
James Hay	Ensign	Pitsligoe's	Aberdeenshire
(Robert) Nairn	Deputy Paymaster		Edinburgh
George Law	Chaplain to the Pretender		Aberdeen
George Gordon	Lieutenant	Glenbucket's	Perthshire
Alexander Buchannan	Captain	Perth's	do.
Donald Ferguson	Sergeant	do.	do.
Roger MacDonald	Private	Clanronald's	Skye
John MacDonald	do.	do.	Inverness-shire
George Addison	Bawman[7]	Pitsligoe's	Aberdeen
Donald MacQueen	do.	do.	Argyleshire
Donald Levistone	Private	Ardshiel	Argyleshire
William Walker	do.	Colonel Crichton	Aberdeenshire
Alexander Smith	do.	Lord Ogilvie's	Angus
Thomas Armstrong	do.	do.	do.
James Drummond	do.	Duke of Perth's	Perthshire
Donald Fraser	do.	Master of Lovat's	Inverness-shire
Andrew Smith	do.	Colonel Crichton	Aberdeenshire
John Gollon	do.	do.	Inverness
Andrew Catanoch	do.	Stonywood's	Aberdeen
Alexander Thomson	do.	do.	do.

Men and materials captured at Culloden

Men's Names	Station	Regiment	County
George Gordon	do.	do.	do.
Alexander MacIntosh	do.	Colonel MacIntosh	Inverness-shire
John Sim	do.	do.	do.
Alexander White	do.	MacIntosh	do.
James MacKenzie	do.	Colonel MacGillavrae	do.
Alexander Davidson	do.	Colonel Farquharson	Aberdeenshire
Lachlan MacIntosh	do.	Colonel MacIntosh	Inverness-shire
Robert Grant	Private	Lord Lewis Gordon	Aberdeenshire
Andrew Mill	do.	Colonel Crichton	do.
John MacAndrew	do.	Colonel Farquharson	do.
John MacIntire	Bawman to the Pretender	Argyleshire	
Alexander Cameron	Private	Lochell	Inverness-shire
Andrew Geddes	do.	Lord Ogilvie	Banffshire
Charles Graham	do.	Glengary	Ross-shire
John Morison	do.	Sir Alexr. Bannerman	Banffshire
John Mason	do.	Stonywood	Aberdeenshire
William Traill	do.	Lord Ogilvie's	Banffshire
Alexander Campbell	do.	Duke of Berwick's	Inverness-shire
Alexander Young	do.	Duke of Berwick's	Inverness-shire
John Smith	do.	Lord Ogilvie's	Angus
William Grant	do.	John Roy Stewart's	Inverness
Dugwal MacLeod	do.	Clanronald's	do.
William Munro	do.	do.	Inverness-shire
David Crab	do.	John Roy Stewart's	Mid-Lothian
Lachlan MacLean	do.	do.	Argyleshire
John Beverly	do.	Stonywood's	Aberdeen
Dugwal MacKenzie	do.	do.	Inverness
William Roy	do.	John Roy Stewart	Lanark

215

Men's Names	Station	Regiment	County
John MacLachlan	do.	Colonel MacLauchlan	Argyleshire
John MacBain	do.	do.	Inverness-shire
James Gordon	do.	Glenbucket's	Banffshire
William Farquharson	do.	do.	do.
James Middleton	do.	do.	do.
John MacLachlan	do.	do.	do.
John MacDonald	do.	do.	do.
William Fraser	do.	Master of Lovat	Inverness-shire
George Forbes	do.	Abbochy	Aberdeen
James Campbell	do.	do.	Inverness
Hugh MacKenzie	do.	do.	do.
Donald Cameron	do.	Lochyel	Inverness-shire
John Guissock	do.	Abbochy	Aberdeenshire
John MacLean	do.	do.	Argyleshire
Hugh Fraser	do.	Lord John Drummond	Inverness-shire
James Ronaldson	do.	Sir Alexr. Bannerman	Aberdeenshire
Donald Ross	do.	Stonywood's	do.
William Robertson	do.	Duke of Athol	Perthshire
William Couts	do.	Colonel Farquharson	Aberdeenshire
Donald MacRea	do.	do.	Sutherland
Malcolm Stewart	Servant to Col. Stewart		Argyleshire
John MacAurie	Private	Colonel Farquharson	do.
Thomas Gillespie a Boy		Colonel Warrant[8]	Midlothian
Walter Gordon	Life Guards	Lord Elcho	Midlothian
John Airth	Private	Colonel Crichton's	Aberdeenshire
Angus MacDonald	do.	Glengary's	Inverness-shire
James Davidson	do.	do.	do.
Donald MacLean	do.	Lochyel	Argyleshire
John MacDonald	do.	Glengary's	Inverness-shire
John Heggans	do.	Lord John Drummond	Lanark

Men and materials captured at Culloden

Men's Names	Station	Regiment	County
John MacDougal	Lord John Drummond's Piper's Servant		Inverness-shire
John MacDonald	Private	Colonel Chisholm's	do.
Robert MacKay	do.	Abbochy	Sutherland
Thomas Nairn	do.	Glenbucket's	Aberdeenshire
John Buchannan	do.	do.	Inverness-shire
William Durrat	do.	Colonel Farquharson	Aberdeenshire
Duncan Catanach	do.	do.	do.
George Murdoch	do.	do.	do.
Archibald Colquhon	do.	Appin's	do.
John MacLean	do.	do.	do.
John MacLean	do.	Colonel MacLean's	do.
Duncan Stewart	do.	Appin's	do.
John Smith	do.	Colonel Farquharson	do.
Archibald MacDonald	do.	Clan Ronald	Inverness-shire
Donald Sutherland	do.	do.	Sutherland
William MacIntosh	do.	Master of Lovat	Inverness-shire
Robert Johnston	do.	Sir Alexr. Bannerman	Mearns
Francis MacIntosh	do.	Colonel MacGillavrea	Inverness-shire
Malcolm Masterton	do.	do.	do.
John MacKenzie	do.	do.	do.
John Kennedy	do.	Keppoch	do.
William Chisholm	do.	Colonel Chisholm	do.
Archibald Cameron	do.	Lochyel	do.
Alexander MacLeod	do.	do.	do.
Farquhar MacGillavrea	do.	Colonel MacGillavrea	do.

217

Men's Names	Station	Regiment	County
James Drummond	do.	Lord Lewis Drummond	do.
Donald Grant	do.	Glengary's	do.
Alexander Morison	do.	Colonel MacLean	Argyleshire
Alexander Duncan	do.	Master of Lovat	do.
Donald Ross	do.	do.	do.
Lauchlan Ritchie	do.	do.	do.
James MacPherson	do.	do.	do.
William MacKenzie	do.	do.	do.
Andrew Mouchall	do.	do.	do.
John Grasick	do.	do.	do.
John Gray, a native of France, come express from the French King.			
Dougal Soutor	Private	Keppoch	Mid-Lothian
Angus Campbell	do.	Master of Lovat	Inverness-shire
Jascol MacKay	do.	do.	do.
Murdoch Cameron	do.	do.	do.
Allan Stewart	do.	Airdshiel's	Perthshire
John MacRobbie	do.	Duke of Perth's	do.
William Anderson	do.	Lord Ogilvie's	Angus
Duncan Campbell	do.	Lochyel	Argyleshire
John Robertson	do.	Keppoch	Perthshire
John Buchannan	do.	Airdshiel	Argyleshire
Archibald MacInnes	do.	do.	do.
Thomas Fraser	do.	Master of Lovat	Inverness-shire
Jan Boy	A Native of France	Fitzjames's	
John MacDonald	Private	Clan Ronald	Inverness-shire
Neil MacGoary	do.	Master of Lovat	do.
John Sim	do.	Lord Nairn's	Perthshire
Evan MacKenzie	do.	Master of Lovat	Inverness-shire
John Ferguson	do.	Lord George Murray	Perthshire

Men and materials captured at Culloden

Men's Names	Station	Regiment	County
George Merry	do.	do.	Aberdeenshire
Evan MacCulloch	do.	Airdshiell	Argyleshire
William Chisholm	do.	Col. Chisholm	Inverness-shire
John MacDowgall	do.	Clan Ronnald	Argyleshire
David Ramsay	do.	Stonywood	Angus
John Nicol	do.	Lord Ogilvy	do.

Although no doubt correct as of the 19th April, this list[9] is far from complete in that it does not include former British army personnel (see below) or the many wounded officers and men then lying on the moor who are known to have been included in later prisoner lists. Conversely no fewer than 101 out of the 154 men and boys who are named, either died in captivity or else simply vanish from the records. This clearly indicates that the majority of those listed here were wounded men who patently had not been bayoneted on the moor.

A List of Englishmen now Prisoners at Inverness, Deserters from several British Regiments to the Rebels; and who, 'tis supposed, will be shot at the Head of their respective Corps.

Mens Names	Regiment	County
Thomas Lebon	Ligonier	Bedfordshire
John Allan	Lt Gen Howard	Northampton
Abraham Kitchens	Ligonier	Cheshire
William Lawson	Guise	Durham
John Roberts	Ligonier	Devonshire
Philip Mons	Blakeney	do.
William Howel	Ligonier	Cambridge
William Lilly[10]	Col. Murray	Essex
Charles Davie[11]	Lt.Gen. Howard	Lestock
Hugh Holland	do.	Warwickshire
John Tarlton	Guise	Lancaster
William Allan	do.	Gloucester
Richard Oldridge	do.	do.
John Jones	do.	do.
Henry Davis	do.	Dorset
Thomas Man	do.	Newcastle
John Bramely	do.	Warwick
John Smith	do.	Derbyshire
Samuel Hawkins	do.	Wiltshire
Abel Brierly	do.	Lancashire

Mens Names	Regiment	County
Richard Robin	do.	Warwickshire
Thomas Picks	do.	do.
Philip Prendergrass	do.	London
Richard Bail	do.	Yorkshire
Alexander Small	do.	Leicestershire
Richard Browne	do.	Derby
Samuel Warnbey	do.	Norfolk
Edward Collier	do.	Cheshire
James Worsley	do.	Yorkshire
John Hawkins	do.	Lancashire
Robert Pool	do.	Warwickshire
Samuel Price	do.	Gloucester
Joseph Hosey	do.	do.
John Dey	do.	Dorchester
Henry Davis	do.	Warwickshire
Robert Johns	do.	Stafford
Richard Hicksham	do.	Warwickshire
Thomas Kesbridge	do.	do.
George Carpenter	do.	Lancashire
Charles Williams	do.	Wiltshire
Samuel Square	Col. Ligonier	Suffolk
John Bull	Col. Murray	Essex
Charles Newton	Pulteney	Kent
Benjamin Lees[12]	Col. Cotterel	London
Robert Hale	Late Monroe's	Wooller
Charles Horsley	do.	Nottingham
William Armstrong[13]	Royal Scots	Cumberland
George Williams	Battereau	Cheshire
Charles Grasely	Price	Lincolnshire

There are also 32 Scots and Irish Deserters, Prisoners there, who, 'tis expected, will share the same fate.[14]

Return of Ordnance and Stores taken at and since the Battle of Culloden. Inverness April 18.

Brass Ordnance	1lb	3
	3lb	11
	4lb	4
Iron Ordnance	4lb	4
		22

Men and materials captured at Culloden

Brass Swivels	6
Iron Ditto	2
	8

Firelocks of different Kinds	2320
Broad Swords and Blades	190
Musquet Cartridges	1500
Shot for Ordnance of different Natures	1019
Musket Shot, C.	5
Barrels of Powder	37
Ammunition Carts	22

Besides small Stores, some Tents, Cantines, Pouches and Cartouch Boxes, Pistols, Saddles, &c.15

There were also a number of colours:

'Received from Lieutenant Colonel Napier the following Rebel colours, viz:-
1. On a staff a white linen colours belonging to the Farquharsons.
2. On a staff a white linen colours, motto *Terrores Furio*, Chisolmes.
3. On a staff a large plain white colours, said to be the standard.[16]
4. On a staff a blue silk colours, *Sursum Tendo*.[17]
5. A staff the colours tore off.
6. Do.
7. On a staff a white silk colours with the Stewarts Arms *God Save King*.18
8. On a staff a white silk colours, in the canton St.Andrew's cross.
9. On a staff a white silk with a red saltire.
10. A blew silk colours with the Lovat arms *Sine Sanguine Victor*.19
11. A white silk with a blue saltire.
12. Piece of blue silk with a St.Andrew saltire *Commit the Work to God*.20
13. A white linen jaik with a red saltire.
14. One of Lord Lovat's camp colours.

Which colours I am to deliver to the Lord Justice Clerk at Edinburgh.
 Hu Wentworth
Inverness May 11th 1746[21]

Sources:

1. Not as is usually stated by Lieutenant-Colonel Stapleton, who had already been taken prisoner on the battlefield.
2. Stapleton was in fact mortally wounded and died shortly afterwards.
3. His prominence in the list is explained by his also being the French 'ambassador' to the rebels.
4. ie: the *Royal Ecossois*.
5. Drummond, who was about to lose a leg, was in fact the Lieutenant-Colonel of the *Royal Ecossois*. Most of the officers belonging to his regiment were at Ruthven Barracks on the 18th, which is why so few of their names appear on this parole list.
6. Presumably Lachlan MacLachlan of Castle Lachlan. Usually said to have been killed on the battlefield by a cannon-shot, however his presence on the early lists indicates that he died of his wounds while in captivity.
7. A 'bawman' was a grazier, which in this context might mean a groom.
8. Colonel Richard Warren had been a captain in the Regiment Clare and ADC to the Duke of Perth, before being sent to France with dispatches. He later commanded the French expedition which rescued the Prince. The 13-year old Thomas Gillespie's prison career can be traced only as far as Tilbury Fort.
9. Allardyce, p. 611–4.
10. Appears on the 'Oath of Abjuration Roll' for the Duke of Perth's Regiment.
11. Executed on the 28th of April 1746.
12. A very determined deserter indeed. Cotterell's Provisional Battalion, made up of Additional Companies spent the duration of the rising in garrison at Portsmouth. He was eventually released on the 30th of November 1747.
13. Probably the William Armstrong of Guise's executed on the 28th of April 1746. The reference here to the 'Royal Scots' may indicate that he was serving in the *Royal Ecossois* when captured.
14. *Newcastle Journal* In actual fact only two of those listed can positively be identified as having been executed, although 28 others whose names do not appear here are known to have been hanged after Culloden. At least 11 of Guise's were in fact 'begged off' by an Inverness minister named Alexander MacBean who was aware of the circumstances of their enlistment into the rebel service. Inter alia it is interesting to note the number of men from the Midlands serving in what would eventually become the Warwickshire Regiment.
15. *London Gazette*.
16. According to John Daniel (*Origins*, p. 177–8) the original standard, raised at Glenfinnan, was accidentally 'broken' at Derby.
17. This colour is unidentified, but the motto belongs to the Kinloch family. It may therefore have been carried by a company of Lord Ogilvy's regiment as Sir James Kinloch commanded the second battalion. On the other hand it is perhaps more likely to have been lost by Captain Charles Kinloch of the Atholl Brigade.
18. Unidentified. Probably John Roy Stuart's Regiment, although another possibility might be Lord Kilmarnock's Footguards.
19. The motto is not Lovat's, and the arms may therefore have been those of Fraser of Inverallochie.
20. Possibly the most intriguing of the colours as the motto belongs to the Sinclair family, none of whom took an active part in the rising.
21. Warden, A *Angus or Forfarshire*, Vol. III, p. 252.

Bibliography

Advice to the Officers of the British Army, with the Addition of some hints to the Drummer and Private Soldier, (1782), (2nd Edn London 1948).

Allardyce, J. *Historical Papers relating to the Jacobite Period*, (2 vols New Spalding Club 1895).

Anderson, Peter *Culloden Moor and the story of the battle*, (2nd Edn Stirling 1920).

Anon. *History of the Rebellion in the Years 1745 and 1746*, (ed. H. Tayler for Roxburghe Club 1944).

Atkinson, C.J. *Jenkins Ear, The Austrian Succession War and The Fortyfive*, (Journal of the Society for Army Historical Research vol. 22 1943–4).

Bailey, D.W., *British Military Longarms 1715–1865*, (London 1986).

Bell, R.F., *Memorials of John Murray of Broughton*, (Scottish History Society 1898).

Blackmore, H.L. *British Military Firearms 1650–1850*, (2nd Edn London 1994).

Blaikie, W.B., (Ed.) *Itinerary of Prince Charles Edward Stuart*, (Scottish History Society 1897).

Blaikie, W.B., (Ed.) *Origins of the '45*, (Scottish History Society 1916). Includes narrative by John Daniel.

Black, Jeremy, *Culloden and the '45*, (Stroud 1990).

Bland, Humphrey *Treatise of Military Discipline*, (1727).

Bruce, A., *The Purchase System in the British Army*, (Royal Historical Society 1980).

Bulloch, J.M., *Territorial Soldiering in North-East Scotland*, (New Spalding Club 1914).

Bumsted, J.M., *The People's Clearance: Highland Emigration to British North America 1770–1815*, (Edinburgh 1982).

Caledonian Mercury, 1745 & 1746.

Campbell of Mamore Papers, (National Library of Scotland NLS 3733–35).

Chambers, Robert *Jacobite Memoirs of the Rebellion of 1745*, (Edinburgh 1834). Includes Lord George Murray's *Marches of the Highland Army*, Harry Ker of Graden's account of Culloden.

Chambers, Robert *History of the Rebellion in Scotland in 1745*, (Edinburgh 1869).

Chandler, David *The Art of Warfare in the Age of Marlborough*, (London 1976).

Charles, George *History of the Transactions in Scotland in the years 1745–*

46, (Leith 1817). Includes Lord George Murray's letter of 16th May 1746.

Daniel, John, *IN* Blaikie, *OriginsDarling, A.D. Redcoat and Browne Bess*, (Ottawa 1970).

Dennistoun, James (ed.) *Memoirs of Sir Robert Strange* . . . (London 1855).

Elcho, David, Lord *A Short Account of the Affairs of Scotland*, (Edinburgh 1907).

Fergusson, Sir James, of Kilkerran *Argyll in the Fortyfive*, (London 1951).

Forbes, Duncan *Culloden Papers*, (1815).

Forbes, Rev. Robert *The Lyon in Mourning: or, a Collection of Speeches, Letters, Journals etc. relative to the Affairs of Prince Charles Edward Stuart*, (3 vols. Scottish History Society 1895).

General Wolfe's Instructions to Young Officers, (London 1768).

Gentlemen's Magazine 1745 & 1746 *Gentleman Volunteer's Pocket Companion describing the various motions of the Foot Guards in the Manual Execise*, (London 1745).

Gibson, John S. *Ships of the '45*, (London 1967).

Gibson, John S. *Lochiel of the '45*, (Edinburgh 1994).

Gordon, Sir Bruce Seton & Arnot, Jean Gordon *Prisoners of the '45*, (3 vols. Scottish History Society 1928–9).

Grant, George *The New Highland Discipline*, (London 1757).

Guy, A.J. *Oeconomy and Discipline: Officershi̶p ̶a̶n̶d̶ ̶A̶d̶m̶i̶n̶i̶stration in the British Army 1714–63*, (Manchester 1985).

Guy, A.J. *Colonel Samuel Bagshawe and the Army of George II, 1731–1762*, (Army Records Society 1990).

Henderson, Andrew *The History of the Rebellion, 1745 & 1746* (2nd Edn 1748).

Hewins, W.A.S. (ed.) *The Whitefoord Papers* (1898).

Home, John *The History of the Rebellion in the Year 1745* (1802).

Houlding, J.A. *Fir For Service: The Training of the British Army 1715–1795*, (Oxford 1981).

Hughes, B.P. *Firepower: Weapons Effectiveness on the Battlefield 1630–1850*, (London 1974).

Jarvis, R.C. *Collected Papers on the Jacobite Risings*, (2 vols. Manchester 1972).

Johnstone, James *Memoirs of the Rebellion in Scotland*, (Folio Edn. 1970).

Ker, Henry, of Graden *IN* Chambers, *MemoirsLeask, J.C. & McCance, H.M. The Regimental Records of the Royal Scots*, (Dublin 1915).

Lenman, Bruce *The Jacobite Clans of the Great Glen*, (London 1984).

Lens, Bernard *The Grandiers Exercise 1735* (London 1967).

A List of the Colonels, Lieutenant Colonels, Majors, Captains, Lieutenants, and Ensigns of His Majesty's Forces, (1740).

Bibliography

Livingston, A., Aikman, C.W.H. & Hart B.S., *Muster Roll of Prince Charles Edward Stuart's Army 1745–46*, (Aberdeen 1994).
London Gazette, 1745 & 1746.
London Magazine, 1745 & 1746.
MacDonald, Donald, of Lochgarry IN Blaikie *ItineraryMacDonnell, Colonel Sir John, IN* Tayler, A & H. *1745 and After*
MacKay, W. *Urquhart and Glenmoriston*, (Inverness 1914).
Mackintosh, Alex. *The Forfarshire or Lord Ogilvy's Regiment*, (Inverness 1914).
McLynn, Frank *France and the Jacobite Rising of 1745*, (Edinburgh 1981).
McLynn, Frank *The Jacobite Army in England 1745*, (Edinburgh 1983).
Maxwell, James, of Kirkconnell *Narrative of Charles Prince of Wales' Expedition to Scotland in the year 1745*, (Maitland Club 1841).
Mounsey, George G. *Authentic Account of the Occupation of Carlisle in 1745*, (1846).
Murray, Lord George *Marches of the Highland Army IN* Chambers, *MemoirsMurray, Lord George Letter of 16th May IN* Charles, *TransactionsNewcastle Courant*, 1745 & 1746.
Newcastle Gazette, 1745 & 1746.
Newcastle Journal, 1745 & 1746.
O'Callaghan, J. *History of the Irish Brigades in the service of France*, (Glasgow 1870).
Orderly Book of Lord Ogilvy's Regiment, (Journal of the Society for Army Historical Research vol.2, 1927).
Prebble, John *Culloden*, (London 1961).
Prebble, John *Mutiny*, (London 1975).
Proceedings of the General Court Martial held for the Trial of Lieutenant Colonel James Durand the 15th and 16th of September 1746.
Public Record Office (Kew) WO.10/28–34 *Royal Artillery Pay and Muster Rolls*, WO.25 *Commission Registers* WO.120, *Chelsea Hospital Registers*
Reid, Stuart *18th Century Highlanders*, (London 1993).
Reid, Stuart *Like Hungry Wolves: The Battle of Culloden Moor*, (London 1994).
Reid, Stuart *King George's Army*, (3 vols. London 1995–6).
The Report of the Proceedings and Opinion of the Board of General Officers, on the examination into the conduct, behaviour and proceedings of Lieutenant General Sir John Cope, Col. Peregrine Lascelles, and Brig. Gen. Thomas Fowke from the time of the breaking out of the rebellion in North Britain in the year 1745 til the action at Preston-pans (1749).
Rosebery, Lord & MacLeod, W. (Eds.) *List of Persons concerned in the Present Rebellion*, (Scottish History Society 1890).
Scholey, Anne (Ed.) *A Jacobite Anthology*, (1745 Association 1995).
Scots Magazine, 1745 & 1746.

Scott-Moncrieff, Lesley *The '45: To gather an image whole*, (Edinburgh 1988).

Speck, William *The Butcher: The Duke of Cumberland and the Suppression of the '45*, (Oxford 1981).

Stewart, David *Sketches of the Highlanders of Scotland*, (2 vols. Edinburgh 1822).

Sullivan, Colonel John William SEE Taylor A & H *1745 and After* Tabraham, C. & Grove, D. *Fortress Scotland and the Jacobites*, (London 1995).

Tayler, A & H. *Jacobites of Aberdeenshire and Banffshire in the Forty-five*, (Aberdeen 1928).

Tayler, A & H. *Jacobite Letters to Lord Pitsligo*, (1930).

Tayler, A & H. *1745 and After*, (London 1938).

Terry, C. S. (Ed.) *Albemarle Papers*, (2 vols. New Spalding Club 1902).

Terry, C. S. *The Fortyfive*, (1922).

Tomasson, Katherine *The Jacobite General*, (Lord George Murray) (1958).

Tomasson, K. & Buist, F. *Battles of the '45*, (2nd Edn. London 1967).

Whitefoord, Lieutenant-Colonel Charles SEE Hewins.

Whitworth, Rex *William Augustus, Duke of Cumberland*, (1992).

Willson, Beckles *Life and Letters of James Wolfe*, (London 1909).

Woosnam-Savage, Robert (Ed.) *1745: Charles Edward Stuart and the Jacobites*, (Edinburgh 1995).

Index

Index